The Romantics

THE CONTEXT OF
ENGLISH LITERATURE

The Romantics

EDITED BY
STEPHEN PRICKETT

HOLMES & MEIER
PUBLISHERS, INC
NEW YORK

*First published in
the United States of America 1981 by*
HOLMES & MEIER PUBLISHERS, INC
30 Irving Place, New York, N.Y. 10003

*Copyright © 1981 by Stephen Prickett, Colin Brooks,
T. J. Diffey, Marcia Pointon*

Library of Congress Cataloging in Publication Data
Main entry under title:

The Romantics.

   (The Context of English literature)
   Includes bibliographical references and index.
   *Contents: Introduction / Stephen Prickett – England, 1782-1832
/ Colin Brooks – Romanticism in English art / Marcia Pointon –
[etc.]*
   *1. English literature – 19th century – History and criticism.
2. Romanticism – England. 3. English literature – 18th century –
History and criticism. 4. Great Britain – Civilization – 19th
century. 5. Great Britain – Civilization – 18th century. I. Prickett,
Stephen. II. Series: Context of English literature.*
PR457.R645   1981   820".9".007   81-6564

ISBN 0-8419-0723-4   *AACR2*
ISBN 0-8419-0724-2 (pbk.)

Printed in the United States of America

Contents

Illustrations

Acknowledgements

The authors would like to acknowledge with gratitude the help, advice and criticism they have received from each other. This book is the product of regular meetings and discussions over the course of a year by four colleagues at the University of Sussex – one of whom described the experience (afterwards) as being like that of a student in a nightmare tutorial with three tutors. All have gained greatly in the process, and it is their hope that the readers will also profit, more painlessly, by their labours.

The editor would also like to thank Professor J. F. C. Harrison who kindly allowed him to read the proofs of his book, *The Second Coming*, while he was at work on chapter 3, and Professor Josef Atholz of the University of Minnesota who helped him unravel some of the intricacies of Evangelicalism.

Introduction

STEPHEN PRICKETT

Unlike other volumes in this series, whose titles denote periods of time with more or less arbitrary boundaries, we see the 'Romantics' as characterizing a distinctive age, or even a 'movement'. The period between, say, 1770 and 1830 had, or was believed to have, an internal consistency and rationale uniquely its own. Our problem is how to define it.

There is, in fact, remarkably little agreement on what constitutes 'Romanticism'. The original meaning of 'romantic' was simply 'as in the old romances'. It first came to prominence as one of a group of similarly derived words in the 1650s – along with such forms as 'romancical' (1656) 'romancial' (1653) and even 'romancy' (1654). It was nearly always used in an uncomplimentary sense, as in the case of 'romancer' (1663), meaning 'liar'. If not always so bluntly disreputable, the suggestions of fable, fairy tale and even dream were never very far from the word throughout most of the eighteenth century. We find references to 'childish and romantic poems', 'romantic absurdities and incredible fictions', and even to 'vile and romantic' deceptions. As late as 1803 Mrs Trimmer, a stalwart of the Society for Promoting Christian Knowledge (SPCK) Tract Committee and indefatigable do-gooder, published in her magazine, *The Guardian of Education*, an attack on a recently published collection of fairy stories, describing them as 'full of romantic nonsense'. Coleridge himself in *Biographia Literaria* (1817) tells us that in the *Lyrical Ballads* he had undertaken to write of 'persons and characters supernatural, or at least romantic'. But even from the middle of the eighteenth century another tone had crept into the word. For some the very element of unreality or even of the supernatural was strangely attractive. Sometimes indeed it is not easy to detect the exact flavour of the word as it was used, and this may even suggest an ambiguity in the mind of the user. Thus Thomas Percy, the antiquary, in his 'Essay on the Ancient Minstrels in England' described King Richard I simply as 'romantic'. Percy's essay was published as a preface to his enormously influential *Reliques of Ancient Poetry* in 1765, and he was writing of Richard in the specific context of medieval metrical romances. Nevertheless, the adjective seems to imply something more than a mere story-book quality, and it is not difficult in the case of Richard the Lion-heart to see how 'romantic', the antiquarian and poetic adjective, could come almost insensibly to convey another much more exciting meaning, a meaning that was to be fully explicit by the time of Scott's novel *Ivanhoe*, on the same theme, which was published in 1819, only twenty-five years later than the fourth and final edition of Percy's *Reliques* (1794).

The first clearly unambiguous examples of the new sense of the word, however, came not from England but from Germany in the opening years of the nineteenth century. According to Goethe, he and Schiller were the first to use it as the opposite of 'classical'. For August Wilhelm von Schlegel the 'modern' (which generously embraces the entire Christian era) is 'romantic' in contrast with the classic spirit of the ancient world. 'The term', he continues,

> is certainly not inappropriate; the word is derived from
> *romance* – the name originally given to the languages
> which were formed from the mixture of the Latin and the
> old Teutonic dialects, in the same manner as modern
> civilization is the fruit of the heterogeneous union of the
> peculiarities of the northern nations and the fragments of
> antiquity; whereas the civilization of the ancients was much
> more of a piece.[1]

For Schlegel the characteristic quality of 'romanticism' is this union of opposite or discordant qualities. It is dialectical, whereas 'classicism' is homogeneous. In this is expressed the predominant sensibility of his own time. 'Romantic, for Schlegel,' writes A. K.

Thorlby, 'meant more than a modern style, it meant a modern manner of experiencing reality.'[2]

Yet the very breadth of Schlegel's category of the 'modern' must give us pause in trying to narrow down the Romantic era to a mere sixty years. Schlegel, after all, thought of Shakespeare as the greatest 'modern' writer and the supreme example of a 'romantic' artist. If the qualities we characterize as 'Romantic' have been with us for two thousand years, is it not more plausible to see them as *permanent* aspects of the human spirit? Should we not, perhaps, abandon Schlegel's idea that romanticism replaced classicism with the coming of Christianity and agree that *both* elements are to some extent present as perpetual 'contraries' in every period? In the Greek world, for instance, it is not difficult to see Aeschylus as 'romantic' and Sophocles as 'classic'. In England the Elizabethan was surely as much a 'romantic' age as was the end of the eighteenth century. Augustanism was, by its own claim, an essentially neoclassic ideal. So some writers have argued. F. L. Lucas, for instance, has plausibly suggested that the essential difference between romanticism and classicism is not aesthetic, but psychological – reflecting 'the strictures with which . . . the reality-principle and the super-ego control . . . emanations from the unconscious mind'.[3] The former word attracts such adjectives as 'wild', 'natural', 'spontaneous', and is in Nietzsche's language 'Dionysian', while the latter implies control, order, reality and the 'Apollonian' qualities.

Faced with such a broad use of the term, yet other critics have reacted by becoming sternly nominalist, and insisting that we restrict the use of 'Romantic' to no more than the last thirty years of the eighteenth century and the first thirty of the nineteenth. In other words, that we should stipulatively *define* the word simply and sweepingly as 'that which was thought, felt, and written between 1770 and 1830'. But though this may introduce some kind of order into semantic confusion, it raises, of course, even more severe problems than it solves. Can we *really* class together Crabbe and Wordsworth, Scott and Jane Austen, Peacock and Shelley like this without drawing further distinctions?

Partly in face of such dilemmas, one eminent twentieth-century American scholar, A. O. Lovejoy, has argued with great contro-versial panache that the term 'Romanticism', *in the singular*, has no meaning at all.

What is needed is that any study of the subject should begin with a recognition of a *prima-facie* plurality of Romanticisms, of possibly quite distinct thought-complexes, a number of which may appear in any one country. . . . There is a movement which began in Germany in the seventeen-nineties – the only one which has an indisputable title to be called Romanticism, since it invented the term for its own use. There is another movement which began pretty definitely in England in the seventeen-forties. There is a movement which began in France in 1801. There is another movement which began in France in the second decade of the century, is linked with the German movement, and took over the German name. There is the rich and incongruous collection of ideas to be found in Rousseau. There are numerous other things called Romanticism by various writers whom I cited at the outset. The fact that the same name has been given by different scholars to all of these episodes is no evidence, and scarcely even establishes a presumption, that they are identical in essentials. There may be some common denominator of them all; but if so, it has never yet been clearly exhibited, and its presence is not to be assumed *a priori*.[4]

Lovejoy's argument is a salutary reminder of the dangers of national parochialism or of too neat a system of classification. Other scholars, however, have accepted his challenge and attempted to show that just such a 'common denominator' or denominators exist – and with some success. René Wellek, for instance, argues that in spite of obvious differences:

If we examine the characteristics of the actual literature which called itself and was called 'romantic' all over the continent, we find throughout Europe the same concept-ions of poetry and of the workings and nature of poetic imagination, the same conception of nature and its relation to man, and basically the same poetic style, with a use of imagery, symbolism, and myth which is clearly distinct from those of eighteenth-century neoclassicism. This conclusion might be strengthened or modified by attention to other frequently discussed elements; subjectivism, mediaevalism, folklore, etc. But the following three criteria should be particularly convincing, since each is central for one aspect of the practice of literature: imagination for the view of poetry, nature for the view of the world, and symbol and myth for poetic style.[5]

This attempt to find in Romanticism certain characteristic ways of looking at the world, distinctive to the period, represents a kind of half-way house between those who would see it in terms of specific beliefs, and those who would emphasize merely common states of mind. Certainly it is true that, say, Blake, Wordsworth, Coleridge and Keats did appear to share broadly similar concerns in their lives, their art and in their attitude to their 'environment' (itself, in this sense, a late Romantic word actually coined by Carlyle). Yet as Wellek half-admits by his caution and studied generality, this similarity tends to be one of terminology rather than of substance. Wordsworth and Coleridge, for instance, commonly used 'imagination' to describe a *psychological* activity, whereas for Blake and Keats (in very different ways) the word carried a transcendent or visionary connotation.

But perhaps the biggest criticism that can be made of Wellek's broad 'criteria' is that they explicitly leave out of account the wider non-literary aspects of Romanticism. Not merely did it affect literature but all the arts. Our criteria must include Turner and Beethoven as well as Coleridge. Furthermore, Romanticism was a political, religious and philosophic phenomenon. With this in mind, some have sought a common factor in the prevailing metaphysical ethos, rather than within the principles of any one art form or movement. T. E. Hulme, the philosopher (1888–1917), for instance, argued that in a curious kind of way Romanticism was fundamentally a religious phenomenon.

They had been taught by Rousseau that man was by nature good, that it was only bad laws and customs that had suppressed him. Remove all these and the infinite possibilities of man would have a chance. This is what made them think that something positive could come out of disorder, this is what created the religious enthusiasm. Here is the root of all romanticism: that man, the individual, is an infinite reservoir of possibilities; and if you

> can so rearrange society by the destruction of oppressive
> order then these possibilities will have a chance and you will
> get progress.[6]

The inevitable result of this kind of facile optimism, he goes on, was
disillusion and despair.

> Just as in the case of the other instincts, Nature has her
> revenge. The instincts that find their right and proper
> outlet in religion must come out in some other way. You
> don't believe in a God, so you begin to believe that man is
> a God. You don't believe in Heaven, so you begin to
> believe in a heaven on earth. In other words you get
> romanticism. The concepts that are right and proper in
> their own sphere are spread over, and so mess up, falsify
> and blur the clear outlines of human experience. It is like
> pouring a pot of treacle over the dinner table. Romanticism
> then, and this is the best definition I can give of it, is spilt
> religion.[7]

Though, as the style suggests, this is a tactical and polemical
definition from a writer whom many might consider to be a highly
romantic thinker himself, this notion of Romanticism as 'spilt
religion' is a useful one – and not only because it helps us to shed
narrowly literary definitions. In spite of the fact that, as we have
seen, the origins of the word are indeed literary, literature was no
more than one of a number of interconnected areas where the new
mood revealed itself. For those who had lived through the French
Revolution, the philosophical revolution initiated by Kant and the
Idealist philosophers, together with the transformation of biblical
studies by the Higher Critics in Germany; in England, the
Evangelical Revival and the Oxford Movement (with their counterparts in a resurgent Catholicism in France and Germany), and the
varying moods of elation and despair that accompanied the world's
first industrial revolution; or the Europe-wide transformation of
neoclassical ideals in the visual arts – it was clear that literature
stood in a highly complex relationship to a world caught up in an
unprecedented process of *change*.

Here, at least, is a simple but fundamental point over which there
is little dispute. We may put it like this: up until sometime in the

middle of the eighteenth century it was possible for a great many people to believe (however falsely) that they lived in a world dominated by great unchangeable permanencies – in agriculture, in the means of production, in religion, in social and political relationships. By 1820 it was impossible to think in this way. We can focus this very neatly in a single literary example from Gray's *Elegy*, published, conveniently for our argument, at the mid-point of the eighteenth century, in 1751.

The early part of the poem is specifically devoted to a celebration of the unchanging pattern of village life. This Gray achieves through a dense network of classical quotations and allusions familiar to any educated reader of the day. Such lines as:

> For them no more the blazing hearth shall burn,
> Or busy housewife ply her evening care:
> No children run to lisp their sire's return,
> Or climb his knees the envied kiss to share.
>
> (lines 21–4)

were not merely a conscious echo of Lucretius' *De Rerum Natura* (Book III, lines 894–6),[8] but were specifically meant to *remind* the reader of that fact – just as the following stanza was intended to recall Virgil's *Georgics*. Gray is calling attention to his borrowings not to parade learning but to appeal to a common consensus on the familiar and unchanging rhythms of rural existence. This was how it had *always* been. The life of the Roman peasant, it is implied, was in its essentials no different from the cottager of Stoke Poges in Gray's own day. That this was in many ways untrue is beside the point. What matters is Gray's confident sense of that unbroken continuity and the fact that he can so effortlessly and (as we know from contemporary references) so successfully assume that his readers will share that sense.

What follows is, in the light of this, the more extraordinary:

> Perhaps in this neglected spot is laid
> Some heart once pregnant with celestial fire;
> Hands that the rod of empire might have swayed,
> Or waked to ecstasy the living lyre.
>
> But knowledge to their eyes her ample page
> Rich with the spoils of time did ne'er unroll;

Chill penury repressed their noble rage,
And froze the genial current of the soul   (lines 45–52)

The elegiac mood is unbroken. Gray is ostensibly doing no more
than extend the commonplace moral that whatever our station in
life we are all equal in death – and, incidentally, once more
demonstrating how rich with the spoils of time his own lines are by
yet more allusions to Lucretius, Milton and Pope. They serve to re-
affirm how far from his mind any thought of originality was. Yet his
argument at this point is not based, as one might expect, upon conventional notions of 'degree', the Chain of Being, or any kind of
divinely endorsed social order, but simply upon *poverty*. Earlier
poets, as late as Pope in Gray's own century, had taken it for granted
that the inequalities of the social order, with its complex hierarchies
of rank and privilege, were part of the unalterable nature of things
– ordained, if not by God, then at least by necessity, and for many
the latter was merely an expression of the former.

There is not the slightest evidence to suggest that Gray would
have wished consciously to disagree, yet simply with that bald
statement, 'Chill penury repressed their noble rage', we have
passed almost insensibly into a world governed by a quite different set of rules. If *all* that holds these villagers back from the
fruits of education, and inhibits the growth of other Miltons or
Hampdens, is money, then that is a problem with an easy solution. We are a hairs-breadth away from a call for universal primary
education.

A hairs-breadth – and yet that is enough. There is, as we have
just said, not the slightest evidence to suggest that this thought
consciously ever occurred to Gray. We are a full generation away
from the French Revolution and its slogan *la carrière ouverte aux
talents*. What makes the *Elegy* so fascinating for us is the very
sensitivity with which it exhibits the delicate balance of forces for
change and stasis within Gray's own intellectual milieu. The year
1751 was perhaps the last moment in English history when a major
author could so unquestioningly assume the permanent shape of
rural life, and, simultaneously, so phrase it as to ensure its eventual
transformation. Within a few years almost every part of the country
was feeling the effects of the enclosure movement and the
accompanying agrarian revolution. A population explosion, an

increasing drift of labourers to the towns and even the construction of new canals and turnpike roads were to transform not merely Stoke Poges (where tradition, at least, places the poem) and tens of thousands of other villages like it, but also the *attitude* of people towards that way of life. One might rejoice in progress, or, more likely, deplore it, as Goldsmith, Crabbe and Wordsworth all did, but no one any more was going to say that village life was fixed in a Lucretian permanence.

Moreover, the literary mould that shaped the *Elegy* was also shattered. Though, as we have seen, Gray's particular way of putting things had social and even political implications, the very form he had chosen for his poem, the pastoral elegy, would have helped to prevent him from seeing them. By its own convention, such a poem was about the unchanging verities, not a questioning of the social order. But for those who came after Gray such questions could no longer be avoided. Literature was not an activity separate from politics, philosophy or religion.

At no time in literary history have the boundaries between one field of activity and the next been more blurred or difficult to define as in the Romantic period. Wordsworth, in a very real sense, came to poetry *through* politics. For Coleridge, he was the man uniquely fitted to write the first great 'philosophic' poem; for Shelley, he was the 'subtle-souled psychologist'. Wordsworth's subject was mankind – not a subject neatly divisible into self-contained disciplines. And what of Coleridge himself? Nowadays we tend to think of him primarily as a poet, yet few of his contemporaries would have done. In effect, his poetic career spans no more than six years out of a life of over sixty. He was a political journalist, preacher and lecturer, philosopher, theologian and literary critic, yet what strikes the reader is not this amazing diversity but the essential *unity* of his thought. All his multifarious activities can be seen as parts of a single, organic and constantly developing whole. Similarly, what of Blake – poet, political thinker, philosopher and theologian, as well as artist, engraver and painter? We could multiply examples (Turner wrote a poem called 'The Fallacies of Hope'), but the point is clear. The response to a quite new quality of change experienced for the first time in England towards the end of the eighteenth century, and only slightly later in Germany and France, meant also an inevitable destruction of the old categories of knowledge and even the actual ways of knowing. The cataclysmic nature of these changes meant also that literature, and in particular, poetry, ceased to be a decorative and peripheral thing, and became central in a quite new way as people looked for a focus for the new pictures of man* that seemed to be emerging. As Coleridge wrote to Wordsworth 'the night after his recitation of a Poem [later to be called *The Prelude*] on the growth of an individual mind':

> Into my heart have I received that lay
> More than historic, that prophetic lay
> Wherein (high theme by thee first sung aright)
> Of the foundations and the building up
> Of a Human Spirit thou hast dared to tell
> What may be told. . . .

For this very reason, if for no other, it is impossible to think of Romanticism solely within the confines of literature, any more than we can think of it solely as an artistic, philosophical, political or religious phenomenon. That, in essence, is the justification for the kind of multidisciplinary approach we have attempted in this book.

If at its centre lies this notion of change, it will be seen that we have not altogether lost sight of some of the other definitions of Romanticism discussed earlier. A. W. Schlegel's conviction, for instance, that his age was characterized by unresolved contradictions is crucial to any understanding of the period. It would, for example, encapsulate the essential difference between Gray and Wordsworth. Both, while valuing the fruits of education and of the literary tradition into which they have been initiated, extol also the solid qualities of the rural poor who are excluded from that world. For both there is here a real conflict of values. But whereas for Wordsworth this sense of conflict is one of the mainsprings of both his aesthetic theory and his poetry, in Gray the conflict is never brought into the open. It remains latent – and visible only to the eyes of a later generation who have *also* known Wordsworth. To a contemporary it simply would not have been there. Such a development can be seen, too, in the work of Constable, who combines with an immense respect for Rubens, Rembrandt and Poussin a deep awareness of the change in attitudes to nature that separates him from them.

* In many instances throughout this book 'man' and 'he' have been used, for simplicity, when 'man/woman' and 'he/she' are meant.

If Schlegel saw such contradictions as typical of the entire Christian era, we must go on to say that the *awareness* of those contradictions is typical of the Romantic sensibility in the narrower sense.

Wordsworth's feelings about the deprivation and ignorance of the agricultural labourer are, in their own way, as ambiguous as those of Gray. Because he does not sentimentalize the labourer through classical stereotypes of the 'happy peasant', he expects more from him as a person. One thinks of the innate nobility and endurance of Michael in the poem of that name. Thus Wordsworth is simultaneously more disgusted by the boorish reality, when he encounters it, and more bitter against the society he saw as responsible for that brutalization.

'Is this the whistling plough-boy whose shrill notes
Impart new gladness to the morning air!'
[. . .]
And mark his brow!
Under whose shaggy canopy are set
Two eyes – not dim, but of a healthy stare –
Wide, sluggish, blank, and ignorant, and strange –
Proclaiming boldly that they never drew
A look or motion of intelligence
From infant conning of the Christ-cross-row
Or puzzling through a primer, line by line,
Till perfect mastery crown the pains at last.
What kindly warmth from touch of fostering hand,
What penetrating power of sun or breeze,
Shall e'er dissolve the crust wherein his soul
Sleeps, like a caterpillar sheath'd in ice?
This torpor is no pitiable work
Of modern ingenuity;
[. . .]
This Boy the fields produce;
His spade and hoe, mattock and glittering scythe,
The carter's whip that on his shoulder rests
In air high-towering with a boorish pomp,
The sceptre of his sway; his country's name
Her equal rights, her churches and her schools –
What have they done for him? And, let me ask,

For tens of thousands uninform'd as he?
In brief – what liberty of *mind* is here?

(*The Excursion*, VIII, 398–433)[9]

This is a much more disturbing passage to read than that of Gray. For one thing, it seems to be on the *wrong* side. Wordsworth, it is true, has put this speech into the mouth of his 'Solitary' – a disillusioned wanderer who takes a sour and cynical view of his society – but though it is an extreme case, the description has an unmistakable ring of truth about it. Though not great verse the passage has a certain vituperative vitality just because of the poet's indignation. But indignation against *whom*? Whose side, we want to ask, is Wordsworth on? Yet the vitality of the passage is directly related to this disturbing ambiguity of tone. It is, we feel, a peculiarly honest piece of writing. Wordsworth is indignant precisely because he doesn't sentimentalize or patronize the plough-boy. He treats him as he might any other human being – and finds him impossible to like. That is the true measure of what his society has done to him.

Obviously it would be grossly over-simple to say that the difference in tone between this extract from *The Excursion* and Gray's *Elegy* is characteristic of 'Romanticism', but it would, I think, be true to say that while both passages are complex and even contradictory, Wordsworth seems to be *aware* of the contradictions in his writing in a way that Gray is apparently not. There has been a shift in artistic self-consciousness. As we shall see, that shift, so typical of both the literature and art of the period, is closely paralleled by even more radical shifts of sensibility in philosophy and theology, as the whole of the thought processes of the age are forced to come to terms with this new awareness of contradiction as a basic condition of human experience.

John Beer, a modern critic of Coleridge, has suggested that Romanticism is better understood as a response to common problems rather than as a set of common beliefs.[10] While this may be over-cautious, and though, as we have seen, it is certainly possible to find in Romanticism positive affirmations, there is much to be said for the initially more modest and explorative aim of trying to understand it in terms of the responses of certain individuals to what they rightly perceived as a quite new order of problems, or, as in the examples of Gray and Wordsworth, to problems that are perceived in a quite new way. In this volume, therefore, the aim is not to attempt an exhaustive description of Romanticism either as a period or as a mood, but to show it as a response to certain characteristic questions – aesthetic, philosophical, religious and political – that were being asked increasingly towards the end of the eighteenth century.

For convenience, we shall be focusing in particular on four main topics as areas of debate where the argument – then and subsequently – highlights problems central to the consciousness of the period. Clearly, not all the topics will be of equal significance from the point of view of the literary critic, the philosopher or the historian of religion, art and society, but the observant reader will notice how they occur and recur in endless variations in every one of the fields we have chosen to discuss. We can summarize them as follows:

1 Growth and change. What are the best models for understanding the processes of growth and change in individuals, in society, in artistic tradition?
2 Nature. What is the relationship of man to his environment? What do we mean by 'nature'?
3 Feeling and reason. What is, and should be, the relationship between head and heart? How much of human awareness is actually conditioned by unconscious forces?
4 Subjectivism. How do we know if what the imagination creates is 'true'? What is the relationship between art and life?

The Romantic period, however we define it, is one of the richest, most complex and most rewarding in English literature. It would be both presumptuous and of little value to attempt a comprehensive or authoritative survey of it here. Our brief has been the much more interesting one of discussing the context of events and ideas that infuse it. We aim to show how some of the above questions arose, why they were felt to be important, and the kinds of answers that, consciously or unconsciously, the Romantics provided. Even in the final chapter, on the literature of the period, we have concentrated less on particular works than on the way in which certain key words reveal in their development the intellectual and critical currents of the day, and the accompanying changes in sensibility and climate of feeling. In a field where many of the central issues remain matters of scholarly debate, we try to incorporate some of the latest ideas and research, and to show how arguments of the period are still living ones for us today.

Notes

1 August Wilhelm von Schlegel, *Lectures on Dramatic Art and Literature*, trans. J. Black, London, 1846, 21–2.
2 A. K. Thorlby, *The Romantic Movement*, Longman, 1966, 2.
3 F. L. Lucas, *The Decline and Fall of the Romantic Ideal*, 2nd edn, Cambridge University Press, 1948, 33.
4 A. O. Lovejoy, 'On the discrimination of Romanticisms', *Essays in the History of Ideas*, Johns Hopkins Press, 1948; reprinted in M. H. Abrams (ed.), *English Romantic Poets*, Oxford University Press, 1960, 8–9.
5 René Wellek, 'The concept of Romanticism', in Stephen G. Nichols, Jr (ed.), *Concepts of Criticism*, Yale University Press, 1963, 160–1.
6 T. E. Hulme, 'Romanticism and Classicism', in Herbert Read (ed.), *Speculations, Essays on humanism and the philosophy of art*, 2nd edn, Routledge & Kegan Paul, 1936, 116.
7 ibid., 118.
8 *Iam iam non domus accipier te laeta, neque uxor optima nec dulces occurrent oscula nati praeripere et tactita pectus dulcedine tangent.* (No longer now will your happy home give you welcome, no longer will your best of wives and sweet children race to win the first kisses, and thrill your heart to its depths with sweetness.)
9 Wordsworth was an inveterate reviser of his poems with the result that nearly all his major poems exist in published form with wide variations. The common practice among later editors to not always reveal which text they are using has not improved matters. Until the new Cornell University Press edition of Wordsworth is fully published, it is not possible to refer consistently to a single edition of his works. In general, quotations from *The Prelude* are taken from the Penguin Parallel text (1971), edited by J. C. Maxwell. *The Excursion, Expostulation and Reply* and *Tintern Abbey* are from *Poetical Works*, five volumes, edited by E. de Selincourt, Oxford University Press, 1940–9 (Oxford English Texts).
10 John Beer, *Coleridge the Visionary*, Chatto & Windus, 1959, 14.

1 England 1782–1832:
the historical context

COLIN BROOKS

Introduction

Romantic England was an England of wars and rumours of wars. Embattled or expansive, seeking opportunity abroad or anxiously watching the need for military force at home, England felt the impact and the various possibilities of war, of invasion, defeat, triumph and militarism. To some war was necessary; to others it was symptomatic of what was rotten in the English polity.

1783 saw the end of the American War of Independence, but the next decade was punctuated by 'incidents' – on the Canadian border, the Pacific coast, the Black Sea, in India. Ironically it was in 1792 that Pitt was able to declare that 'unquestionably there never was a time when a durable peace might more reasonably be expected than at the present moment'.[1] A year later began the wars against Revolutionary and Napoleonic France that were to continue, with but brief respite after the Peace of Amiens in 1802, until 1815.

The impact of the war was great. 250,000 men were under arms in 1812; some 100,000 were to remain after 1815. The barracks built in and after the 1790s could hold 150,000 troops. Naval manpower rose from 36,000 to 114,000 between 1792 and 1812. The financial impact of the war is hinted at in Table 1. Government expenditure peaked in 1815 at £112.9 million. In 1811 the war took 16 per cent of gross national income, the same proportion as in 1915.[2]

Table 1

Year	Govt income £m	Govt expenditure £m	National debt £m
1770	11.4	10.5	130.6
1780	12.5	22.6	167.2
1790	17.0	16.8	244.0
1800	31.6	51.0	456.1
1810	69.2	81.5	607.4
1820	58.1	57.5	840.1
1830	55.3	53.7	798.2

The burden of war meant that the age was of necessity interested in quantification, in the possibilities of statistics. Political arithmetic, drowsing for three generations, reawakened. Government commissions became characteristic vehicles for the making of policy and the airing of grievances. The potential of statistics was realized. An adequate census was taken for the first time in 1801. It helped to settle the contemporary argument as to whether the population was rising or falling. Repeated decennially, the census revealed the momentum of population growth (see Table 2).

Table 2

	England and Wales	
	m	% increase
1770 estimate	7.48	
1780 estimate	7.95	6.3
1790 estimate	8.68	9.2
1801 census	8.89	2.4
1811 census	10.16	14.3
1821 census	12.00	18.1
1831 census	13.90	15.8

The population of Scotland grew from 1.61 million in 1801 to 2.36 million in 1831. And the occupational structure was changing, as shown in Table 3.

Table 3

% of families	1811	1831
Agriculture	35.2	28.1
Trade, manufacture, handicraft	44.4	42.0
Other	20.4	29.8

New manufacturing towns embodied the dynamism and the instability of the age. They were emphatically outside of the traditional social structure. The increase in expenditure on poor relief was dramatic. This rise substantially outstripped the growth in population. From some £1½ million per year in the mid 1770s, the amount spent on poor relief reached £4¼ million per year early in the 1800s, £6½ million a decade later, and over £7¼ million by 1820.[3] The facts of finance and population show that this was an age of wrenching changes and an age in which government, as employer of men and extractor of money, as oppressor and as saviour, played an ever more important part in national life.

This was an intensely political age. It ended with the prolonged, maybe even potentially revolutionary crisis over the need for a reform of the franchise and of the number and distribution of parliamentary constituencies. This crisis was resolved, though the problems which created it were not solved, by the Reform Act of 1832. The age had opened too with the question of parliamentary reform being aired, and with the crisis over the conclusion of the American war and the resignation in 1782 of Lord North, Prime Minister since 1770. The ministries of Shelburne and Rockingham were short-lived. The Fox–North coalition saw a major constitutional crisis over the conduct of George III, who brought pressure to bear on the House of Lords to reject Fox's India bill (which, George believed, would throw Indian patronage into Whig hands). Fox and North bitterly attacked George's choice of William Pitt the Younger to be First Lord of the Treasury (December 1783). Until after the election of 1784, Pitt led a minority government. The events of 1782–4 both flabbergasted and alienated the Whig party. For most of the following half century, the Whig party was the party of opposition. As such it had to mediate – a desperately difficult task – between its aristocratic fastness and the radicals who surrounded it clamorously and indecently as well as honestly and tenaciously.

Throughout the years 1782–1832 the political system was under stress. The demands upon it were immense. It had to organize the fighting of the wars against France. It had to comprehend the condition of the economy (even to 'solve' its problems). It had to maintain public order whilst insisting upon individual responsibilities.

And the whole government, the establishment which it represented and embodied, was under challenge. Its legitimacy was doubted, asserted, and doubted again. These debates were rooted in eighteenth-century political culture – in the arguments over political power, its forms, control and limitations which had marked the reigns of William III and Anne, the hegemony of Walpole and then the first troubled decades of George III's reign. This crisis of authority *within* the established political system set King against (self-styled) aristocracy, George and Pitt against Charles James Fox and the Whigs. Political argument was given added edge by the coincidence of changes in the economy and by the assertion, apparently confirmed in revolutionary France, of the possibilities of establishing a radically different polity. From outside – or from the fringes of – the political nation, new tones, often angered by economic change and transported by the vistas of justice held to inhere in the notion of 'rights', were increasingly voiced. Against this cacophony the political nation split and two tunes alone were heard – that which announced the *anti-French* theme and that which proclaimed a fanfare for *reform*. All these lines of argument, passion and conviction came together and separated. As they did so the typical eighteenth-century preoccupation with 'the state of the nation' changed indefinably into the typical nineteenth-century concern with 'the condition of England'. In the process, the realm of the thinkable was greatly extended, and what was thought was quickly published, urged, debated, overthrown. These thoughts and arguments I hope to illustrate in what follows.

Students of literature are wary of claiming that a text is a reflection of society, even of the opinions of the person responsible for it. Historians too must be very cautious in arguing that a letter or a speech reveals more than its author's mere perception of the needs of the moment, of the state of an argument, or an audience. I do not intend to pin writers or politicians to the remains they have left behind in letter, speech, poem, novel or conversation. Rather I hope to use contemporary evidence to show just how much could be thought, argued and believed, to indicate not the concentration of opinion, not a typical point of view, but rather the range of possibilities.

Doubt rather than confidence, debate rather than deference, involvement rather than indifference: these were characteristic. Perception of change was not yet appreciation of progress. The penetration of the culture by 'improvement'[4] brought confrontation as much as celebration: in 1831 troops were rushed by steamship to quell a popular rising in Merthyr Tydfil; tricolours were waved at the opening of the Liverpool and Manchester Railway. It was only later that 'improvement' became 'progress' and, for a time, became common rather than contentious.

Man in the economy

The land and 'the alteration in the times'   England was the first country to experience an Industrial Revolution. Perhaps 'an' rather than 'the': the forms have been so diverse, even while the basis remains the same. Emphasizing similarity and discounting variation, some historians have been tempted to speak, on the one hand, of a general process (now world-wide and certainly not specifically capitalist) of 'modernization' and, on the other, of pre-industrial or traditional society. But such societies were many and various: England in the mid-eighteenth century was a far more 'developed' country than many others have been when on the verge of their, more recent, industrial revolutions. England was not a 'backward' country in 1750. Finance capitalism, market agriculture and so on were well developed before then. But this does not mean that the general transformation of the economy – of which the process of industrialization was a part – was accomplished smoothly. The transformation came suddenly, its impact unpredictable, its implications unforeseen.

The agricultural wage labourer was not created in that transformation, yet it profoundly and traumatically affected him, as it affected the proprietor and the tenant farmer. 'In general eighteenth century conditions encouraged a persistent bias towards larger farms occupied by tenants rather than freeholders.' Increasing size of farms changed the position of the labourer; the consolidation of ownership struck at the small proprietor, 'although there were areas of small-scale farming where the numbers of owner-occupiers were little affected by the processes of change'.[5] In the *structural* sense, there was no old order in England. Long-term changes in the pattern of land ownership had precluded that. Yet the *cultural* relation of gentry, farmer and farmworker in the 1720s or 1730s was very different from that prevailing a century later. And – by improvement, enclosure and a sheer sense of possibility – the face of England was irreparably changed, even dehumanized:

> Scarce could any trace of man descry,
> Wastes of corn that stretched without a bound,
> But where the sower dwelt was nowhere to be found.
>   (*Salisbury Plain*, 1793–4, lines 43–5)

Between roughly 1750 and 1850, a tradition of paternalism was severely eroded. Relationships based upon money became correspondingly more important and, crucially, more uncertain. These years see, in the sweeping words of Hobsbawm and Rudé, the end of the 'ancient belief that social inequality could be combined with the recognition of human rights'. A witness before a parliamentary enquiry in 1830 looked back to the previous state of things:

> When I was a boy I used to visit a large Farmhouse, where the Farmer sat in a room with a Door opening to the Servants' Hall, and everything was carried from one Table to the other. Now they will rarely permit a Man to live in their Houses; and it is in consequence a total Bargain and Sale for Money, and all Idea of Affection is destroyed.[6]

On the estates of the Stafford family in the West Midlands the farmer no longer had direct access to the Marquis – he went to the agent ('the regular channel').[7] This was a change in attitudes to both *persons* and *property*. Of course, sheer lust for ownership played a continuing, crushing part – the more visible in previously sheltered areas, as Wordsworth believed his Lake District to be:

> No Joy to see a neighbouring house, or stray
> Through pastures not his own, the master took;
>   (*The Female Vagrant, Lyrical Ballads*, 1798, lines 41–2)

This depressing and oppressing phenomenon was a common topic of conversation in the Lakes:

> John Fisher overtook me on the other side of Rydale. He talked much about the alteration in the times, and observed that in a short time there would be only two ranks of people, the very rich and the very poor, for those who have small estates says he are forced to sell, and all the land goes into one hand.[8]

The market economy – especially in war time – offered new

opportunities to the farmer and proprietor; the culture allowed them to be seen as such and grasped. The landed interest – the farming interest – was rethinking its role, its duties and its responsibilities. Enclosure was perhaps the most obvious, most visible, most easily publicized form of improvement. Alongside enclosure we might place the threshing machine, whose apparently inexorable taking over of man's work 'prompted' the riots of 1830. No doubt the changes in agrarian organization and technology had long been in process and no doubt the net, long-term effects were beneficial. In fact the number of people employed on the land often rose as a consequence. But many contemporaries saw the matter differently. The aristocratic traveller John Byng reported conversation on the consequences of enclosure which he had with a cottager in Meriden, Warwickshire in 1789:

> Ah, lackaday, Sir, that was a sad job; and mind all us poor volk: and those who then gave into it, now repent it. . . . Because, we had our garden, our bees, our share of a flock of sheep, the feeding of our geese; and could cut turf for our fuel – now all that is gone! – Our cottage, as good a one as this, we gave but 50s a year for; and for this we are obliged to pay £9 10s; and without any ground: and coals are risen upon us from 7d to 9d the hundred. My cottage with many others is pull'd down; and the poor are sadly put to it to get a house to put their heads in!!! Heigh ho!
> HEAR THIS, YE PITIERS OF MONEY-BEGUMS
> HEAR THIS, YE FREERS OF BLACK-SLAVES
> HEAR THIS, YE REPRESENTATIVES OF THE PEOPLE.

The spirit abroad in Meriden was captured by Byng when he went off to an archery ground nearby:

> The place . . . has been lately enclosed, turf'd, and planted, by Lord A[ylesford] in the style of an extended bowling-green; and there is a rustic building erected by the club, for their meetings, dinners etc. which are provided by the ruin.[9]

Improvement could enhance pleasure as well as profit. That enclosure 'might lead to more and more regular local employment – at least for a time – did not compensate for the poor man's loss of independence'. But independence can hardly be measured. In their book *Captain Swing*, which investigates the background to and circumstances of the rural discontent of 1830, Hobsbawm and Rudé themselves admit that 'in a rapidly changing society, the labourers themselves were often no longer so ready to accept the traditional discipline of the domestic servant'. There were also several traditions of independence: the annual hiring of labour and subsequent 'living in' was one, access to the common another.[10] Demand for agricultural labour might have risen in the war years, but the labourer was himself a consumer. The instability of bread/grain prices hit both the urban and the rural labourer, for whom, consequently, recourse to poor relief became essential in bad years. Before 1815 this was prompted by occasional high prices as in 1795–6 and 1799–1801; after 1815 by the greatly reduced demand for labour. Here were two quite different attacks on 'independence', prompting the labourer to identify two quite different 'enemies'.

The same difficulties confront us when evaluating the impact of industrialization and of the great transformation on the town or village worker or labourer: indeed on *everybody*. Some who initially benefited from the transformation – the handloom weavers, for example – were later 'overtaken' and left stranded by mechanization. For many, industrialization *per se* was a disaster. We may explain the predicament of the handloom weaver – insufficient mechanization retarded industrial rationalization – but we must not explain away his sense of grievance, of being trapped. Historians must resist the temptation to advise the dead to take the long view. Yet what was disruption and abomination to an individual represented, from another perspective, 'the responsiveness of English agriculture . . . [which] was approximately successful even when most strained by the inflation, population pressure, and glowering blockades of the Napoleonic Wars'.[11]

Rational recreation and customary conduct Writers who are persuaded of the truth and relevance of the notion of 'modernization' subsume within it many changes of ideas and values – the triumph of calculation, uniformity, rationality, achievement. The Second Marquis of Stafford might be held typical here. A traveller reported that he was 'a man of taste, virtue, reserved and very well bred, he does not like the bagpipe and says so and shews it indeed, for he has converted the piper into a porter'.[12] No one could accuse Stafford of being other than an aristocrat. The great transformation of the century 1750–1850 transcended class. It was not a matter of mere social structural change, of any simple rise of a bourgeoisie. Yet the bourgeoisie – always present yet always 'rising' – was central to that transformation, helped though it often was by the revived sense of duty and sobriety among the aristocratic evangelicals. The 'middling classes' became the 'middle class'. Its values were stamped on much of the legislation, the culture and the concerns of the age – on, for example, labour discipline, town planning and humanitarian reform.

In no sphere of life was the change of values and the concurrent impact of the middling classes more apparent than in that of sport and recreation. The story has been well told by R. W. Malcolmson in his *Popular Recreations in English Society, 1700–1850* (Cambridge, 1973). In 1807 Robert Southey declared that 'all persons . . . speak of old ceremonies and old festivities as things which are obsolete'. Urban life could not follow traditional rural rhythms. 'In large towns the population is continually shifting . . . all local differences are wearing out.'[13] Southey here suggests that old customs were going; not that *popular culture itself* was being undermined. Obsolescence was one thing. But positive suppression was often nearer the mark. Professionalization would soon be contributing; duties long performed by clergymen, for example, would become secular, professional responsibilities. Between the two, customs were simply swept aside. Enclosure, for example, in changing the distribution and layout of land, curtailed recreational possibilities. New values were eagerly publicized. More respectable recreations were urged on an unwilling population. Keep out of the ale-house. Stay indoors. Cultivate domesticity. What had been rural innocence became slothful sin. 'The summit of human happiness', opined Wilberforce while attacking bull-baiting in 1801, lies 'not in picnics, but in the cottage of the peasant, surrounded with his smiling family'.[14]

Similar crusades had been launched by magistrates during the Puritan 'Reformation of Manners' in the late 1640s and 1650s. And in the Jacobin France of the 1790s there was a corresponding, if more thoroughgoing, attempt to contract the area of indifference, to give all activities a moral value, to extend the supervisory role of 'authority'. In these two examples, the momentum soon ran down: men returned to billiards and the wife. But in Romantic England the evangelical thrust was maintained. It marked indeed the whole century after 1740. Custom became unworthy. Rules and organizations became essential. Of course these were often imposed from outside and above, but it is important that these could represent self-discipline rather than social control, could reflect the expression not the imposition of values. By 1815 the evangelicals were subjecting to close scrutiny the practices of the new urban populations, free at once from the routine ritual of custom and the restraints traditionally exercised by squire and parson; and they also reached out into the countryside, adding moralistic fervour to the forces which were redefining the community of the land. It was in the new towns though that the problems were greatest. Already in 1789 a vicar was quoted as saying, while 'we know of none who openly profess a disregard for Religion . . . there are many who in fact do disregard it, and wholly absent themselves from all public worship – as in all places where large manufacturers are established'.[15] The situation did not improve over the next generations.

By contrast to the cultural implications of the apparent instability and rootlessness of urban life, the immobility of rural life long delayed the disappearance of custom, as Hardy insisted in the preface to *Far From the Madding Crowd* (1895–1902). As the squire often gave succour to custom, the evangelical attack could be seen as threatening the relationship of squire and community. Some reformers drew back from the onslaught on society *tout court* which this could imply. Charles James Fox thought that if the recreation of the labourer were to be denounced, then so too ought the approving role of the gentry: 'In a letter writing mood wrote to Dr. Bardsley of Manchester on his pamphlet against bull-baiting. Not against it himself; thought the outcry against the common people unjust while their betters hunted and fished. Was decidedly in favour of boxing.'[16]

Indeed the recreation which was closest to the heart of landed society – fox-hunting – well displays the ambivalence, the determination yet the doubts, of our period. On the one hand, it was characterized by a search for 'the new ecstacy', by the rowdy amorality and spendthrift inconsequence of the Melton Mowbray set; 'hunting to ride' combined Regency manners and romantic defiance. On the other, hunting was brought under the rubric of 'improvement'. Hounds were bred 'scientifically', meets organized, territories defined and the potential application of the law of trespass clarified, the sport publicized, professional correspondence encouraged. Withal the solidarity of the rural community was emphasized. Hunting 'links all classes together from the Peer to the Peasant'. Viewed in this light, men 'rode to hunt'. Here hunting was a distinct and deliberate counter to Regency manners, for it 'prevents our young men from growing quite effeminate in Bond Street'. Duty and Stewardship in social relations and the control of land were accentuated by the community's hunt. Influence was rationally and beneficially exercised.[17]

Aristocratic improvement   Improvement was not the monopoly of the middling classes. But could the aristocrat, the landed gentleman, sustain a role both as landowner – as traditionally conceived – and as improver? A recent book by E. S. Richards, *Leviathan of Wealth: The Sutherland Fortune in the Industrial Revolution*, allows us to look at one example of the opportunities offered to the landowner and of the pressures upon him.

The Second Marquis of Stafford, a considerable landowner in the north-west Midlands and beneficiary of the will of the Duke of Bridgwater (the family inherited the famous canal in 1803), had in 1785 married the Countess of Sutherland. Her estates in the far highlands of Scotland amounted to almost one million acres. Stafford was inextricably involved in the transformation of the economy. And inevitably he was dependent upon his estate manager. By 1800 this job had become a profession, involving far more than the old tasks of collecting rent and pacifying tenants. Stafford's manager was James Loch, and Loch was a major national figure. His decisions and recommendations affected not merely the Stafford family, not merely their estates, but the changing country at large. Born in 1780 to a Scottish gentry family in reduced circumstances, Loch studied law at Edinburgh and practised in London in the first decade of the new century. He became intimate with the leaders and intellectuals in the opposition Whig party. In 1812 Loch went to work for Stafford who was, as his family had been since early in George I's reign, a Whig. He remained in the service of the family until his death in 1855.

Loch considered himself a *liberal*. He saw liberalism as following two paths to the future. One was that of concession, concession both to the squirearchy (the system of legislative protection for agriculture ought to be demolished *gradually*) and to the middling classes (*judicious* parliamentary reform was essential). The other path was more direct, purposive in a Benthamite way, taking in ideas which came from his student days in the coterie of the Edinburgh Reviewers. Knowledge must be spread, improvement justified. Thus he supported the Society for the Propagation of Useful Knowledge and helped to found London University. These characteristically Benthamite activities did not alienate Loch from the aristocracy: far from it, though there were, of course, aristocrats and aristocrats.

> The property of a great English Nobleman must be managed on the same principle as a little kingdom, not like the affairs of a little merchant. The future and lasting interests and honour of the family as well as their immediate income must be kept in view – while a merchant thinks of his daily profits and his own immediate life interest.

Thus Loch in 1816, in language that would not have disgraced a Tory of a century previously.

Stafford's wealth freed him, and his status obliged him, to take the long view. This was not merely a matter of fixing rents at a paternalistically low level ('It is fit and proper that those who hold of a great man' should receive such benefits). It was a matter of positive, deliberate, planned improvement. Loch's career and his self-justification are symptomatic of an important change in this period. The Whig aristocrat imaged by Burke in the 1770s and 1780s had been essentially a public figure, a man of authority and influence, of a stability rooted in the predominance of land in the rentroll. The magnate whom Loch served owned land enough. But his concern was also for coal, canals and railways. He helped to incarnate the doctrines of classical economics. 'The utility of the Gentlemen of England', to Loch, was that they managed, *without state aid*,

> all the local affairs of their district, such as roads, bridges, drainage etc. To this we think is owing in a great degree

the prosperity of our nation, as it gives the management of these matters to them both the most capable and the most interested in their being well and economically executed and always kept in repair. [1820]

This abhorrence of state aid arose no doubt in part from a belief in the free market and 'the dispensations of Providence'; but it also had a more political origin, in concepts of legitimate influence. The hostility was directed rather at *state* aid than at *aid* itself. Private intervention was legitimate influence. That was positively encouraged. On one occasion, 'Parliament itself asked the King to advance money from the Civil List to aid the East End of London, where there was no great magnate to undertake the role of local benefactor.' [18]

Loch's ideas mixed eighteenth-century whiggery and nineteenth-century political economy. He re-emphasized the primacy of land – a notion reinforced perhaps by the teachings of Ricardian economics, that land would benefit in the long run, given the increase of population and of the gross national product. A commitment to *laissez-faire* involved a commitment to planning and to education, in their widest senses, fusing the instrumentally and the morally right. A key text here is provided by Lord William Bentinck, in evidence to a Select Committee on India in 1837: 'The great want of the Eastern world may be comprehended in a single word "knowledge". I look to steam navigation as the great engine of working moral improvement.' [19] This whole association of ideas was caricatured by contemporaries – the 'Steam Intellect Society' was Thomas Love Peacock's name for it. [20] But it must be distinguished from cruder assertions of the sanctity of self-interest, which also claimed descent from Adam Smith. 'How, in serving himself, does the merchant greatly serve society! How wonderful is the scheme of things produced by the desire for gain!' marvelled one such debaser of the Smithian currency. [21]

The 'desire for gain' did not mean that lunches were free: of that Loch had no doubt. Everything had its cost. To do one thing was not to do another. Education was essential. It trained men to weigh up options, to plan, to discriminate, to impose order. Loch advocated a standard gauge for the newly developing railway lines which would soon become a network. And he chastised Lord Clive, who had refused to discuss, plan and compromise the interests of a canal of 'his' with a Stafford promoted railway, for displaying 'a blindness to enquiry which I have always seen attend the losing party'.[22]

But the Stafford plans for their Scottish estates went grievously awry. Their attempts to check the increasing under-employment and degrading poverty of the Highlands by the shifting of the population to the coastal areas and the introduction of large-scale sheep farming resulted in some of the most notorious of the Highland Clearances. Again the eighteenth and nineteenth centuries struggle for the soul of James Loch. When berated for his role in the clearances, he responded by denouncing those who made it 'a necessary part of their patriotism to abuse loudly all alterations that are made for the improvement of their country', and those 'English philanthropists who like any story, if it consists of lamentable details of cruelty and oppression, especially if occasioned by the better orders of society'. There, in 1820, spoke the rationalizer, the manager, the improver, holding in contempt the sentimentalist and the conservative, the radical and the do-gooder. One commentator aptly applauded Loch for siding with the economics of Adam Smith as against those of Oliver Goldsmith. Yet this same Loch was heir too to that eighteenth-century political economy which had concerned itself with the stages of civilization and the relationship between economy and culture as mediated by politics and law. He knew that 'the ancient customs of a people are not to be rashly innovated upon'. The issue – development or expropriation, reconstruction or destruction – was brought to a head not by Loch but by the family's great sheep farming tenant, Patrick Sellar, who wrote his name clearly in the annals of infamy by the crass vigour, to put it no stronger, with which he 'cleared' Strathnaver in 1814. It was bad enough that – as one 'sentimentalist' put it – 'a pastoral and poetical people' had been recreated as 'a plodding and commercial race': worse were Sellar's methods and, in the long run, even more confusing (and financially costly) was the continuing failure of Sutherland to develop into a second Lancashire.

The whole story has a sad conclusion. The Second Marquis, himself a reformer, lost his nerve as a public figure. Whereas many a nobleman continued to look down from his castle on to the town below, Stafford was not able to face up to the challenge of Stoke and the Potteries from his nearby Trentham. He withdrew from politics.

Then, faced by troublesome industrial relations, he abandoned direct working of the colleries. 'The roles of aristocrat and captain of industry had become incompatible,' notes Dr Richards. Stafford's son was to take the process a stage further, threatening the estate by lavish expenditure which frequently outran income and forced the sale of land. The consumer and the rentier had triumphed.

Postwar depression and uncertainty   The sheer scale of Stafford's estate and the diversity of his interests allowed him to tide most of his farms over the years of depression after the end of the Napoleonic wars. But many others were not so fortunate. Their resentment and sullen confusion was mercilessly captured by Byron:

> Alas, the country! How shall tongue or pen
> Bewail her now *un*country gentlemen?
> The last to bid the cry of warfare cease,
> The first to make a malady of peace.
> For what were all these country patriots born?
> To hunt, and vote, and raise the price of corn?
> But corn, like every mortal thing, must fall,
> Kings, conquerors, and markets most of all.
> . . . . [Bonaparte] amplified to every lord's content
> The grand agrarian alchymy, high *rent*.
>   (*The Age of Bronze*, 1822–3, st. 14)

The farmers became disgruntled. They turned their energies from scientific farming to political agitation. Such alienation could lead men to support a parliamentary reform which would (among other things) increase county representation at the expense of rotten boroughs monopolized by executive minded, rootless administrators.

The government was no mere tool at the disposal of the landed interest. It saw its essential task after 1815 as being to maintain public order and to ensure food supplies. Beyond that it had no comprehensive policy and no ideological commitment one way or the other, to free trade or to protection. It did appreciate the interdependence of the various sectors of the economy. So did some of the spokesmen for the landed interest, but their conclusions were very different. The interdependence they envisaged merely confirmed the priority of the land. All agreed that the French wars had created an *artificial* economy. They did not speak in terms of *development*. Lord Liverpool emphasized the artificiality of the agricultural boom: 'I am fully satisfied that the [great] principal cause of that distress was the quantity of land that was brought under the Plough in the last years of the war in consequence of the [very] high prices of Corn.' Old land ought to be improved; but attempts to maintain income by increasing output, to bring marginal and waste land into cultivation, aided by government grant, would only exacerbate the problem. On the other hand, Lord Kenyon, a Lancashire landowner, identified the uncertainty and depression as originating in the war's stimulus to 'so vast a population to be employed in manufacture'. Now the market was glutted but the poor rate system encouraged employers of labour to keep on too many hands: an 'artificial state'.[23]

I will return later to notions of 'artificiality'. The point here is that government sought desperately to stabilize the economy. The general opinion was that the entrepreneur had over-extended himself. He must learn patience, insisted Lord Redesdale, in 1828: 'our old traders did not make fortunes *in a minute* but they generally died rich, the result of constant moderate gains on regular trade'. This was not true, of course, but it was reassuring, that one might go back to what the imagination insisted was a more predictable age. And the ideas of learning by, and of salvation through, suffering were correspondingly widespread: 'we shall be the better', thought Gladstone's father in 1826, 'for passing through the ordeal'. There was little comfort for the labouring classes during the painful period of redeployment, of a 'shake-out' of labour. Prime Minister Liverpool's opinion in 1827 was that

> there is no prospect of the hand-looms ever being able to compete again with the power-looms. This must throw an immense population out of employment, and be the cause of appalling distress till the individuals interested shall have been dispersed and engaged in other pursuits.

So the country passed through the traumatic years from the Luddites to Captain Swing. Voices as callous as that of the office-holder Charles Arbuthnot – who opined that scarcity 'would not be thought to exist at all, were it not necessary for every one in this country to be swelled out with beef and pudding and strong liquors'[24] – were seldom heard in the making of economic policy, but this was no comfort to even the most loyal weaver or agricultural labourer. Yet there could be no going back to the pre-war economy, though it may have been less 'artificial'. Social ideology, political power and the sheer fact of economic and demographic change dictated that. There was to be no return to a tradition of government intervention in the economy, no reintroduction of the paternalist legislation that had been hacked away during the wars. In the uncertainty and resentment of the depression the grudges and bitterness of the labourer were liable to be equated with the determination and rancour of the radicals. So it is to the relations between the working man and the state – and to what E. P. Thompson sees as 'the making of the English working class' – that we now move.

The consciousness of the labourer   The contribution of the working man to the England of these years – his initiative and his response – has been variously interpreted. It changed through time: the experiences of a labourer born in 1780, as he moved through the life cycle, were very different from those of another born in 1800. It was dependent upon tradition – of life as it had been on the farm in the old village, in Ireland. It echoed individual temperament. It could depend upon the state of the economy:

> He had, by his industry, been able to earn about £3 or £4 a week, and while this was the case, he never meddled with politics; but when he found his income reduced to 10s a week, he began to look about him. . . . And what did he find? Why, men in power, who met to deliberate how they might starve and plunder the country.[25]

Once information had been obtained, ideas implanted, the radical *potential* was rarely lost. Individual education played its part in awakening interest in the world outside one community, in a world as it had been, might yet become, or as it could be imagined: Cobbett's reading of Swift's *Tale of a Tub* revealed to him a world of possibility. The structure of the local community was crucial in encouraging or in confounding the initiative of the working man, and in determining the forms of association. Birmingham, dominated by an artisan tradition, was no Manchester, where the factory predominated. The options for the labourer and the artisan were many. Some, threatening arson or murder, insisted that 'we are fully Determin'd to Destroy Both Dressing Machines and Steam Looms'. Others looked beyond machine-breaking: 'We know that every machine for the abridgement of human labour is a blessing to the great family of which we are a part.'[26] Some looked to Owenism and co-operation, others to violence – and a *coup d'état*.

The atmosphere became highly charged. On both the national and local levels, in political and in economic arenas, divergent class interests and cultures were becoming deeply rooted. The nervousness of a frightened middle class and the policies of a determined government continued to add to the sense of unstable friction. When Prime Minister Perceval was assassinated in 1812, many felt a sense of release, now that the battle lines were clearly drawn. One could speak in fear of, or look in hope to, an overturn of government. Anything appeared possible. But I am less confident than Thompson of the relevance of the term 'insurrectionary' to describe much of the activity, confused and despairing, purposive and resilient, of these years.[27]

Thompson describes the germination of a working-class consciousness within an 'opaque society', a society that was barely accessible or even visible to outsiders. The New Connexion Methodists, 'tinged with Jacobinism', met in Leeds 'in the midst of a dense, poor, and unruly population, at the top of Ebenezer Street, where strangers of the middle class could not reasonably be expected to go'.[28] How could such a society be won over, reintegrated? The national government and the evangelical reformers wished to divert its attention, 'put it back on the rails'. And then the relative economic prosperity of the 1820s after the lean years of the 1810s completely altered the picture. Would a man with a full stomach become an agitator? The political radicals of the middle class wished to bend the energies of labourers and artisans to their own ends; Francis Place led a sustained campaign to win the allegiance of the labourer for what he saw as constructive, *useful*, Benthamite radicalism. The labourer must place himself under the educational and moral tutelage of the middle class. 'It is to the *middle* class now, as at *other* times, that the salvation of all that ought to be dear to Englishmen ought to be confided. . . . It is from *this* class . . . that whatever of good may be obtained must proceed.' The Benthamite concern for structural reform of the instruments of power and government – the law not least – had much to commend it. But it did not appeal to the emotions of the working man. And its spokesmen – Brougham, in particular, and Place's friend, Joseph Hume – were tainted. 'Mr. Hume opposed our Bill on Dr. A. Smith's grounds of letting Trade alone' reported the Nottingham radical, Grosvenor Henson, after one parliamentary passage of arms. Benthamite radicalism rejected a sense of history, of community roots: 'we really think we cannot better advance the cause of reform than by excluding from the consideration of the subject, all allusions to a former state of society'. Nor was it comforting to the labourer to be told that the supposedly paternalist legislation whose going was so lamented had in fact itself been directed *against* the working man.[29]

Rightly suspicious of outside aid, the labouring man could look to his fellows. This could be through the mediation of a man like Cobbett, whose role in the creation of 'a common discourse' Thompson has brilliantly delineated. It could come through the local community – through benefit societies, trades unions and discussion groups. There was a premium on conversation in Rochdale and in Barnsley as much as there was in fashionable circles. Historians have lavished much attention on denying or affirming the existence and 'meaning' of those 'nocturnal meetings' to which the informations and letters in the Home Office papers make so many allusions; but as interesting are the equally frequent stories which begin along the lines of 'I fell in with three men on the road from Manchester to Bolton and soon we got talking about the times. . . .' And the labourer could look to God and to his Methodist teachers, whose searching and insistent message was that the listeners' energies must be 'displaced from expression in personal and in social life and confiscated for the service of the Church'. From Hazlitt at the beginning of the nineteenth century – the Methodists are 'a collection of religious invalids' – to Lecky towards the end of the century – 'a more appalling system of religious terrorism, one more fitted to unhinge a tottering intellect and to darken and embitter a sensitive nature, has seldom existed' – and on to E. P. Thompson, the Methodist character has been dissected by historians. That it responded to the preachers' call for obedience and cut itself off from much radical activity seems clear.[30]

To Thompson Methodist anti-intellectualism, on the one hand,

and the clique of Benthamites epitomized by Francis Place, on the other, represented the great threats to a developing working-class culture. The key was in Benthamite political economy, insidious and degrading. In the 1810s and 1820s there had been some evidence that the establishment, or rather the political nation, was divided: the Whig Fitzwilliam, for example, resigned from the Lord Lieutenancy of Yorkshire after Peterloo. The life of Fox was still relevant. The Whigs stood out for civil liberty, for legal reform, maybe even for peace. But the working man never really got the benefit of *this* aristocratic, libertarian, eighteenth-century 'liberalism'. The Whigs in power in the 1830s were taken over by economic 'liberalism', by a 'middleocracy . . . the sham-liberal pauper-starving Malthusian crew' who 'may . . . be very friendly to Reforms of all sorts and sizes, both in church and state; they may also be in favour of the abolition of all monopolies except their own, those of mill-men and placemen'.[31] They were typified by the two MPs elected for the new constituency of Leeds in 1832: T. B. Macaulay (journalist, historian-to-be and immediate past client of Lord Lansdowne, whose family seat at Calne he had occupied in the previous Parliament) and John Marshall Jr, son of the great flax-spinner and 'in-comer' to the Lake District.

And so by the mid 1830s, a case was made out for Tory radicalism:

> I admit the Tory stands opposed to you as Radicals, but the Whig stands opposed to you as poor men. The Tory pities and would fain remove in his own time and way that poverty and distress which, in their own times and ways, the Whigs endeavour at once to increase, to perpetuate, and to punish.[32]

But in the meantime, England had had to face a far more abrupt challenge to liberties and liberty, from the actions of its government in the repressive policies designed 'to maintain public order'. The episodes are well known: Spa Fields and Peterloo, the use of informers, the Six Acts. And as Thompson points out, 155 barracks were erected in England before 1815: a visible, looming presence, an embodiment of one kind of order. Barrack building was but one aspect of the reordering of the townscape; and it is to the ambiguity – control and release, repression and energy, knowledge and profit, submission and incarceration, change and stability – of urban 'improvement' that I wish now to turn.

Order and energy: the ambiguity of improvement The eighteenth century – often thought of as, *par excellence*, the aristocratic century, the century of the landed interest – had seen a boom in culture for the urban middling classes. It saw the dawn of the development of leisure activity, of enjoyment, on the one hand, and of an obsession with voluntary association, with self-sacrifice and dedication to charitable work, to purposive, public activity, on the other. These characteristics survived after the 1780s, into an age of greater political tension and social division.

The provinces were becoming alike. A nationwide culture of the middling classes long preceded that of the working man. The theatres in Penzance and in Richmond, Yorkshire, appear to have had the same designer. Assembly Rooms, Philharmonic Societies, Infirmaries, Circulating Libraries dotted the land. They were nearly all urban enterprises (perhaps the Assembly Rooms were more likely to be the forum for a 'landed invasion': the York Assembly Rooms, for example, were central to the dominance of first the Marquis of Rockingham and then his heir, Earl Fitzwilliam, in county politics). Civic improvements were forerunners of the great townscapes of the Victorian era. Assembly Rooms were to the eighteenth century what Town Halls would be to the nineteenth. Typically, as the century closed, the balance between localism and conformity was a fine one. Local designs for town and shire halls fell out of favour. To prove the worth of one's town, an architect of national repute had to be called in and this implies an acceptance of professional judgement and of national experience.

Carlisle's experience of improvement is instructive.[33] Economic development came slowly to this border town, only really at ease after the failure of the Jacobite invasion in 1745. The government's need to control the border led to the completion of a road network east to Newcastle and south to Lancaster. Then after the turn of the century, the local élite called in Thomas Telford to redesign the city centre (Telford had previously been employed by the government to consider anew the national communications – not least after the 1798 rising in Ireland). Carlisle had looked jealously at improvements in Chester and Lancaster, just as Chelmsford had looked over its shoulder at Hertford. So we have economic development, communications (prompted by military need), civic pride – and an individual line in radical expression: when Richard Southey visited the town, the curtains around his bed were decorated with radical icons. Much improvement in the city was to be done by Robert Smirke, who had previously been employed by Lord Lonsdale at Lowther Castle. The city walls ('now, it is hoped, for ever useless') were to be demolished. They were 'a circumscribing nuisance, confining the air . . . and fostering diseases'. Their destruction angered Sir Walter Scott, who lamented in 1828, 'I have not forgiven them for destroying their quiet old walls and building two lumpy things like madhouses.' These 'lumpy things' were the bastions of the new citadel, which was part of a 'sufficient and proper Shire Hall, Court House, or Court Houses and other offices for holding the Assizes'. Improvement implied the distinct assertion of the physical presence of law and order. Was it something to be proud of? William Cobbett was scornful of the jails:

> Nothing speaks the want of reflection in the people so much as the self-gratulation which they appear to feel in these edifices in their several towns. Instead of expressing shame at these indubitable proofs of the terrible increase of misery and of crime, they really boast of these 'improvements', as they call them.[34]

Everywhere these developments were imposing: 'handsome . . . though rather out of scale with the rest of Carlisle', comments Pevsner.[35] Precisely. Shire Hall, Assize Courts and jail remain the most imposing pre-Victorian secular buildings in many a county town. In Exeter and Lincoln the close association of justice and the military was alarming and symptomatic, even though the new law was housed within the mere ruins of a castle. And in working-class 'memory' the associations of order remained, the state's impact interwoven with the 'triumph' of the capitalist: 'All reet and left, up away to bastile and barracks was all common. . . . They built barrack at one end and church at 'tother' – and mills, too.[36]

Carlisle's entrepreneurs were active at the same time: there was one bank in 1798 and four by 1811, a savings bank, the Solway Canal, gas lighting (crucial for the policing of the town), new bridges and (at the close of our period) a rapidly constructed railway over the Pennines to Newcastle (1829–38) and the then (1836) largest cotton mill in England. This expansive spirit was matched by the city's cultural and philanthropic presence: a newspaper in 1798, three in the 1820s, a Female Visiting Society, an Infants Clothing Society, schools, a theatre, a Fine Art Academy.

In characteristic nineteenth-century fashion the political, the economic and the cultural merge at the end of our period with the opening of the Mechanics Institute in 1824 and a News Room in 1837. Progress, in Carlisle as in the nation, was about to triumph; energy was about to dismiss overt controls. The eye is now caught as much by the railway station (1847) as by the citadel. But the relationship of order and improvement remained to be clarified and – as Carlisle's history illustrates – the victory of economic energy over political control was close indeed.

Man in the polity

Whiggery and the French Revolution   The ideological and the physical war against Revolutionary France came to dominate English public life. But 1789 was not a gulf, cutting off all that went before. Rather arguments of the eighteenth century – and especially of the 1780s – continued through the 1790s and beyond. The French Revolution was a bridge, over which people passed into a new age, continuing their old disputes on the way.

For the Whig leaders the fateful years were 1782–4. Then George III had decisively, contemptuously, rejected them and had installed the young William Pitt as Prime Minister, in despite of the Whig majority in the Commons. Executive monarchy, court influence triumphed. State, it appeared, held society in thrall. Pitt had no feeling for his heritage. He surrounded himself by a mere 'subservient squad'.[37] The Whigs engaged in a sustained attempt to refurbish the term 'aristocratic' and to oppose the monarchy of George and the ministry of Pitt.

Debate about the state of France and Anglo-French relations was intense in the 1780s. Shelburne and his friends (including Priestley and Bentham) enjoyed close links with the leaders of the late Enlightenment in France. Burke's hatred for Shelburne, ripened in 1782–4, helped to prompt his critical scrutiny of France in and after 1789. Yet Paine had been writing to Burke as late as 1788 in optimistic vein about the possibilities for a better understanding between the two countries. The *ancien régime* could change itself; all would benefit. The optimism, even internationalism, underlying the Anglo-French trade treaty of 1786 were to reappear later; England would prosper with, not at the expense of, other nations: 'Any measure which tended to increase the wealth of foreign nations was calculated to produce an increase of our own.'[38] It was also plausible to argue that in 1789 the French were doing what the English had done in the seventeenth century, particularly in 1688; that is, they were ridding themselves of absolute monarchy, plumping for constitutional, balanced government. The theme for the Latin Essay Prize at Cambridge in 1790 was: 'Whether the French Revolution is likely to prove advantageous or injurious to this country?' Advantageous thought the winner. The optimists were making the running.

But Burke's *Reflections on the Revolution in France and on the Proceedings in Certain Societies relative to that Event* – the latter is as important a concern as the former – changed the debate immediately it was published in November 1790. Where Burke led, many were to follow. George III thought the tract one which all gentlemen ought to read. Wordsworth was to find his way back to Burke's path:

> Genius of Burke! forgive the pen seduced
> By specious wonders . . .
> > > (*The Prelude*, 1850, VII, lines 512–13)

After reading the Reverend Richard Price's *Discourse on the Love of our Country*, Burke had determined to 'set in a full View the danger from [the] wicked principles and [the] black hearts' of the dissenting radicals and French sympathisers.[39] Burke's pamphlet won him new allies; it lost him old friends in the Whig party. Few Whigs followed, few understood. This was most distressing. The sedition of the artisan was perhaps to be expected. And Burke knew that there was an unfortunate tendency to remember the Civil Wars of the 1640s rather than the Glorious Revolution of 1688 as the key event in England's seventeenth-century history. Men like Richard Price had even essayed a different, radical, interpretation of 1688. But what was not predictable was the willingness of so many of Burke's

Whig colleagues to take the 'popular' line, to renege on all Burke believed that they and their late leader, the Marquis of Rockingham, had represented. This was a bitter personal blow for Burke, who sensed and knew that the French Revolution of 1789 and all it foretold mocked everything about the English Revolution of 1688 which the Whigs claimed to personify. So Burke, in his *Letter to a Noble Lord* (1795), attacked the sheer foolishness of radical chic: the French revolutionaries 'are the Duke of Bedford's natural hunters; and he is their natural game'.[40]

Of this Burke was sure: that it was Fox and his friends, not he, who had changed, who were the deserters. So Burke could not be happy at Pitt's side. Pitt was doing a vital job, yes. But his administration lacked the spontaneous integrity, the 'clubability' of the Rockingham Whigs of old. And to the Duke of Portland (in characteristic language of property and inheritance) the government lacked moral force, 'consistency of conduct as a security as a title for confidence'.[41] But Portland came to see the necessity of Pitt and joined his ministry in July 1794.

On the other hand, Fox found it difficult to maintain what he considered was the central Whig ideology. Fox emphasized the struggle with George and with Pitt in 1782–4 as the key experience in the Whig past. More general, more positive justifications of whiggery were now less easy to construct without giving hostages to a radical fortune. Paine, Thelwall and others were already taking over and transforming much Whig *language* to help establish their own radical position. Here is one reaction to Fox's behaviour at a Whig Club dinner in December 1792:

> he explain'd the grounds of his constitutional creed by comments upon the ordinary toasts of the Club, the wording of which, when taken abstractedly, we all might, and all do cordially subscribe to, but I must say, when coupled with the times, and with the constructions and uses, these statements and sentences have continually put upon them by others, his commenting on them at all does not meet with my approbation.[42]

Fox's 'attachment' to the Revolution in France was mocked by Burke: it 'has been great and long and, like a cat, he has continued faithful in the house long after the Family has left it'.[43] The French

Revolution had, from 1789 to the September Massacres, the execution of Louis XVI and the Terror, changed; and so had British politics. Fox tried not to acknowledge this, tried to subsume both changes, impossibly, into traditional whiggery.

Whiggery retained its social base through to Victoria's reign – from Fox to Holland, Grey, Durham, Althorp. But it lost much of its language, its own means of expressing its cause. It is this, and not the vagaries of his behaviour or the deviousness of his evil mind ('I have a natural partiality for what some people call rebels' [44]), though both were considerable, that explains Fox's hapless move to the 'left' in the 1790s. Fox's Whig party was an aristocratic party set over against the king and his tools, a party *for* not *of* the people. But opposition to the king and his administration became every day less the prerogative of the 'aristocracy', more that of the people, of those outside the political nation. And the transformation of political *participation* was matched and intensified by that transformation of the *matter* of politics which the processes of industrialization and of population growth were ensuring.

Pitt moved to efficient administration; Portland, as Home Secretary, to internal security; Burke to international reaction. Fox dangled his feet in the bracing/chilling waters of radicalism, but kept his (substantial) bulk firmly on the bank of the aristocratic eighteenth century. Pitt, he wrote petulantly, 'is not a man capable of acting fairly, and on a footing of equality with his equals'.[45] Fox's approach to politics, not that of the dilettante yet not that of the professional, he passed on to his successors, Grey and Holland. The Whigs were apparently indifferent to – even disdainful of – office right through to the Reform Crisis of 1829–32. The administrators, the men of business, were Tories.

Fox believed the French Revolution to be 'the greatest event that ever happened for the happiness of mankind'. But, he argued, the French must work out their own destiny. 'I can never allow that while we agree about what ought to be the constitution of our own country, it can be of any importance how far we do so about what passes in France.' [46] So much for Burke. Fox's revulsion against Pitt's war was deep: it had *created* in France the kind of government, the 'principles' of conduct, which it claimed to be attacking. To Wordsworth, in a variant of this line of argument, Pitt's war thrust legitimacy upon a base regime:

> In France, the men, who, for their desperate ends,
> Had plucked up mercy by the roots, were glad
> Of this new enemy.
>
> (*The Prelude*, 1805, X, lines 308–10)

The war brought disorder and terror to France, corruption and tyranny to England: 'When it does not find sedition, it creates it,' said Sheridan of Pitt's regime.[47] Fox fretted against Pitt. He could not abide George. Yet he found Paine's call for an entire change of system an irrelevance. Paine believed that events in America and France emphasized that England had no constitution, was ruled by naked power. Burke believed that the evils of revolutionary France highlighted the blessings of the British constitution and quite overshadowed the old meanness of George and Pitt. Fox believed that the struggle against the new regime in France underlined the corruption of the good old British constitution by Pitt and George. What had been remained of prime importance. Visiting France after the peace of Amiens (1802), Fox did not study the Napoleonic regime; he read in the diplomatic archives, accumulating material for his history of England in the late 1680s. For him, George III was James II reincarnated. Paine – and the publication statistics bluntly show this – created and captured the spirit of the age. Fox could only toy with it. His followers remained trapped by their past:

> to describe . . . Whig Principles . . . in general would be easy enough. Economy, retrenchment, enquiry into the abuses of Power, a salutary principle of reform applied to the corruptions of the Government and the Parliament, and a resistance to wild and impracticable theories, which are equally incompatible with the British constitution, and with a settled government. But the details of a regular [system?] founded on these principles will I fear be found very difficult, perhaps almost impossible for an Opposition to lay before the publick, and at all events, perhaps, impolitick and inconvenient.[48]

Changes in the economy and in economic ideology had penetrated the citadels of Whiggery: among the 'wild and impracticable theories' were attempts to intervene in the market. In his *Memoirs* Lord Holland, the Whig patron and cousin of C. J. Fox, poured scorn on the rearguard action of the paternalists in this new age, on those men like Lord Kenyon who 'always foster the narrow minded maxims of past times'[49] (Kenyon we have met denouncing the preponderance of manufactures). The Whigs were trying to convince themselves that theirs was not a creed of the dead past; that the battle against executive monarchy, and all its corruption, was a continuing one, relevant, even paramount. But before 1830 that creed had not showed itself to be one attuned to an industrial future. In the 1830s a new creed was to do this with a vengeance.

Order   Argument over the ordering of society was fierce and fundamental. Ought individuals to be released to follow their own interest, or restrained and guided towards a 'national' interest? How could public order be maintained outside traditional communities, in the teeming metropolis and in the new manufacturing town with no resident Justice of the Peace?

There were those who saw fulfilment in the release of economic energies and not in their containment. The *release* of energy, the lauding of the individual, acting freely in the marketplace, indirectly benefiting all, became a prime ideological concern.

> Selfishness, the care of self – both in high and low is the only effectual Motive which causes or can cause the well being of all the orders of Society – and . . . what is called Liberality . . . must for the same reason go to ruin all human well being.[50]

But while some were to be freed, others were to be regimented. Hence another ideological (and practical) priority was the *disciplining*, the ordering of men for their economic tasks. Labourers indeed knew that equation between 'time, work-discipline and industrial capitalism' about which E. P. Thompson has written.[51] 'Clockwork' received its modern meaning late in the eighteenth century. Reacting against this mechanistic ideology, Blake denounced Newton, and the Romantics adopted the imagery of wind and water. Capitalism was at once aggressive, rampant, a matter of risk – and cautious, a matter of the margin, of calculation. 'Calculation, when founded upon knowledge of the subject, prepares a man for losses, and puts anxiety, in a rational mind, at great distance.'[52] Predictability is one order of the day. Man calculates, reasons, dominates. Custom is superannuated; ordered, rational recreation is required. A new breed of managers were created and themselves created a 'work force'.

The question of order was given an acutely *public* turn by the French Revolution; after 1789 the matter of order, public order, could never be separated from the matter of Jacobinism. It became specifically political, explicitly ideological. The contribution of the 'new political economy' also warped old traditions, old understandings. Paternalism was out: it was unnatural interference. It encouraged licence. Crowd activity was now seen clearly as 'a violent and unjustifiable attack on property pregnant with the most fatal consequences'. Selling grain below the 'market price' and other such traditional, no doubt temporary, expedients 'cannot in the nature of things be justified'.[53] Precisely how Portland, the Home Secretary, whose language has been quoted here, came to this view of 'the nature of things' we do not know: the ideology and practice of order has, unfortunately, barely been investigated.

Old legislation encouraging intervention in the market was repealed according to the dictates of the new political economy; whilst order necessitated a whole range of repressive legislation at various times through the 1790s for a generation: freedom of speech was restricted and freedom of association, habeas corpus, suspended, and so on. Ought not the sale of beer after 6 p.m. be prohibited, ventured one Midland Justice of the Peace. And what of parliamentary debate and its publication: 'was it a desirable thing that the public at large, that the lower classes of the community from one end of the kingdom to the other, should, from day to day, be told' of the disagreements about the conduct – even the very necessity – of the war against France?[54]

And so concern for discipline and predictability – essentially economic and cultural matters – joined a determination to maintain public order to produce an uncertainty about the right to associate, either for economic purposes or for political. The appearance of an *orderly crowd* was most perturbing:

> that very ORDER they cried up before
> Did afterwards gall them the thousand times more,
> When they found that these men, in their 'Radical Rags',
> March'd peaceably on, with their Banners and Flags.[55]

Such challenging self-restraint notwithstanding, the men of the day arrived at the notion of order as *control*, by law and by military force, in ways often alien to the whole English tradition. And this control was backed up by suasion, blackmail, vigilantism, violence and guilt by association. In Wilberforce's words, 'it ought never to be forgotten, that men who expose themselves to suspicion must often incur the disadvantages of guilt'.[56] The Yeomanry backed their horses through the windows of a radical's shop; followers of John Reeves's Association for the Preservation of Liberty and Property against Republicans and Levellers (1792–7) played on, as well as created, community hostilities; radicals were watched (for example, Coleridge and Wordsworth in the Quantocks in 1798; Blake had been arrested on the Medway during the American War). Worse was the use of informers and agents provocateurs, about whose role Thompson has written so eloquently. Yet, on the one hand, this was more than a mere 'panic of property'. It was the expression of a deep revulsion against revolutionary France as well as of a fear, reasoned as well as unreasoning, of the labourer and the manufacturing town in which he lived. And, on the other, order had to be kept by a government whose powers remained restricted and whose agents were few in number and limited in resources.

Later, the eighteenth-century commitment to decentralization – now tinged with the ideology of self-help – reasserted itself:

> We must have an army in peace to protect the Metropolis, including as it does, the King, the Parliament, and the Bank. We must have a regular force likewise for the protection of our Dock Yards, and other great public depots – but the Property of the Country must be taught to protect itself. . . . I should be sorry therefore to think that any thing that is now doing should induce the Magistrates of the West Riding of Yorkshire to place their whole, or even their principal, Reliance upon Government. Government may and will assist them, but their chief support must be from Themselves.[57]

Hence the local control of our police forces. But in the 1790s the Home Office had moved from sending out agents to take the provincial temperature to urging the construction of barracks; this building programme began in 1792. Barracks overawed a town and isolated soldiers from the contagion of radicalism. All this raised the spectre of a standing army, a fear of two centuries, still alive in the 1840s when rural police forces were likened to 'the worst kind of standing army'.[58] The very atmosphere of England was contaminated by the military: the artist Haydon noticed it at Dover:

> the respect and awe every person had for the military, as if they were tinctured by the opposite coast. 'You mustn't walk there, or here, or to this place' was in every body's mouth.[59]

And Wordsworth felt a perversion of the purpose of government:

> Our Shepherds, this say merely, at that time
> Thirsted to make the guardian crook of law
> A tool of murder. . . .
> . . . they leagued
> Their strength perfidiously to undermine
> Justice, and make an end of Liberty.
> *(The Prelude*, 1805, X, lines 646–58)

Yet as Wordsworth declared in Book X of the 1805 *Prelude* (excised by 1850), the very decision for war against France could be seen as

> the unhappy counsel of a few weak men   (line 293)

and not as the work of a united nation. Throughout the years of repression, individual responsibility could be assigned and individual 'shepherds' singled out. One such was the Reverend W. Hay ('instigator' of the Peterloo massacre). Another was Liverpool's Home Secretary of 1819:

> I met murder on the way –
> He had a mask like Castlereagh.[60]

Critics of E. P. Thompson, like A. D. Harvey, have insisted that really rather few men were involved in scaremongering in the provinces. Certainly the counter-revolutionary intensity of France had no parallel in England: there was no Vendée, no Gard. Women played no prominent 'conservative' role. There was no equivalent to the hold of the Roman Catholic Church on much of the French population; the anti-radical, loyalist Priestley rioters (Birmingham,

1791) with their slogan, 'No Philosophers – Church and King forever', had few successors. Though there were tentative hints, especially from Home Secretary Sidmouth around 1810, of plans to restrict the rights of Dissenters, they came to nothing. The state was – and long had been – simply 'too weak to put down dissent',[61] and the state and the established Church were not ready to produce much of a positive response to the demands and opportunities of social change. The answer could only lie, not in enforced uniformity or chaotic individualism, but in voluntary association.

Order, it could be argued, did not necessitate reaction, even repression. Voluntarism would be the principle for the willing. For the nation as a whole, strong administration was the key; this was the line taken by the Tory governments of the 1820s and exemplified by Robert Peel. The 'liberal Toryism' of that decade was helped by the more buoyant state of the economy. To minds like Peel's, what the government did was more important than how parliament was constituted. And from the 'other side', the Whigs, came the view that parliamentary reform would allow influence to be placed on a more honest, reasonable basis. The idea of parliamentary reform could, by the late 1820s, be discussed and taken seriously as it had been in the early 1780s before 1789 had forced it off the agenda of British politics. No great change was anticipated in what a reformed parliament would actually do. John Marshall of Leeds noted that his 'chief motive for having a seat in the House of Commons is a wish to see the mechanism by which the affairs of a great nation are conducted and to study the characters of the men who take the lead in public life, and the principles on which they act. I also desired it as being creditable to my family and an introduction to good society.' An observer not a mover, he had, the *Leeds Intelligencer* was to note, 'little capacity for mixing in the arena of legislative and party politics'.[62]

None the less, there was some broadening of horizons. As fear of the monarch – and memory of 1782–4 – receded, so the Whigs looked more sympathetically, more positively, at the urban bourgeois and professional élites. And so too reform proposals came to envisage increasing the urban electorate and strengthening urban rather than rural representation. The schemes of the 1780s had sought to expand the role of the counties, whose electorates were thought of as independent and not susceptible to executive blandishments and threats. In the 1820s the towns and their 'rulers' were accepted more on their own terms: 'The people have far more wealth and far more intelligence now, than they had in former times, and therefore they ought to have, and they must have, more political power.'[63]

For many – advocates and beneficiaries alike – this was to be a symbolic rather than a severely practical matter. Benthamite reformers, looking to a reformed House for radically revised and economical government, remained a distinct minority. Influence not opinion, interest not policy, continued to hold the ring. Symptomatically, the Reform Act of 1832 was quickly followed by procedural changes which, by restricting the time for the acceptance and discussion of petitions, reduced popular influence on parliament and strengthened the position of front as opposed to back benchers. Order would out.

Political dissent   In 'closed' villages, where one or a group of like-minded and resident proprietors owned all the land and scrutinized all employments, there were few echoes of radicalism. Such a village was Raveloe, to which George Eliot's Silas Marner was admitted ('the old linen-weaver in the neighbouring parish . . . being dead, [Silas's] handicraft made him a highly welcome settler'). In Raveloe, life went on: 'there were several chiefs . . . who could farm badly quite at their ease, drawing enough money from their bad farming, in those war times, to live in a rollicking fashion . . . and the poor thought that the rich were entirely in the right of it to lead a jolly life'. The Anglican Church went unchallenged, spiritual life languished. Raveloe's 'careless abundance' was only to be checked after 1815, by that 'fall of prices' which so stirred the landed interest and confused and contorted politics for a generation.

The peace of thoughtless unanimity was no characteristic of the 'open' village. Here there was no resident proprietor; instead, much common, waste and wood, many smallholdings, widely distributed ownership of land, separated, straggling settlement and rapidly increasing population. Agricultural earnings were supplemented by domestic handicrafts and industrial 'by-employments'. The Dissenting chapel often competed with and frequently outbid the Anglican church. Here were to be found the radical shoemaker, the visionary, the millenarian, ready in the 1790s as they had been in the 1640s. Moral and political heterodoxy were interwoven. In the north Leicestershire village of Shepshed, the Lords of the Manor had not been resident since 1683. By 1800 men and women were marrying in their early twenties, some five years earlier than had their grandparents. Here flourished the purest radicalism of the war years and, later, 'physical force' Chartism.

Two other societies which bred dissent must be mentioned. First, unknown England – the community of the miner, the tinner, the forester. The Kingswood colliers, but a step from Bristol, were notorious. Their moral isolation now came under renewed and successful attack, with Methodism in the vanguard. Cornish Methodism was a highly distinct, totally patterned, phenomenon. Second, a society like that of Cumbria lauded by Wordsworth in his emphatic restatement of one option – 'mountain liberty' – in the long debate on the effect of climate and geography on social structure and manners:

> Born in a poor district, and which yet
> Retaineth more of ancient homeliness,
> Manners erect, and frank simplicity,
> Than any other nook of English land,
> It was my fortune scarcely to have seen
> Through the whole tenor of my school-day time,
> The face of one, who, whether boy or man,
> Was vested with attention or respect
> Through claim of wealth or blood
>
> (*The Prelude*, 1805, IX, lines 217–25)

But this was to *forget* the Lowther family, who dominated the area. Later, Wordsworth's determination to help repulse the 'democratic torrent' led him to *forgive* and to applaud the perpetuity of that family's presence and the shadows it threw. That these were protective and not menacing was also the result of the different character of the new head of the Lowther family. Wordsworth's 'small independent *proprietors* of land . . . men of respectable education who daily labour on their own little properties' were a reminder, no more.[64] But the men from 'unknown' England would long remain at the heart of radical politics.

In the open villages and in the manufacturing towns and the

trading boroughs, alternative values and codes of conduct lay, resilient, adaptable, close at hand. Arguments between freemen and corporation, between freemen and outsiders, attained an almost medieval intensity in the eighteenth century in, for example, Nottingham and Liverpool. The term 'liberties' was kept in common currency, ready for that slight clipping which would turn it into 'liberty'. Charters were not now declarations of independence. Our radicals viewed 'charters and corporations' from below and outside: 'Every chartered town is an aristocratical monopoly in itself. . . . An Englishman is not free of his own country.' This is from *The Rights of Man*. Its author, Tom Paine, contrasted England unfavourably with Revolutionary France and with independent America (where the town of Boston, cherishing its Town Meeting, had long resisted incorporation). Paine's assessment of English urban life was sombre enough, but it lacked the bitterness of Blake in his shattering revision of *London*:

> I wander thro' each charter'd street,
> Near where the charter'd Thames does flow.
> And mark in every face I meet
> Marks of weakness, marks of woe.[65]

'A town without a charter is a town without a shackle,' believed William Hutton, the chronicler of Birmingham.

It was in this school of ideas – intensely local yet universally resonant – that the great radical Thomas Spence of Newcastle learnt his politics. He yearned for local, community control, and insisted on the moral priority of access to the land. The key issue in the public life of eighteenth-century Newcastle was control of the town moor. Spence saw the world as Newcastle writ large. 'Corruption' chipped away at liberty. That its forces were systematic was a perception which urban radicals in England shared with the patriots of America. 'Improvement' threatened independence, meant alienation and worse. The Jacobin novelist Bage had one of his characters argue that 'nature created no other evil for man but pain; all things else, which we call evil, spring from improvement'.[66] Alienation implied indifference; Spence would restore responsibility and reactivate citizenship; in 1801 he said, 'I would not have the Land national, nor provincial, but parochial property; that the people might be as much interested as possible, both in the improvement[!] of their Estate, which would always be under their eye, and in the expenditure of all public monies, which would be straight out of their Revenues.'

What was, what had been, was no guide to what ought to, or could be, Burke notwithstanding. A not dissimilar way of thinking led Thomas Jefferson, future American President and then American Ambassador in Paris, to muse on the desirability and practicability of the notion that 'the earth belongs to the living'. Legislation ought only to last as long as a majority of the generation enacting it was alive; one generation could not bind another. Jefferson was particularly worried by the licence for war which a 'national debt' had given the rulers of Europe. Distaste – yet fascination – for the 'national debt' was common in radical circles at the end of the eighteenth century, as it had been among Tory gentlemen at the beginning.[67]

The American conflict had not excited such a depth of feeling, such a revulsion, against war as did Pitt's:

> Say, rulers of the nations, from the sword
> Can ought but murder, pain, and tears proceed?
> Oh! What can war but endless war still breed?
> (*Salisbury Plain*, 1793–4, lines 507–9)

Thus Wordsworth in 1793–4 shared the revulsion of Blake, of the cartoonist Gillray and of many others; a revulsion which was not to be paralleled in the Napoleonic war a decade later. For in the 1790s people had looked forward, if not to the millennium, at least to the *shock* of Enlightenment:

> Let foul Error's monster race
> Dragged from their dens start at the light with pain
> (*Salisbury Plain*, 1793–4, lines 544–5)

Light was almost synonymous with reason and with truth. It was a key word, a key notion in the transmutation of eighteenth-century thought. Here is John Hurford Stone, writing from Paris to Joseph Priestley in 1790: 'It requires no uncommon degree of sagacity to foresee, that an *Ideot King*, a *slavish Hierarchy*, a *corrupt Administration*, & the *delusion of the people*, will melt like snow before the sun of truth.'[68] The italicized phrases, though forcefully put, are eighteenth-century commonplaces, but the resolution is not. It cuts through the long debate as to whether a vicious executive had corrupted the people, or whether a debauched populace was getting the rulers which it deserved. Truth reveals, extends, rights. By the 1790s this was more to the point than the notion that the study of history would recover them. Freedom from history was a possibility. William Godwin thought in terms of perfectability, not perfection. Paine put this into the terms of 'generation' so important to our age: 'Every generation is, and must be competent to all the purposes which its occasions require.'[69] This line of argument led Godwin to reject the idea of inherent natural rights.

The impact of war, the power of light – these are the keys to the radical mind. Those who emphasized the 'sun of truth' tended to political quietism. Godwin was of this persuasion: 'Discussion, reading, enquiry, perpetual communication: these are my favourite methods for the improvement of mankind, but associations, organized societies, I firmly condemn.'[70] And to the horror of his friends, Godwin disavowed open opposition to the repressive legislation of 1795. Hazlitt wrote of Godwin's friend, Thomas Holcroft, that:

> He believed that truth had a natural superiority over error,
> if it could only be heard; that if once discovered, it must,
> being left to itself, soon spread and triumph; and that the
> art of printing would not only accelerate this effect, but
> would prevent those accidents, which had rendered the
> moral and intellectual progress of mankind hitherto so
> slow, irregular, and uncertain.[71]

Printing: the word could be spread, the eager land flooded. The impact of the steam press was enormous. Passengers on London's first 'omnibuses' (1829) were given newspapers to read. Information was vital. One of the first radical societies was the Society for Constitutional Information. T. B. Oldfield, one of its officials, produced in 1792 a survey of the electoral system which underpinned much subsequent radical criticism. Information was, to paraphrase Bacon, like muck – no good lest it be spread: 'The public mind being suitably prepared by reading my little Tracts' was how Spence put it. The printers of Bath gloried in their trade: 'Hail to the Press! to thee we Britons owe / All we believe, and almost all we know.'[72] Hence 'the war of the unstamped', the crusade to force the repeal of taxes on the press, was a vital part of public life at the end of our period; hence too the attempt by Benthamite radicals to ensure that the knowledge thus spread was 'useful knowledge'. Information went to individuals, to reading rooms, benefit societies, trades unions. Burke himself had set people thinking. His *Reflections* (price, three shillings) sold 30,000 copies in a couple of years; Paine's reply, *The Rights of Man* (part one) sold 50,000 in 1791, while part two sold perhaps 200,000 in 1792–3 (that is, getting on for one household in ten). When issued in a cheap reprint, it brought down government wrath on its author. Paine was prosecuted, but the administration could leave Godwin alone as his *Political Justice* sold at three guineas.

But ought the response of order to be repression – or education? Although John Reeves of the 'Association for the Preservation of Liberty and Property . . .' insisted that his branches 'are not open Societies for talk and debate, but for private consultation and real business', the real business turned out to be not so much the prosecution of sedition as the proselytizing for order and loyalty through such tracts as 'Village Politics' by 'Will Chip', i.e. Hannah More.[73] The people had to be introduced, enlightened even, educated as to the benefits and necessity of obedience and loyalism.

Information, education, these were tough enough issues. The impact and burden of war were worse: direct, unavoidable. Everybody paid. Trade, industry, the availability of food (a problem exacerbated by bad weather) – all were grievously affected by the uncertainties of war. By 1795 'a new instructor was busy among the masses – WANT'.[74]

War necessarily prompted self-scrutiny. The labouring poor were to transform themselves into a working class not least as a result of that scrutiny. Traders and manufacturers were provoked by the unpredictability of war to look again at the political system. War involved an extension of the executive, and that meant more grist for the mill of 'old corruption'. So the investigation in 1809 of accusations that Mary Clarke, the Duke of York's mistress, was involved in 'selling' army offices was a key to future opposition/radical attacks on the government/administration. Here again our age built on an eighteenth-century tradition going back to the Public Accounts Commissions of the late seventeenth century. One of Pitt's many dying words was to the effect that Englishmen would forget the battle of Austerlitz sooner than they would the conclusions of the Accounts Commissions. And this kind of enquiry led on to thoughts of parliamentary reform; 1810, in the wake of the Mary Clarke affair, saw the first Commons motion for reform since 1797. Francis Place looked for 'good and cheap government' from a reformed parliament: policy making would be more rational, military establishments and military commitments minute.

The burden of war and what this suggested about the need to alter the structure and purpose of government, the power of light and what this suggested about the importance of political rights and education: these dominated radical discussion, and prompted organization and publication. The literature of dissent and dissatisfaction is vast. Some is exceptionally sophisticated. Some is clearly based on opposition rhetoric from earlier in the eighteenth century. Some is imbued with the language of the sentimental era. Blunt, witty, malicious, threatening: it is the sheer variety of approach, the vitality of the culture thus revealed, which is impressive. To my mind it is a pity that E. P. Thompson allows himself to speculate on how close the country was to revolution: 'if' appears too often in his book. I do not find the possibility of insurrection a helpful yardstick in discussing these years. But, on the other hand, Thompson's critics exaggerate the transitory, even the irresponsible, unorganized nature of much of the protest. That that protest grew naturally and unforced from the conditions of the day and from the political experience of the eighteenth century does not mean that it was sporadic or thoughtless. Far from it, protest was central to the whole tradition. And often in the writings of Thompson's adversaries there is an implied comment on the superior political consciousness of our own day, which seems to me disputable, to put it mildly. Thompson is right to quote Cobbett on the agricultural labourers: 'I have always maintained, that they well understood the *nature of their wrongs* and the *causes of their misery.*' [75]

This awareness and realization is sufficiently secure to resist the 'enormous condescension of posterity' (Thompson's expression) just as in its own day it resisted the patronage of the urban radical, like he who urged the Swing rioters to 'give up all these petty outrages against property, so unworthy of you, and unite for a Glorious Revolution'.[76] No doubt the sheer effervescence of the radicalism of our period could attract men for the worst of reasons.[77] No doubt attendance at meetings, at midnight cabals and so on, was exaggerated – by both sides. No doubt many agitated as a result of hunger and were satisfied with (if they could get) a full stomach. No doubt many appeared vague and unspecific: 'they seemed to be looking generally for a better state of things . . . I cannot recall their exact expression'. But the long term and the immediate *could* be fused. The burden of the past could be removed, horizons could be seen and reached for. Petty local grievances, the more irritating for being petty and local, could be redressed by collective action; the small debts courts in both Birmingham and Merthyr Tydfil were a local focus of riot yet symbolized a whole unjust polity. There was a sense of combined, converging possibilities. A hum of expectation characterized our period, as it had the 1640s and 1650s; it was evident in Sheffield, Manchester and Norwich, in Merthyr and Wem. In Merthyr the Eisteddford medals were struck off by a Jacobin from the Paris mint; in Wem Hazlitt's father told him in 1790, 'If we only think justly we shall always easily foil all the advocates of tyranny.'[78] The country had known nothing like it for a century and a half.

Man in society

Right conduct   The ideological struggle went deeper than the military. 'An army of principles will penetrate where an army of soldiers cannot' was Paine's opinion (1797). Of Paine in turn it was said that he had overthrown 'all the armies of Europe with a small pamphlet'. The anti-Jacobin resisted Jacobin principles and Jacobin arms with equal determination. The future 'would not ascribe the annihilation of thrones and altars to the armies of France'; rather it would indict 'those principles which, by dissolving domestic confidence, and undermining private worth, paved the way for universal confusion'.[79]

The anti-Jacobin stood for the *family* and for normal sexual relations. Persecution of homosexuals, in London in particular, intensified in our period; the extent of buggery in the Navy caused alarm. The radical did not necessarily see the family as the basic human unit, nor did he share Burke's enthusiasm for local attachment. Godwin fretted over the (irrational) depths of local and familial loyalty; one sharp young lady cautioned him: 'Are you sure in this case that my affections [for my family] are not the result of reason?' Godwin 'shrugged disbelief'.[80]

In the future, 'family attachment would . . . be weakened or lost in the general principle of benevolence, when every man would be a brother'.[81] And the very word 'brother', indicative of the rejection of automatic respect for the past generation, received new significance when the Anti-Slavery Society in 1787 adopted as their motto, 'Am I not a man and a brother?' Radicals revelled in denouncing parental opposition to young romance and in equating the parent with the old regime. This was to bring home the message of America's Declaration of Independence. 'Too peremptory a tone cost us America,' one of Bage's characters warns his aristocratic foe.[82] What the radical saw as the establishment of a reasonable and understanding relationship, the conservative saw as an unnatural repudiation of patriarchal control. C. J. Fox 'used always to say that he did not like to discourage the young ones'.[83] In Old England as in the new United States, this age saw the coinage of the term 'fogey' and, perhaps, the increasingly disrespectful use of 'gaffer'. Dress came to fit the young rather than to reinforce the dignity of the venerable. And, quite simply, there were more young people around, as shown in Table 4.[84]

Table 4

	England and Wales					
	Male		Female		Total	
	1791	*1821*	*1791*	*1821*	*1791*	*1821*
% under 20 yrs	42.1	49	42.5	47.6	42.3	48.3
% 20–39 yrs	26.8	28.3	26.7	28.8	26.7	28.6

Paine, as against Burke's appeal to the past, announced that 'every age and generation must be free to act for itself in all cases as the ages and generations which preceded it'. The distinction between 'age' and 'generation' is interesting, as is the relation between such claims (compare the idea that 'the earth belongs to the living') and the plea that 'posterity is vitally involved'. That confusion led Paine into tangles over the validity of contracts.[85]

These are essentially *secular* terms. The enthusiast and the millenarian were more likely to write in terms of the new day:

Bliss was it in that dawn to be alive.
But to be young was very heaven!

and

> the times are ended . . . the morning 'gins to break.[86]

Emphasis on rights tended away from concern with historical process: 'man has rights which no statutes and usages can take away'. Radicals repudiated the past: 'that which I glory in, in the French Revolution is this: that it has been upheld and propagated as a principle . . . that ancient abuses are not by their antiquity converted into virtues'. Less was heard about the glories of the Anglo-Saxon constitution. This was aimed in part at Burke. Nor were radicals satisfied with the present even as manifested in France. Indeed the present in France did not, could not, represent the true Revolution; for in France the impact of the *ancien régime* was too great to shrug off simply, and the result had been the unwilled eruption 'of the old leaven of revenge, corruption and suspicion which was generated by the systematic crudities of the old despotism'. France was struggling to create a nation founded on liberty, while England, argued C. J. Fox, would find it difficult to throw off its chains precisely because it *had* known and thought it still experienced liberty.[87]

Revolution meant the freedom of a society and also of the individual. Mary Wollstonecraft's life could be seen in its mobility and variety as signifying opportunity as well as revealing her plight. And this held for many another woman: entry into the 'free' capitalist labour market (it is argued) at once liberated the girl from the multitude of constricting community controls in the old village, and prompted the 'wish to be free'. Yet it also redoubled the difficulties of forming permanent relationships and making a living. The bourgeoisie, ideologues of the family, were destroying it – by fuelling the wish to be free and by a political economy which led inexorably to a vision of people as objects. There was a rise in the rate of illegitimacy. Wordsworth well knew how fragile was a family before the vagaries and pressures of the marketplace (and of the state); the 1801 letter to Fox, *Michael, Guilt and Sorrow, The Last of the Flock* . . . all show this to have been a continuing concern. The labouring poor – to whom the family was so frequently commended – found its security and predictability dashed away from them.

Something of the same tension between an awareness of people as individuals and an awareness of their market value can be seen in the response to children. J. H. Plumb has described 'a new world of childhood'. The young were *valued* as having their own tastes, delights, vanities, needs, as a readily exploitable market, *and* as 'counters in the parents' social aspirations'.[88]

Industrialization, modernization, democratization, the French Revolution – each in its own way altered social relations, dissolved old ties, softened old antagonisms, forged new links, provoked new animosities. A caricature of the 'new' sees it as leaving the power of class naked and unmediated:

> The mechanic and his master were left, as it were to them-
> selves. . . . It was not as in the agricultural counties where
> the peasant looked up to the farmer, the farmer to the
> landlord, the proprietor to the peer, and the peer to the
> Crown, thus forming a chain which bound together the
> highest and lowest classes of society together – on the
> contrary, the operative saw no gradation.

And the speaker, Stuart Wortley, MP, lamented the 'nonresidence of wealth and rank'.[89]

But, as we have seen, agricultural social structure, the very purpose of agriculture, was changing. And the towns – old and new – were not all of a piece. Whereas disorder in Manchester was fostered by the gulf between master and man, in Sheffield,

> the manufactures . . . are of a nature to require so little
> capital to carry them on, that a man with a very small sum
> of money can employ two, three or four men; and this
> being generally the case, there are not in this, as in other
> great towns, any number of persons of sufficient weight
> who could by their influence, or the number of their
> dependents, act with any effect in case of a disturbance.[90]

And worse, 'in the town itself there is no civil power'. That is, class hatred was provoked in such towns as Manchester, dissent in such as Sheffield: from the point of view of the Home Office what was there to choose between them? In political terms the attempt to create a deferential urban community failed, just as did the attempt to bring religion to the people. The nineteenth century was to see a battle in urban politics between the purchase of a vote and the sale of an opinion, which the latter was finally to win. But there was to be little dissent from the view that the right community was that based on the family, and it was at the end of our period that right conduct became ritualized as respectability.

Exhilaration and despair In the early 1790s prophecy was a characteristic type of thought, optimism a characteristic tone. There was a sense of the lifting of burdens, the straightening of backs. But then it became clear that political revolution was not necessarily for the best, and that economic change would not reduce the burden of labour. By the end of the Napoleonic wars, reinterpretation was the characteristic purpose of discourse, and a sense of the misapplication of those earlier possibilities a characteristic complaint or regret. To Wordsworth in 1817,

> the principal ties which kept the different classes of society in a vital and harmonious dependence upon each other have, within these thirty years, either been greatly impaired or wholly dissolved. Everything has been put up to market and sold for the highest price it would bring.

To this had the *ancien régime* and the democratic revolution alike been brought. From his vision and his confident appraisal of himself in the early 1790s ('Hence it follows that I am not among the admirers of the British constitution'), Wordsworth came through to a perception of the utter necessity of (as went the metaphor) roots or pillars:

> what else but the stability and might of a large estate, with proportional influence in the House of Commons, can counterbalance the democratic activity of the wealthy, commercial, and manufacturing districts. It appears to a superficial observer, warm from contemplating the theory of the constitution, that the political power of the great landowners ought . . . to be strenuously resisted . . . [but is there] any arrangement by which Jacobinism can be frustrated except by the existence of large estates continued from generation to generation in particular families.[91]

E. P. Thompson has spoken of 'the decline of the first Romantics into political "apostasy" – most abject in Southey, most complex in Coleridge, most agonizing and self-questioning in Words-worth'.[92] Yet this was not the apostasy of reaction. Rather it was a return to the Burke of the 1770s and 1780s, with his emphasis on the responsibility of the public person to defend *interests* against *opinions*. Thus Southey, become 'an honest alarmist . . . though he may have changed his opinions concerning governments and dema-gogues, he retains his love of mankind and zeal for the best interests of humanity'. The revolutionary decades had taught these men complexity. By 1815 Crabb Robinson thought the sentiments of the Liverpool radical, William Roscoe, 'were those of unthinking vulgar democracy, abusing Governments, and uttering general truths, which are, it is true, incontrovertible, but unmeaning without other qualifying truths added to them'. While the alarmist and notions attributed to Pitt could still be opposed (Coleridge in 1811 spoke of 'a mere panic of property'[93]), men looked back on what they had done in the 1790s with fascination and with horror – 'I aided the Jacobins. . . .'[94] The retreat from radicalism and Jacobinism was not merely a response to the promptings of class fear and personal distaste. Hope was lost, the young aged, the climate changed. Godwin used that metaphor: 'The human intellect is a sort of barometer, directed in its variations by the atmosphere that surrounds it.'[95]

The French attracted some support as silly and as unthinking as some of the hostility which they provoked (for example, those feminine raptures over the possibility of a Napoleonic invasion of England so avidly reported by Crabb Robinson). Quite apart from the destabilizing influence of the French Revolution, the mental climate in England was very variable and unpredictable.

> The great national events which are daily taking place, and the increasing accumulation of men in cities, where the uniformity of their occupations produces a craving for extraordinary incident which the rapid communication of intelligence gratifies,

had contributed to a blunting of 'the discriminating powers of the mind'. To this tendency, 'the literature and theatrical exhibitions of the country have conformed themselves'. These comments of Wordsworth, in the Preface of 1800 to the *Lyrical Ballads*, are a challenge as much to historians as to his readers. Historians have barely risen to it. I would suggest that the roots of the taste decried by Wordsworth lie deeply embedded both in a gradual revulsion among the educated élite from the rationalism of the Enlightenment *and* in a long germinating culture of commercialized leisure. These led, on the one hand, to a sapping of the moral certainty of the *ancien régime*; on the other, the turn from rationalism was itself part of a spurning of critical enquiry. Conservatism and credulity could go together at the end of the eighteenth century. And (here was work for a Coleridge) language lost its sensitivity: a revolution could be equated with an ephemeral pamphlet, as in Jane Austen's *Northanger Abbey* (ch. 14).

We know little either of the social springs of paranoia – or of nervousness. And examples of nervous illness – and of the combination, fatal to reason, of physical debility and religious hysteria – are frequent in our age. Elton Hamond, son of a city tea dealer, found his enthusiasm for 'virtue' and 'happiness' to be misplaced: 'he was at length compelled to conclude that the progress of mankind towards a state of virtuous benevolence was an almost imperceptible movement, despaired, & in his despair, shot himself'. What Wordsworth saw as a 'false sensibility and tendency to tears in the present age' went through self-pity to violent reaction: 'with the purest intentions it has always been my misfortune to be thwarted, misrepresented, and ill used in life' – this is the plea of John Bellingham, the assassin of Spencer Perceval.[96]

The exaltation and the despair of the Revolution brought together the sensibility of the age and its conception of its place in history. An opportunity to escape from history was being offered: 'London disloyal, superstitious, villainous, and infamous. An earthquake prophesied by Brothers. Many leave town'.[97] But there was to be no millennium; the age would have to redeem itself by its own efforts. It is to these that we turn.

Association and the reforming impulse Hazlitt commented upon 'this everlasting, importunate sense of personal identity' characteristic of the age, at once constraining and liberating. It was through an examination of the self that society could be examined and through association that one could act to alter that society. The English became, as never before, a nation of joiners.

Some associations, like the Smeatonian Society of civil engineers, were professional, exclusive. Others were intellectually purposive. The Cambridge Union Society dates from 1815. 1830 saw the founding of the Geographical Society and 1831 of the British Association for the Advancement of Science. Many were the associations, often local in scale, of 'economic' origin and for personal gain or security – building societies, friendly societies, benefit clubs. Some societies, cutting across class and occupation, were essentially cultural. These were frequently fluid, transitory (for example, subscription concerts). In music all were willing to have a go at a transcribed Haydn chamber music piece. Haydn, lionized, participated in London life to the full; his biographer has argued that his Symphony no. 100, first performed in London in 1794, was the last masterpiece of western music to be commonly recognized as such on its first performance.[98] In religion, association was challenging system, voluntarism was threatening establishment. Instruction became a key for evangelicals. Sunday schools proliferated. A typical one proclaimed itself, 'A school for all denominations'.[99] Association was morally purposeful, ranging from the utopian (the Society for the Promotion of Permanent and Universal Peace) to the specific (the Society for the Diffusion of Knowledge upon the Punishment of Death and the Improvement of Prison Discipline). Traditional preoccupations (the Society for the Suppression of Vice) and the concerns of the age (the Society for Superseding the Necessity of Climbing Boys) were equally compelling. Associations gave scope for a national philanthropic effort (the British and Foreign Bible Society) and for the most determined attempt to do good (the Society of Young Ladies to Sell Clothes at Reduced Prices). And association became a characteristic political device, at first of radical and conservative alike. An 'Association for the Preservation of Liberty and Property against Republicans and Levellers' was founded in November 1792. It was enormously successful in mobilizing anti-radical sentiment: 'The whole country is forming itself into associations.'[100] On the radical side the principle of association had developed from the 1760s. The Whig Party itself received much of its impetus from the Fox Clubs which celebrated its leader. Personal demonstration became mandatory: one refused sugar tainted by slave labour.

Moral reform by association and pressure became businesslike. That very word was coined in this period – by Burke in 1791.

He was followed by Treasury Secretary George Rose. The Clapham Sect supported formal training of the clergy. Training involved preparation and knowledge; moral reform was part of a concern for qualification and utility. Written examinations were instituted at Oxford (1800); the foundations of the Royal Military College, Sandhurst, were laid; the term 'general practitioner' came into use, and, with it, an appropriate magazine, the *Lancet*.

The greatest of the moral reform movements was undoubtedly that which led to the abolition of the slave trade in 1806–7, so largely the work of Wilberforce, yet crowning too the career of C. J. Fox. Abolition kept alive the relationship between moral and political reform, for 'the raising of the slavery question in any form necessarily raised the whole question of the limits of authority over other men'.[101] The concerns of the Enlightenment crossed over the bridge of anti-slavery into the causes of nineteenth-century radicalism. The relationship between support for anti-slavery and a commitment to a free labour market at home was close if complicated. 'Slavery' was given renewed relevance as a term in the investigation of domestic social conditions. In *Emma* (ch. 35) Jane Austen equated the 'governess trade' with the slave trade. The penetration of the whole society by slavery was frequently suggested. Thus Fuseli was impressed by the 'improvements' of London (1806), but 'methinks I everywhere smell the blood of slaves'.

> Fuseli: Be Gode its like the smoke of de Israelites making bricks.
> Haydon: It is grander for it is the smoke of a people who would have made the Egyptians make bricks for them.
> Fuseli: Well done, John Bull.[102]

We return to the ambiguity of improvement. Godwin's friend, Holcroft, thought that nature had given pain but that all other evils were the result of improvement. Now cruelty itself was attacked. This was closely related to the very improving urge itself; revulsion against cruelty to animals sprang from distaste for the customs of the perpetrator of that cruelty. He must, as we have seen, be taught rational recreation. Wordsworth well knew what the profession of arms did to a man: see the textual changes which transformed *Salisbury Plain* into *Guilt and Sorrow*. Holcroft, after discussing vegetarianism, argued that the 'habit of putting [animals] to death, probably injures that class of men (butchers whose office it is), and that they communicate the injury in part to society. This evil I think might be greatly remedied.' [103] (Communication is used to signify the passing of disease as of knowledge. Burke uses it as a synonym for sexual intercourse.)

By 1830 the reforming urge was overwhelming. 'Pull down an abuse where you can,' the *Westminster Review* encouraged its readers, 'especially where it is one, like that of slavery in the West Indies, whose supporters support all the rest.' [104] How different from the 1790s when, confronted by the horrors of the new French republican regime, 'a damp and odium has fallen on these collective applications' seeking political change.[105] In the mid 1790s, opposition to 'collective applications' had been generalized. The Association Movement gave over its functions to the government and to the volunteers. Burke's 'little platoon', the family, was 'natural' or had become natural. Prescription and the accretions of time had sanctified the county as a natural unit. Family and county – these communities were involuntary, men were born into them. A family was a family; a county could be properly mustered, as Wordsworth commented about Cumberland in 1808. By contrast, association was voluntary, purposive, selective. An association (to call it 'society' was a perversion of that word) could be anything, could cover a multitude of evil intentions. Thus Wordsworth 'considers the combinations among journeymen, and even the Benefit Societies and all associations of men, apparently for the best purposes, as very alarming'.[106] The very word 'combination' carried seditious overtones: '"Entered into a combination!" "Yes, Mr. Grey! A conspiracy . . ."'.[107] Thus was 'combination' elevated and 'conspiracy' debased, and both hung around the neck of the labourer. Yet professional and morally purposeful association was central to the emerging ideology of respectability; all other associations were regarded with great suspicion. An act of 1829 insisted upon government licensing of benefit societies.

The moral reformers could argue that artificial means were necessary to restore to the helpless and the penitent the blessings of *naturally constructed* society (for example, The Asylum or House of Refuge, for the Reception of Orphan Girls the Settlements of whose Parents cannot be found, 1800) or of *appropriate* society (for example, The Female Friendly Society, for the Relief of Poor, Infirm, Aged Widows, and Single Women, of Good Character, Who Have Seen Better Days, 1802). Burke, writing in his *Thoughts on the Cause of the Present Discontents* for the Whig 'party' of Rockingham against the 'King's Friends' had, as early as 1770, argued that 'when bad men combine, good men must associate'. The vocabulary of the argument was thus set out and its implications indicated: what were the boundaries of legitimate associations, what the valid intentions of associators? And, in setting 'association' against 'combination', Burke was asking: what was the 'natural' and what the 'artificial' state of society?

Natural and artificial society   There had been a continuing and wide ranging debate throughout the eighteenth century about luxury and corruption. How was their extent to be measured, their effects analysed? How were the terms to be defined? Did they refer essentially to the political world – to the work, say, of 'the great man', Walpole? Or to the economic – were they the inevitable consequence of the 'progress' of 'society'? Already in 1771 the Conversation Society of Manchester had decided that 'literature' had 'been more advantageous to Mankind' than had 'commerce'. Adam Smith himself was wary of the effects of commercialism and of the division of labour on manners. The question, 'Had the application of the system of "the Division of Labour" since [1760] been beneficial to the country?', received a unanimous negative from the Cambridge Apostles in 1830.[108] It was often argued (perhaps less often believed; certainly less often tried) that the quality of life was better in America, though the reasons for lauding a life with the Indians, solitude on the Susquehanna, or yeoman farming in plain Connecticut society were very different. The debate over 'primitivism and the idea of progress' was inconclusive; it was possible to argue with facility on both sides of the question. By 1800 the debate had shifted. 'Corruption' became an indictment of the regime. The argument was now about the artificiality of society, an artificiality based upon commerce and now manufacture, and spurred by the massive reallocation of resources necessitated by the Revolutionary wars.

A similar division existed between the proponents of 'honour' and those of 'virtue'. This was almost the equivalent of the aristocratic/bourgeois and artificial/natural polarities. Godwin, attacking honour, held in contempt the custom of using servants to tell callers that the master was not at home. He insisted on complete candour.[109] Jane Austen had more sense of the need for discretion, to avoid wounding others. Yet she too was determined to expose the falseness of 'manners':

> he is quite an MP, very smiling, with an exceeding good address and readiness of language. I am rather in love with him. I dare say he is ambitious and insincere. He had a wide smiling mouth and very good teeth.[110]

Here, by contrast, in *Emma* (ch. 42) *is* right conduct: Mr Knightley's 'idea of the simple and the natural will be to have the table spread in the dining room. The nature and the simplicity of gentlemen and ladies, with their servants and furniture, I think is best observed by meals within doors.' Behaviour and physical setting were appropriate. And, as Emma comes to realize, Donwell Abbey 'was just what it ought to be, and it looked what it was'. The very name Donwell reinforced this. Jane Austen was also prompted by the diffuse evangelical austerity to be tougher in *Mansfield Park* and in *Persuasion* on the licence which was accorded to, and claimed for itself by, the establishment.

Wordsworth was, in his own way, as sensitive to inappropriate behaviour, especially in his Lake District, as was Austen. His concern too was for society. He may have seen virtue in simple societies, but his primitivism was social not reclusive, his concern was for the contribution of individual well-being to the whole community. He worried about that 'most calamitous effect [of] the measures which have lately been pursued . . . a rapid decay of the domestic affectations among the lower orders of society', especially among those like the 'statesmen' of Cumbria whose 'little tract of land seems as a kind of permanent rallying point for their domestic feelings'.[111]

That supposed society provided Wordsworth's circle with a moral certainty cushioning the shock of disillusion with the French Revolution. It helped to resist the harshness of the 'city sharpened radicalism' of a Godwin (who 'wondered I should think of being out of London; could I be either amused or instructed at Southgate? How did I pass my time?').[112] Of that world of Wordsworth some

had no conception. Dr Burney totally missed the point when he saw
the mind of the *Lyrical Ballads* as 'tinctured with . . . unsociable
ideas of seclusion from the commerce of the world: as if men were
born to live in woods and wilds, unconnected with each other'.[113]

In Godwin, and Burney, there is an optimism fundamentally
opposed to primitivism and the exaltation of rural manners. It is
essentially outside the arguments about social development and
economic improvement. Scottish historians, like Adam Ferguson,
taking up from Montesquieu, had proposed an economic history of
society, passing through hunting, agrarian, commercial and manufacturing stages. A generation later, Ricardo, the political econo-
mist, too saw this progress as irreversible: 'as well complain of a
man's growing old as of such a change in our national condition'.
Like individuals, nations grow old.[114] Others could easily equate age
with decay, even total disintegration, imagining

> future times when this little island shall have fallen into its
> natural insignificancy, by being no longer possessed of a
> fictitious power founded upon commerce, distant colonies,
> and other artificial sources of wealth, how puzzled will the
> curious antiquary be when seeking amidst the ruins of
> London vestiges of its past grandeur.[115]

Sentiments such as these, the contemplation of English civilization in its maturity and decay, were closely related to the fascination
with ruins and with gloom. They brought introspection and melancholy into the mainstream of concern about the progress of society.
Decay was not merely in the general evolution of society (in that
evolution which produced both Old Sarum and the Suffolk
churches),[116] nor solely in the individual consciousness. It was in the
mental, moral and physical impact of manufacturing, and it was
immediate and overwhelming. Shelley saw manufactures and
manufacturers working their evil spell, even in Keswick, as girls in
the cotton twist factory on the banks of the Greta threw their
aborted babies into the river below. The process of industrialization
was symptomatic of wealth and of decay. Here is the Hon. John
Byng at Aysgarth Falls in the West Riding of Yorkshire in June 1792:

> What has completed the destruction of every rural thought
> [begun by the improvement of the bridge at the falls], has

been the erection of a cotton mill on one side, whereby prospect, and quiet, are destroy'd: I now speak as a tourist (as a policeman, a citizen, or a statesman I enter not the field); the people, indeed, are employ'd; but they are all abandon'd to vice from the throng.

If men can thus start into riches; or if riches from trade are too easily procured, woe unto us men of middling income, and settled revenue; and woe it has been to . . . the Yeomanry of the land.

At the times when people work not in the mill, they issue out to poaching, profligacy and plunder – Sir Rd Arkwright may have introduced much wealth into his family, and into the country; but as a tourist, I execrate his schemes, which, having crept into every pastoral role, have destroy'd the course and beauty of nature; why, here now is a great flaring mill, whose black stream has drawn off half the water of the falls above the bridge.

With the bell ringing, and the clamour of the mill, all the vale is disturb'd; treason and levelling systems are the discourse; and rebellions may be near at hand.[117]

Here preconception meets perception and remains too strong for it. The policeman, citizen and statesman overcome the tourist. This tourist adamantly rejects that involvement with the energies of industry – light, noise, control – that so fascinated visitors to Coalbrookdale or Darley. Here the landscape reflects the shabbiness of the mill; the stream is reduced to a trickle. Nature is dominated and destroyed. Byng's is a total condemnation of the mill and all involved in it – master and men alike – but it also holds out the prospect of more discrimination in the description, a greater sense of the respective roles of opportunity, of greed and of necessity, of corruption and innocence, of a discrimination which would follow aesthetic and sociological investigation.

Establishing responsibility was a major task for our age. Whether the manufacturer, the labourer, the statesman or the consumer was to be blamed, one thing was clear to many: the manufacturing 'system' was 'a most menacing evil'; 'things cannot go on in this way'.[118] But was the resolution to be in decay and ruin, in political reform, or in economic transformation? Macaulay looked to political reform to reinforce the immense impact of economic growth. The result would be *amelioration*:

> the higher and middling orders are the natural representatives of the human race. Their interest may be opposed, in some things, to that of their poorer contemporaries, but it is identical with that of innumerable generations which are to follow.[119]

Conclusion

The age was self-conscious, searching for its spirit. It was an age of transition. Constable thought of his friend Leslie's Marylebone house as 'quite the country'. Leslie was just off to Abbotsford to paint Scott's portrait; he was to go by steamboat.[120] Aristocratic *hauteur* blunted improvement. The Whig hostess, Lady Holland, insisted that a train on which she was travelling should be slowed down. Brunel, 'in spite of the protestations of the passengers', concurred.[121] It was an age of paradox and contradiction. Southey noted how the English scorned yet imitated the French, took from them the telegraph, conscription, income tax. The conceptualization of improvement prompted the conviction of deterioration. The search for order and rational influence provoked repression and dissent. The quest for education and literacy perhaps contributed to that blunting of 'the discriminating powers of the mind' which Wordsworth feared in 1800. A generation later J. S. Mill would claim that 'the grand achievement of the *present* age is the diffusion of *superficial* knowledge'.[122] It was an age tense with opportunity, aware, whether alarmed or excited, of possibility. It was ironically aware of what it was doing to language. The Benthamite Charles Buller was to bequeath copies of Adam Smith and Mill to Thomas Carlyle, 'with the hope that he will improve thereby'.[123] It was anxious to assign responsibility for the changes it came to realize that it had nurtured: 'But in truth it should be said, that the working classes did not substitute Rights for Duties, and take the former into their guardianship, till the higher classes, their legitimate protectors, had subordinated *Persons* to *Things*, and systematically perverted the former, into the latter.'[124] Class became an appropriate category for such arguments, though it could be hoped that a society divided by class would be reunited by respectability. The distinctions and equivalences of persons and things were worked out at Chawton and at Rydal, at Halifax and Rochdale, at Birmingham and at Sheffield, in the Fens and the Forest of Dean, in the Paris Sections and at Westminster. The Industrial and the French Revolutions were separate phenomena: but they soon became, and still are, indissoluble in their consequences, threats and promises.

Notes

1 Quoted by J. S. Watson, *The Reign of George III, 1760–1815*, Oxford, 1960, 299.
2 A. D. Harvey, *Britain in the Early Nineteenth Century*, London, 1978, 334.
3 All tables from B. R. Mitchell and P. Deane, *Abstract of British Historical Statistics*, Cambridge, 1962.
4 An excellent example of the physical impact and moral implications of 'improvement' is provided by Humphrey Repton's design for changes to his own property – see L. Parris, *Landscape in Britain, c.1750–1850*, London, 1973, 60–1.
5 G. E. Mingay, *English Landed Society in the Eighteenth Century*, London, 1963, 89.
6 E. J. Hobsbawm and G. F. E. Rudé, *Captain Swing*, London, 1973, xxiii, 23–4.
7 Quoted by E. S. Richards in *Agricultural History Review*, 22 (1974), 102.
8 *Journals of Dorothy Wordsworth*, Oxford, 1971, 19 (18–5–1800).
9 C. B. Andrews (ed.), *Torrington Diaries*, London, 1934–6, II, 108–9.
10 Hobsbawm and Rudé, *Captain Swing*, 16, 26.
11 E. L. Jones (ed.), *Agriculture and Economic Growth, 1650–1815*, London, 1967, 20–1. 'Social issues', the editor warns, p. 23, 'are . . . aside from our purpose.'
12 E. S. Richards, *Leviathan of Wealth: The Sutherland Fortune in the Industrial Revolution*, London, 1973, 166.
13 R. Southey, *Letters from England*, London, 1807, letter no. 58.
14 Quoted in R. W. Malcolmson, *Popular Recreations in English Society, 1700–1850*, Cambridge, 1973, 104, n. 63.
15 The Vicar of Middleton, Lancs, quoted by E. Stigant in his unpublished paper, 'Religion and social control: Methodism, 1790–1830'. Such vague or wilful behaviour was no new thing: but the scale and concentration of it was now alarming (cf. K. S. Inglis, *Churches and the Working Classes in Victorian England*, London, 1963).

16 S. Rogers, *Recollections*, London, 1859, 45.

17 R. Carr, *English Fox Hunting*, London, 1976; D. C. Itzkowitz, *Peculiar Privilege: A Short History of English Fox Hunting, 1753–1885*, Hassocks, 1977.

18 Harvey, *Britain in Nineteenth Century*, 317–18.

19 J. Rosselli, *Lord William Bentinck*, London, 1974, 285–92.

20 T. L. Peacock, *Crotchet Castle*, London, 1831, ch. 2, 'The march of mind'.

21 Quoted from the *Christian Teacher* (1839) by C. Elliott in R. M. Hartwell (ed.), *The Industrial Revolution*, Oxford, 1970, 163.

22 1830, in F. C. Mather, *After the Canal Duke*, Oxford, 1970, 71.

23 British Library, Add. MSS 38287, f. 347–8, 363–6, December 1819; important discussion in B. Hilton, *Corn, Cash, Commerce: The Economic Policies of the Tory Governments, 1815–1830*, Oxford, 1977. Deletions of 'great' and 'very' by Liverpool.

24 Hilton, *Corn, Cash, Commerce*, 229–30, 228, 83–4, 278.

25 John Brunt, shoemaker, after his conviction for taking part in the Cato Street Conspiracy, 1820 – E. P. Thompson, *The Making of the English Working Class*, London, 1963, 704.

26 Quotations from Thompson, *English Working Class*, 567, 597 (both 1812).

27 Cf. Thompson, *English Working Class*, 616: 'Nor should it be assumed that an insurrectionary movement in 1812 or 1819, might not – if it had gained sufficient impetus – have achieved at least a temporary success.'

28 Thompson, *English Working Class*, ch. 14, section 2; 420–1; 44–5.

29 Quotations from Thompson, *English Working Class*, 613 (1817); 517 (Grosvenor Henson of Nottingham, 1812); 770 (John Wade in *The Gorgon*, 1818); ch. 16, section 2.

30 Thompson, *English Working Class*, 368, 369, 374. 'Clear' in the short term: in the longer term radical, non-violent political organizations may have owed much to Methodist training and association.

31 Bronterre O'Brien (?1835) in J. Wiener, *War of the Unstamped*, Ithaca, 1969, 221–2; Thompson, *English Working Class*, 825, quoting a radical Leeds paper, *The Cracker*, 1832.

32 *Nottingham Journal*, 21–11–1834; in M. Thomis, *Politics and Society in Nottingham, 1785–1835*, Oxford, 1969, 248.

33 John Cornforth, 'Carlisle's years of improvement', *Country Life*, 11–5–1978.

34 W. Cobbett, *Rural Rides*, G. D. H. Cole (ed.), London, 1930, 163.

35 N. Pevsner, *Cumberland and Westmorland*, London, 1967, 101.

36 Feargus O'Connor, 1844, in Thompson, *English Working Class*, 231.

37 Earl of Carnarvon, quoted by A. D. Harvey, '. . . the Whigs in office . . . 1806 to . . . 1807', *Historical Journal*, 15 (1972), 621.

38 Lord Liverpool, 1822 in B. Semmel, *The Rise of Free Trade Imperialism*, Cambridge, 1970, 136. Note the dual meaning of *calculated*.

39 Burke to P. Francis, 20–2–1790 in A. Cobban and R. A. Smith (eds), *The Correspondence of Edmund Burke*, Cambridge, 1967, VI, 88–92.

40 P. Fussell, *The Rhetorical World of Augustan Humanism*, Oxford, 1965, includes a discussion of the 'Letter'. Bedford had affected a 'radical' style of life.

41 October 1793, in F. O'Gorman, *The Whig Party and the French Revolution*, London, 1967, 157–8.

42 Fitzwilliam, in L. G. Mitchell, *C. J. Fox and the Disintegration of the Whig Party, 1782–94*, Oxford, 1971, 201.

43 Rogers, *Recollections*, 81–2.

44 Fox to Mrs Armistead, 7–10–1792, in Mitchell, *C. J. Fox*, 192.

45 Fox to Grey, 19–4–1804, British Library, Add. MSS 47565, f. 125.

46 16–3–1792 in Mitchell, *C. J. Fox*, 176.

47 *Parliamentary Debates*, 1 series, 31, 1067, 5–1–1795.

48 Grey to Howick, British Library, Add. MSS 51546, f. 63–5, 24–10–1819. Cf. Windham to Grey, 29–9–1809, quoted in A. D. Harvey, 'Whigs in office', *Historical Journal*, 1972, 647: 'It is indeed difficult to say what good we could do if we had the affair all in our own hands. . . . I am not sure that we should be better . . . than our neighbours [i.e. opponents, the Tories!]. And for great and beneficial measures I know not what they are to be.' Here the old politics confesses its bankruptcy.

49 Lord Holland, *Memoirs of the Whig Party*, London, 1853–4, I, 166–8.

50 John Rickman (administrator of the 1801 Census) to Southey, 10–11–1817, in G. Carnall, *Southey and his Age*, Oxford, 1960, 195.

51 In *Past and Present*, no. 38 (1967), 56–97; cf. S. Pollard, *The Genesis of Modern Management*, London, 1965.

52 Arthur Young, 'The pleasures of agriculture', 1784, discussed in R. Feingold, *Nature and Society: Later 18th Century Uses of the Pastoral and Georgic*, Hassocks, 1978, 57.

53 E. P. Thompson, 'The moral economy of the English crowd in the 18th century', *Past and Present*, no. 50 (1970), 129, 130, 131 (last two quotations from the Duke of Portland).

54 Joseph Willday to Sidmouth, 31–5–1817, in A. Aspinall (ed.), *The Early English Trades Unions*, London, 1949, 233; William Windham, 1798, in Harvey, *Britain in Nineteenth Century*, 45.

55 Quoted from a radical publication in Newcastle, 1821, by Thompson, *English Working Class*, 681.

56 J. L. and B. Hammond, *The Town Labourer*, London, 1978, 163 (1st edn, 1917).

57 Liverpool to John Beckett, 25–10–1819, British Library, Add. MSS 38280, f. 205–6, part quoted in Hilton, *Corn, Cash, Commerce*, 81.

Depot had recently been introduced into the language – taken from the French.

58 Quoted by A. J. Peacock in J. P. Dunbabin (ed.), *Rural Discontent in Nineteenth Century Britain*, London, 1974, 55.

59 W. Pope (ed.), *The Diary of B. R. Haydon*, Cambridge, Mass., 1960, I, 9, July 1808.

60 Shelley, *The Masque of Anarchy*, stanza 2, written after Peterloo in 1819.

61 W. R. Ward, *Religion and Society in England, 1790–1850*, London, 1972, 1. This book provides a useful counterpoint to E. P. Thompson's chapters on religion in *The Making of the English Working Class*.

62 W. G. Rimmer, *Marshalls of Leeds, Flax-Spinners, 1788–1886*, Cambridge, 1960, 111, 113.

63 Jeffrey in the *Edinburgh Review*, quoted by J. R. M. Butler, *The Passing of the Great Reform Bill*, London, 1914, 26.

64 Wordsworth, *Lowther* (?1832); Wordsworth to C. J. Fox, 14–1–1801, in E. de Selincourt, A. G. Hill, M. Moorman and C. L. Shaver (eds), *Letters* (of William and Dorothy Wordsworth), 5 vols, Oxford, 1967–80, I, 312–15.

65 T. Paine, *The Rights of Man*, London, 1969 (Pelican edn), 97, 242–5; D. V. Erdman, *Blake: Prophet against Empire*, Princeton, 1969, 276–7. Hutton quoted in J. Money, *Experience and Identity: Birmingham and the West Midlands, 1760–1800*, Manchester, 1977, 11.

66 Bage in 'James Wallace', quoted by L. Whitney, *Primitivism and the Idea of Progress*, Baltimore, 1934, 270.

67 For Thomas Spence, see T. R. Knox, 'Thomas Spence . . .', *Past and Present*, no. 76 (1977), 75–98 (Quotation at p. 89), and T. M. Parssinen, 'The revolutionary party in London, 1816–20', *Bulletin of the Institute of Historical Research*, 45 (1972), 266–82. Jefferson: J. P. Boyd (ed.), *Papers of Thomas Jefferson*, Princeton, 1958, XV, 384–99.

68 Quoted by C. Garrett, *Respectable Folly*, Baltimore, 1975, 165.

69 Paine, *Rights of Man*, 64 (part 1, 1791).

70 Godwin to Shelley, 4–3–1812, in F. K. Brown, *Life of Godwin*, London, 1926, 261–2.

71 W. Hazlitt, *Life of Holcroft*, E. Colby (ed.), London, 1925, II, 12.

72 Spence in Thompson, *English Working Class*, 161; Banner of Bath printers, 1831, quoted by R. S. Neale, *Class and Ideology in the Nineteenth Century*, London, 1972, 53.

73 E. C. Black, *The Association: British Extra-Parliamentary Organisation, 1769–93*, Cambridge, Mass., 1963, ch. 7.

74 Quoted by Thompson, *English Working Class*, 142; Want was not, of course, new, although 1795 was a particularly bad year. But now want was prompting specifically political education / mobilization.

75 In his important review of *Captain Swing*, *New Society*, 13–2–1969, 251–2.

76 Hobsbawm and Rudé, *Captain Swing*, 186.

77 E.g. K. Garlick and A. MacIntyre (eds), *Diary of James Farington*, New Haven, 1978, II, 437, 11–12–1795, for a mercenary bookseller.

78 Testimony from Merthyr Tydfil in G. A. Williams, *The Merthyr Rising*, London, 1978, 121; Hazlitt's father quoted in P. P. Howe, *The Life of William Hazlitt*, London, 1942, 35.

79 Mrs West, 'A tale of the times', 1799, quoted by M. Butler, *Jane Austen and the War of Ideas*, Oxford, 1975, 104–5.

80 Amelia Alderson, 1794 – quoted in Brown, *Godwin*, 79–80.

81 Hazlitt, *Life of Holcroft*, II, 17.

82 Quoted by G. Kelly, *The Jacobin Novel, 1780–1805*, Oxford, 1976, 46.

83 Quoted in Butler, *Reform Bill*, 33–4.

84 W. A. Armstrong, 'La population de l'Angleterre . . .', *Annales de Demographie Historique*, London, 1965, 139–40.

85 Paine, *Rights of Man*, 63; *Common Sense*, 1776, section 'Thoughts on the present state of American affairs'; E. Foner, *Tom Paine and Revolutionary America*, New York, 1976.

86 Wordsworth, *French Revolution*, 1804, published 1809, ll. 4–5; Blake, *America*, 1743.

87 J. Thelwall, 1795–6, quoted in Thompson, *English Working Class*, 158 (cf. *The Prelude*, 1805, x, ll. 745–8); Fox quoted by Rogers, *Recollections*, 12.

88 J. H. Plumb, 'The new world of children in eighteenth century England', *Past and Present*, no. 67 (1975), 64–95.

89 *Parliamentary Debates*, 9–12–1819; part quoted M. I. Thomis, *Responses to Industrialization*, Newton Abbott, 1977, 117–18.

90 De Lancey (a proponent of barracks) to Dundas(?), 13–6–1792, in Aspinall, *Early English Trade Unions*, 4–6.

91 Wordsworth to Daniel Stuart, 7–4–1817, de Selincourt et al., *Letters*, III, 374–6; to Mathews, Whitehouse, 8–6–1794, ibid., I, 123–4; to Lord Lonsdale, 21–1–1818, ibid., III, 412–4. Note that democratic is equated rather with 'non-landed' than with 'popular'.

92 Thompson, *English Working Class*, 176.

93 E. J. Morley (ed.), *Henry Crabb Robinson on Books and their Writers*, 3 vols, London, 1938, I, 189, 192–1816 (note distinction of interest and self-interest); 177, 3–2–1815 (cf. Fitzwilliam on Fox's toasts, above p. 39); 22, 29–1–1811.

94 Coleridge to Sir George Beaumont, E. L. Griggs (ed.), *Collected Letters of S. T. Coleridge*, Oxford, 1956–71, II, 998–1005.

95 W. Godwin, *Thoughts Occasion'd by Dr. Parr's Spital Sermon*, London, 1801, 9; in a paragraph which much impressed Coleridge.

96 Brown, *Godwin*, 252; *Crabb Robinson on Books*, I, 77, 6–5–1812;

Carnall, *Southey*, 144.

97   John Stedman, June 1795, quoted in Garrett, *Respectable Folly*, 203.

98   H. C. Robbins-Landon, *Haydn in England, 1791–5*, London, 1976, 559.

99   W. R. Ward, *Religion and Society*, 14, and ch. 1 generally.

100 A. Mitchell, 'The association movement of 1792–3', *Historical Journal*, 4 (1961), 56–77. Mitchell argues that 'the associations produced a national unity which led indirectly to war' (with France).

101 R. Anstey, *The Atlantic Slave Trade and British Abolition, 1760–1810*, London, 1975, 403–13.

102 Haydon, *Journals and Autobiography*, M. Elwin (ed.), London, 1950, 47.

103 Hazlitt, *Life of Holcroft*, II, 129.

104 Quoted in M. G. Brock, *Great Reform Act*, London, 1973, 81.

105 Capel Lofft, 1793, in Anstey, *Abolition*, 278n.

106 *Crabb Robinson on Books*, I, 90, 26–5–1812.

107 Disraeli, *Vivian Grey*, London, 1826; *OED*.

108 Quoted by R. M. Wiles in P. Korshin (ed.), *The Widening Circle*, Philadelphia, 1976, 112; P. Allen, *The Cambridge Apostles*, Cambridge, 1978, 3.

109 The results may be seen, e.g., in the Coleridge correspondence, II, 782–4, Coleridge to Godwin, 22–1–1802.

110 Letter of 1813 in Q. D. Leavis, 'A critical theory of Jane Austen's writings', *Scrutiny*, 10 (1941–2), 118.

111 Letter from Wordsworth to Fox accompanying a copy of the second edition of the *Lyrical Ballads*, 14–1–1801, in de Selincourt et al., *Letters*, I, 312–15; cf. *Prelude*, London, 1805, IX, ll. 217ff.

112 Amelia Alderson, 1794, in Brown, *Godwin*, 79–80.

113 1799 review, excerpted in A. R. Jones and W. Tydeman (eds), *The Lyrical Ballads: a Casebook*, London, 1972, 55–7.

114 1822 in Semmel, *Rise of Free Trade Imperialism*, 71.

115 Lady Holland, *Journal*, Earl of Ilchester (ed.), London, 1908, *sub*. March, 1800; cf. Haydon at Dover, *Diary*, W. B. Pope (ed.), I, 3, 1807.

116 R. B. Beckett (ed.), *John Constable's Discourses*, Ipswich, 1970, 22–3, 24–5.

117 Andrews, *Torrington Diaries*, III, 81–2; part quoted by Thompson, *English Working Class*, 189.

118 Crabb Robinson reporting Wordsworth, 26–5–1812, *Crabb Robinson on Books*, I, 90; Dorothy Wordsworth to Catherine Clarkson from Halifax, 10–1–1817, in de Selincourt et al., *Letters*, III, 355.

119 Butler, *Reform Bill*, 262, quoting Macaulay in the *Edinburgh Review*, 1829.

120 R. B. Beckett (ed.), *John Constable's Correspondence*, 6 vols, Ipswich, 1962–8, III, 4–5.

121 L. G. Mitchell, *Holland House*, London, 1980, 24.
122 J. S. Mill, 'The spirit of the age', London, 1831, in G. Himmelfarb (ed.), *J. S. Mill: Writings on Politics and Culture*, New York, 1962.
123 Allen, *Cambridge Apostles*, 235, n. 24.
124 A conclusion of Coleridge's, 1832, quoted by J. Colmer in R. L. Brett, *Writers and their Background: Coleridge*, London, 1971, 253–4.

Further reading

General surveys

Baylen, J. O., and Gossmann, N. (eds), *Biographical Dictionary of British Radicals Since 1770*, vol. 1, 1770–1832, Hassocks, 1979.

Briggs, A., *The Age of Improvement*, London, 1959.

Mathias, P., *The First Industrial Nation: An Economic History of England, 1700–1914*, London, 1969.

Palmer, R. R., *The Age of the Democratic Revolution*, 2 vols, Princeton, 1959–64.

Thomis, M. I., *Responses to Industrialization: The British Experience, 1780–1850*, Newton Abbot, 1976.

Thomis, M. I., and Holt, P., *Threats of Revolution in Britain, 1789–1848*, London, 1977.

Watson, J. S., *The Reign of George III, 1760–1815*, Oxford, 1960.

Class and class consciousness

Briggs, A., 'The language of class . . .', in A. Briggs and J. Saville (eds), *Essays in Labour History*, London, 1960.

Briggs, A., 'Middle class consciousness in English politics, 1780–1846', *Past and Present*, no. 9 (1956).

Laqueur, T. W., *Religion and Respectability: Sunday Schools and Working Class Culture, 1780–1850*, New Haven, 1976.

Perkin, H., *The Origins of Modern English Society, 1780–1880*, London, 1969.

Spring, D., 'Aristocracy, social structure, and religion in the early Victorian period', *Victorian Studies*, 6 (1962–3).

Spring, D., 'The Clapham Sect: some social and political aspects', *Victorian Studies*, 5 (1961–2).

Disorder and riot

Rudé, G., *The Crowd in History, 1730–1848*, New York, 1964.

Stephenson, J., *Popular Disturbances in England, 1700–1870*, London, 1979.

The family

Levine, D., *Family Formation in an Age of Nascent Capitalism*, New York, 1977.

Shorter, E., *The Making of the Modern Family*, London, 1975.
Stone, L., *The Family, Sex and Marriage in England, 1500–1800*, London, 1977.
Thompson, E. P., review of Stone, *New Society*, 8–9–1977.

The 'standard of living'
Taylor, A. J. (ed.), *The Standard of Living during the Industrial Revolution*, London, 1975.

Government and administration
Emsley, C., 'The Home Office and its sources of information and investigation, 1793–1801', *English Historical Review*, 94 (1979).
Gash, N., *Mr Secretary Peel*, London, 1961.

Impact of the French Revolution and the French war
Brown, P. A., *The French Revolution in English History*, London, 1918.
Cone, C. B., *The English Jacobins*, New York, 1968.
Emsley, C., *British Society and the French Wars, 1793–1815*, London, 1979.
Goodwin, A., *The Friends of Liberty*, London, 1979.

Parliament and parliamentary reform
Briggs, A., 'The background of the parliamentary reform movement in three English cities, 1830–2', *Cambridge Historical Journal*, 10 (1950–2).
Brock, M. G., *The Great Reform Act*, London, 1973.
Cannon, J., *Parliamentary Reform, 1640–1832*, London, 1973.

The spirit of the age
Altick, R. D., *The English Common Reader: A Social History of the Mass Reading Public, 1800–1900*, Chicago, 1957.
Davis, D. B., *The Problem of Slavery in the Age of Revolution, 1770–1823*, Ithaca, 1975.
Plumb, J. H., 'Reason and unreason in the eighteenth century: the English experience', in his *In the Light of History*, London, 1972.
Webb, R. K., *The British Working Class Reader, 1790–1848: Literacy and Social Tension*, London, 1955.

2 Romanticism in English art

MARCIA POINTON

Rome was at the heart of the classical world as experienced in the eighteenth century; it was there in 1778 that a young Swiss-born artist named Johann Heinrich Füssli (1741–1825) made a drawing which most of his contemporaries would have regarded as an eccentricity but which heralds and typifies much that is readily recognizable but difficult to define in the visual arts of the Romantic period (Plate 1). Fuseli, as he preferred to be called after he had settled in London later in life, depicts two monstrous fragments of sculpture, juxtaposed without rhyme or reason on two plinths against a vertical wall composed of huge stone slabs which are cracked and worn at the edges. One of the fragments is a giant foot, the other a right hand of similar dimensions with the index finger raised in the gesture which traditionally belongs to the Holy Ghost and which signifies the act of blessing. A weed is sprouting from the stonework near the hand and, seated at the foot of the plinth is a figure of uncertain sex, one hand supporting its head and shading its eyes, the other draped languidly over the upper part of the stone foot. Although the artist left no recorded title for this drawing, it has always been known as *The Artist Moved by the Magnitude of Antique Fragments*.[1]

For the late eighteenth-century student of art, the remains of Greece and Rome constituted not merely an aesthetic experience but an authoritative source of ultimate knowledge about art. They represented the height of human achievement and only by close study of such works could the young artist ever hope to become established. As a young art student in Rome, Fuseli would have studied ancient sculpture in considerable detail. The educational value of the encounter with antiquity is typically stated by James Barry, Professor of Painting at the Royal Academy from 1783 to 1799. In his lecture 'On design', Barry says: 'There is in the great monuments of Grecian art, a strain of perfection, beauty and sublimity far beyond anything the moderns have produced.' He then goes on to state that little can be expected from 'mere imitation' and that 'we must investigate the principles upon which those statues were constructed, and adopt the same mode of study in our own pursuit and imitation of nature, or we labour to no purpose'.[2]

The student was, therefore, expected to look, to record, to investigate the principles (that is the general rules which might be seen to be universally applicable) behind the work of art and then to apply these in his own work. Innumerable painstaking drawings of antique sculpture by English, German and French art students from the end of the eighteenth century testify to the seriousness and universality of this approach. Fuseli, however, here does none of these things.

The Artist Moved by the Magnitude of Antique Fragments is neither careful nor painstaking. It is dashed off in ink and watercolour with little regard for composition. The right-hand side of the drawing is unresolved and the spatial relationships between the various objects are undecided. Having run out of space at the bottom of the page, Fuseli distorts the perspective of the end of the plinth in order to get it on to his paper. Not only does he choose not to record and investigate a distinguished example of antique statuary, such as the *Laocoön* group or the *Apollo Belvedere*, both readily available in the Vatican, he defiantly and humorously underlines the fact that his antique fragments are figments of his imagination. The carelessly scribbled letters S.P.Q.R., cipher of the Roman Republic, are a provocative reminder to the viewer that this is the position where the conscientious student of antiquity would have recorded for himself and for posterity the precise identity of the object of his examination.

It might be argued that it is unreasonable to consider so seriously a sketch which the artist clearly tossed off to please himself and which he never planned to exhibit or even, probably, to show outside his most intimate circle of friends. Yet the development of private forms of visual expression that differ radically in character from the artist's exhibited work is an important characteristic of Fuseli's circle (which included artists like Romney, Flaxman and the Scottish artist Alexander Runciman) and was to become a feature of Romantic expression in all media. Reconciling the unorthodox pictorial manifestation of a 'spontaneous overflow of powerful feeling' with the demands and expectations of patron and public, transposing the vision that is recorded in the expressive but ephemeral medium of watercolour into the lasting and monumental medium of oil, remained a problem for the Romantics. It is seen most clearly, perhaps, in the work of J. M. W. Turner (1775–1851) whose discoveries about light and colour in Venice are recorded in watercolour in numerous private sketch-books but do not impinge upon his execution in oil until some twenty years later.

If we turn to Fuseli's writings, we find ample justification for a serious appraisal of a drawing like *The Artist Moved by the Magnitude of Antique Fragments*:

> To have leisure to think of the author, when we read, or of the artist, when we behold, proves that the work of either is of an inferior class; we have neither time to inquire after Homer's birth-place or rank, when Andromache departs from her husband, nor stoop to look for the inscription of the artist's name when we stand before the Apollo.[3]

The artist, if such is the figure in Fuseli's drawing, does not draw, paint or write. He does not even look. Hiding his head in his hand in a pose of melancholy contemplation, he retains tactile contact with the object of his admiration whilst inwardly thinking and feeling the experience. His posture is one of submission, even of obeisance. The sculpture is ancient, fragmented, worn by time. It comprises one hand and one foot severed from their original composition and, therefore, without function. There is no question of repair or reconstruction, both commonplace practices in the eighteenth century; the artist instead humbly accepts the incomplete evidence of the genius of the past. James Barry would have found it hard to 'investigate the principles' upon which this statue was constructed. Yet the artist is blessed by the archaic and powerful hand, and the drawing constitutes, therefore, a kind of manifesto, anticipating the Romantic predilection for unfinished and fragmentary works of art.

Fuseli's drawing also anticipates the European Romantics' pre-occupation with the inner working of the creative mind; it looks forward to the concern with genius and with inspiration that is expressed in the first half of the nineteenth century by, for example, Delacroix in his drawing *Michelangelo in his Studio* (1851, Galérie Bruyas, Musée de Montpellier). Fuseli's spontaneity of handling, the emphasis he places on the emotional encounter as opposed to the connoisseur's investigation, the idea of the artist looking in at himself, the identification of the artist as sensitive human being rather than as craftsman (immediately recognizable by palette and brushes), the imaginative approach to the past, the astute and witty acknowledgement of current academic practice, the treatment of familiar subject matter in an unorthodox way: these are all aspects of Romantic art to which we shall have occasion to refer.

Romantic historicism

In 1749 Horace Walpole, fourth son of the famous British Prime Minister, bought a cottage that had been built fifty years earlier by Lord Bradford's coachman, and which stood in five acres on the banks of the Thames near Twickenham. His intentions were from the first not to create a mansion with which to impress his friends by his rank and status but to express a vision. His friends were, none-theless, impressed, and Strawberry Hill became a major tourist attraction (Plate 2).

Romanticism, by its very name, conveys the world of medieval romance which inspired so many artists from the middle of the eighteenth century. A taste for gothic had never died in England. Inigo Jones had used the gothic style in the chapel he designed for Lincoln's Inn and which was built between 1618 and 1623. Wren, usually thought of as the arch-exponent of English baroque and architect of St Paul's Cathedral – the nearest approximation of any major British monument to the Albertian ideal of a centralized church plan – was constantly in search of variety in architectural style; he built the upper part of Tom Tower, Christ Church, Oxford, between 1681 and 1682, in a gothic so authentic in appearance that 'innocent visitors never notice the difference' between Wren's additions and the original level built in Wolsey's time.[4] The playwright and architect, John Vanbrugh, created for the Marlborough family at Blenheim a palace in the style of international baroque, but when building for himself at Greenwich in 1717 he created a fairy-tale gothic castle.

The antiquarians of the seventeenth century were primarily concerned with family history, topography and ecclesiastical history. Yet their work involved the recording of fast-disappearing medieval monuments of the British Isles. Sir William Dugdale's *Monasticon Anglicanum*, first published in Latin from 1655 onwards, was translated into English in 1693, and contained engraved plates of medieval antiquities. Like Sandford's *Genealogical History of the Kings of England* (1677), it became a source-book for designers in the gothic style and was used by Walpole when he was planning the interior embellishments of Strawberry Hill. Tombs, oratories and chapels were all converted by Walpole into fireplaces, window seats, library shelves and garden bowers.

Although Walpole inherited from the antiquarian tradition of the seventeenth century an interest in genealogy and a predisposition to view the medieval past of England in a nationalistic light (an attitude to the past which becomes an important feature of nineteenth-century historicism), he differed from his predecessors in the emphasis he placed on the evocative qualities of gothic. 'One must have taste to be sensible of the beauties of Grecian architecture', wrote Walpole in his *Anecdotes of Painting*, 'one only wants passions to feel Gothic',[5] – sentiments which closely resemble Goethe's revelation before Strasbourg Cathedral in 1773:

> No wiser than a people which calls ''barbaric'' all the world it does not know, I called *gothic* whatever did not fit my system. I made no distinction between the contorted, painted puppets and decorations with which our noble bourgeois fancify their houses and the awesome relics of our older German architecture. . . .
>
> What unexpected emotions overcame me at the sight of the cathedral, when finally I stood before it! One impression, whole and grand, filled my soul, an impression which, resulting from the harmony of a thousand parts, I could savor and enjoy but neither explain nor understand. They say that such are the joys of heaven.[6]

In the preface to his *Description of Strawberry Hill* (1774),

Walpole says that the house 'was built to please my own taste, and in some degree to realize my own visions'.[7] However much one is tempted to dismiss Walpole's aspirations as naive and to laugh kindly at the stage-set properties of Strawberry Hill, it is important to realize, as Wilmarth Sheldon Lewis has pointed out,[8] that it worked for Walpole's contemporaries, that the 'gloomth' of abbeys and cathedrals which Walpole believed he had imprinted on his house and the 'trophies of old coats of mail, Indian shields made of Rhinoceros's hides, broadswords, quivers, long bows and spears – all *supposed* to be taken by Sir Terry Robsart in the Holy wars' constituted both a witty diversion and a serious emotional reality.[9]

It was the capacity of gothic to convey impressions to the mind that made it so attractive to the Romantics. What seemed to men like Walpole and his friend, Thomas Gray, the very Englishness of gothic, as well as its distance in time, ensured its potential for imaginative expression. Yet, it is important to realize that the first artists to exploit the gothic style in pictorial art were those very artists who had immersed themselves in the culture of classical antiquity. It was the growing curiosity about the intentions of Greek and Roman sculptors, the controversy surrounding the influential writings on art of the German Johann Joachim Winckelmann (1717–68) – who significantly had never seen an original Greek work of art when he wrote his first essay on the subject – which were translated and disseminated throughout Europe, that lent impetus to a nascent sense of curiosity about other 'primitive' cultures. The word 'primitive' had, we must remember, many meanings during the Romantic period, ranging from the ideal of the noble savage that was thought to be manifest in the American Indian to the qualities enshrined in works of art executed in Europe before the Renaissance.

Fuseli, who was responsible in 1765 for translating into English Winckelmann's *Reflections on the Painting and Sculpture of the Greeks* (first published in 1755), also read and illustrated Norse legends – a century before Wagner or William Morris became interested in the ancient culture of the far north. 'We are more impressed by Gothic than by Greek mythology', Fuseli declared, 'because the bands are not yet rent which tie us to its magic: he has a powerful hold on us, who holds us by our superstition or by a theory of honor.'[10]

The English never embraced the strict neoclassical doctrines on art which inspired the drama of Racine or the paintings of Jacques Louis David. Dr Johnson may have complained that Shakespeare was 'more careful to please than to instruct' and that 'he seems to write without any moral purpose',[11] but Fuseli was inspired by his reading of Shakespeare to invent designs, based on the plays, to replace every one of Michelangelo's frescoes on the Sistine Chapel ceiling. Moreover it is inconceivable, for all the Royal Academicians' strictures on High Art, that anyone in England in 1800 could have exhibited the sort of plan shown by a French artist in 1800 for the most efficient way of destroying gothic churches by means of hollowing out the piers at their bases and inserting kindling so that the structure might be guaranteed, once ignited, to collapse in less than ten minutes.[12]

John Flaxman (1755–1826), whose economic and stylized line drawings of subjects from Homer and Aeschylus epitomized the classical revival in the visual arts and were influential in their engraved form on artists throughout Europe in the early years of the nineteenth century, was one of the first to be inspired by the visual qualities of gothic. In 1780 Flaxman gave his future wife a copy of Percy's *Reliques of Ancient Poetry*, a collection of ballads that had first been published in 1765 and which (despite its questionable authenticity) was a major influence in the rediscovery of a medieval chivalric past. The gift was accompanied by a letter in which Flaxman praised the 'heroic virtue, the constant love, and every noble quality which exalts the human soul, which is expressed in a way so simply [that it] cannot fail of pleasing you'.[13] In 1783 Flaxman spent the whole afternoon and evening in Westminster Abbey in the company of William Hayley and George Romney, studying the medieval tomb monuments.[14] Blake, his friend and associate, also drew equally on Hellenistic models and on gothic sculpture with which he became acquainted as a very young man working under James Basire drawing the monuments in Westminster Abbey for Gough's *Sepulchral Monuments of Great Britain* (published from 1786 onwards).

Attitudes to the Middle Ages changed during the early and middle years of the nineteenth century. For Fuseli, Blake and Flaxman the classical and the medieval past coexisted and were equally viable modes of expression. Medieval art as a source of inspiration – in direct opposition to the establishment norm of academic art modelled on antiquity and the High Renaissance – was manifest first in the work of the German Nazarene artists who banded together in 1809 to form the Brotherhood of St Luke. They settled in Rome in a deserted monastery, and imitated both the art and what they believed to be the lifestyle of pre-Renaissance painters. In their adoption of archaic modes of painting and religious subject matter as a means of protest against the principles and practice of academy art, the Nazarenes prefigure the English group of the Pre-Raphaelite Brotherhood, founded in 1848.

It was the essentially Christian quality of medieval art that appealed especially to the nineteenth century. For Augustus Welby Northmore Pugin (1812–52) and later for the Ecclesiologists, the gothic style was the only true Christian style, and it had to be exploited and adapted to the last detail of every church fitment and furnishing. Alexis François Rio, in his influential book, *De la Poésie Chrétienne*, begun in 1836 and translated into English in 1854, said, writing of Fra Angelico:

> Mysticism stands to painting as ecstacy to psychology. It is not enough, then to determine the traditions of the school; it is necessary to associate oneself, with a sympathy strong and deep, with certain religious ideas which preoccupied this artist.[15]

Ultimately such ideas led to Pater at the end of the nineteenth century, but Rio was widely read by non-religious and moderate readers in the first half of the century. W. E. Gladstone, who on his own admission had an undeveloped aesthetic sense and no special pretensions to connoisseurship, was not unusual in reading Rio as he travelled through Germany on his way to Italy in 1838 and in preferring English gothic cathedrals to St Peter's in Rome.[16]

As the Oxford Movement gained momentum, and especially with the second generation of Oxford men (although Pusey and Newman were inclined to ridicule it), medieval art and, indeed, early church music came to be seen increasingly as an inspirational and theologically correct means of reviving the ancient beliefs of the Church of England and of restoring an element of ritual into religious practice. Nicholas Wiseman, writing to the Aberdeen-born artist, William Dyce, in 1834, used the term 'ancients' to describe not the artists of the antique world but the *quattrocentisti*, the fifteenth-century, early Renaissance Italian artists who had until recently been rejected as primitives by comparison with the mature art of Raphael and Michelangelo:

> Your feelings upon religious art . . . I am delighted to see you have cherished within you bright and pure in spite of the smothering atmosphere all around you. When portrait painting and scene painting or what is very akin to it form the surest careers to success for a young artist, to see one who dares to admire and longs to imitate the old, symbolic manner of the ancients is refreshing indeed to the mind; it is like listening to a strain of Palestrina after a boisterous modern finale. I do not know whether the wish to paint your symbolical designs for the Blessed Virgin excludes every other place but Rome for its fulfilment. Here it would be difficult not to say impossible to procure such a commission; but if you have courage enough to make the first step in a new and beautiful track, before the eyes of our own countrymen, and raise a new style and new school in England, where I am sure you would have many admirers, I can from this moment promise you place and opportunity enough to put all your designs in execution.[17]

The comparison that Wiseman made between art and music is also significant, since it was Dyce who, in 1844, founded the Motett Society, named after the form of composition most commonly used by polyphonic composers from the middle of the thirteenth century. Parallel in many ways to the contemporary Percy Society which published medieval poetry, the Motett Society declared itself to be concerned with the publication and distribution of early church music by composers like Tallis and Palestrina, music that was largely forgotten and frequently unobtainable. The Motett Society was non-denominational but was predominantly supported by Tractarians.

The revival of archaic styles in the visual arts during the nineteenth century is invariably to some degree political in motivation. The style and subject matter of Republican Rome were adopted by French artists during the Revolution not merely for aesthetic reasons or as a result of fashion but because artists deliberately sought an apt means of visually demonstrating a historical parallel. In England as in France the present could be read meaningfully only in terms of the past, a heroic past remote in time and place. Walpole's insistence on genealogy, his invention of a pedigree for the objects in his collection going back to the time of the Crusades, is symptomatic of a nationalism which was sustained throughout the nineteenth century. English patrons had generally turned to their native artists only for portraits, and English artists at the end of the eighteenth century were, therefore, unaccustomed to searching for events from British history suitable for pictorial representation. Yet the very fact that regicide French artists like David (in paintings like *The Death of Socrates*, 1787, Metropolitan Museum, New York) laid such stress on the reinterpretation of events from classical history placed an even greater responsibility on English artists at the turn of the century to find edifying scenes from England's great past as subjects for their paintings. In 1788 Benjamin West, the American-born artist who eventually became President of the Royal Academy, painted *The Battle of Crecy* in which the English had routed the French in 1346 (Royal Collection). His picture shows a genuine attempt to capture the spirit of the medieval battlefield, with gleaming armour, foaming horses, archers at the ready, the wounded grovelling in the mud and the whole illuminated by a sun breaking forth from behind a black cloud. English literature provided a wealth of events for the English history painter who was not too scrupulous about authenticity. James Barry, for example, painted *The Death of Cordelia* (1774, Tate Gallery) with a careful reconstruction of Stonehenge in the background for added conviction. West and Barry provided an example which aspiring British history painters at the beginning of the nineteenth century would follow.

One of the chief differences observable between the nineteenth-century artist's treatment of the Middle Ages or even more remote periods of British history and that common at the end of the eighteenth century was the result of the gradual but definite development of interest in the commonplace and the everyday. The hero and the monarch were replaced by the anti-hero and the commoner. The most popular subjects were those from English literature which contained sufficient evidence of actual events to satisfy the desire for an authentic view of the English past without demanding a stringently accurate treatment.

The work of Thomas Stothard fulfilled all these requirements admirably. It is hardly surprising that Cromek, the publisher, having discovered that William Blake was thinking of a large engraving of the Canterbury Pilgrims as described by Chaucer, should have advised Stothard in 1806 to follow suit. He was fully aware of the commercial viability of the project. Blake's *The Canter-bury Pilgrims* (Plate 3) differs greatly, however, from that of Stothard. Blake (who was naturally very angry at being pre-empted by a man whom he had numbered among his friends) described Chaucer as the 'great poetical observer of men, who in every age is born to record and eternize its acts'.[18] Blake's design possesses a hieratic dignity and a strongly archaic quality but there is no attempt at authentic fifteenth-century detail. As David Bindman has pointed out: 'The Pilgrimage is a journey of life and the Pilgrims represent both the components of the human mind and eternal types. . . . The journey is from Experience symbolized by the elaborate Gothic architecture of the Tabarde Inn, into the country-side, over which the sun of Redemption is beginning to rise.'[19] Stothard, on the other hand, depicted, in decorative relief style reminiscent of sixteenth-century German woodcuts, a series of prancing steeds and gesticulating riders, both clad in convincingly medieval trappings. Like those early Victorian artists who were selected to paint scenes from British history on the walls of the newly-erected Houses of Parliament from the late 1840s, Stothard found that archaeological accuracy was a costly business. While at work on his picture, he found the expenses of research and costumes so heavy that he obtained from Cromek the promise of another forty guineas on top of his original fee when the subscriptions came in.[20] Stothard's daughter leaves no doubt that Stothard's *Canterbury Pilgrims* was intended as a history painting, and was read as such by nineteenth-century spectators:

Stothard was truly *the* painter of the oldentime – of early poets and writers; for no artist ever so completely identified himself with the simplicity of their days, with the domestic manners and habits of their period. His mind was familiar with the spirit of those remote ages; he could fall back upon them, and breathe in their air, and move in their warlike, social, rural, or their courtly circles, as familiarly as in his own. His pictures, therefore, of scenes and characters, such

as were recorded by Chaucer or Froissart, had a truth about
them, as well as an imaginative beauty, that gave to each an
individual identity, and wanting which no illustration of
such works, will ever deeply impress the memory, or assist
the mind, in giving, as it were, a bodily and visible existence to the historian and the poet.[21]

If one individual possessed every qualification for the romantic
anti-hero in the repertoire of English artists, it was Thomas Chatterton (1752–70). The author of forged medieval manuscripts the
authenticity of which was still being debated at the end of the nineteenth century, Chatterton's origins were extremely humble. He had
immersed himself in the medieval past of his own locality, St Mary
Redcliffe, Bristol, he was an atheist, and he had risen through his own
creative efforts and died by his own hand before reaching maturity,
reviled and misunderstood by his contemporaries. Chatterton was a
romantic historicist. Through his work, but even more through the
events of his life and especially his death (Ruskin once remarked that
Chatterton's death was the only real thing about him), he became a
symbol of the martyrdom of creative genius.

Henry Wallis's *The Death of Chatterton* (Plate 4) comes late in
our period. It was exhibited at the Royal Academy in 1856 but, as it
encompasses a cult originating at the time of the poet's death in
1770, it provides an appropriate case study for our purposes. The
controversy over the Rowley manuscripts – which Chatterton
claimed to have found in 'Canynge's cofre' in St Mary Redcliffe,
Bristol, but which in fact he had forged – was precipitated by
Horace Walpole and Thomas Gray, but eventually involved many
famous names and raged for most of the succeeding century. Alongside this controversy grew a fascination with Chatterton as an individual, with his short and tragic life, the suicide for which
Walpole was held responsible, his artistic promise and the bizarre
nature and extraordinary intensity of his literary activities. Between
1780 and 1860 at least eleven major biographical studies were published. The British Library possesses, besides these, three large
collections of cuttings from journals and magazines as well as dozens
of different editions of the poet's works. The authoritative edition,
The Works of Thomas Chatterton, was edited in 1803 by Robert
Southey and Joseph Cottle, both of whom had connexions not only

1 J. H. Fuseli, *The Artist Moved by the Magnitude of Antique Fragments* (Kunsthaus, Zurich).

2 Strawberry Hill from the south, from *The Works of Horace Walpole*, London, G. G. and J. Robinson and J. Edwards, 1798.

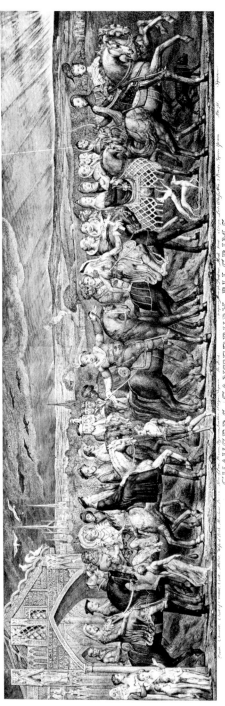

3 W. Blake, *The Canterbury Pilgrims*, engraving (reproduced by courtesy of the Trustees of the British Museum).

4 H. Wallis, *The Death of Chatterton* (The Tate Gallery, London).

5 J. Flaxman, *Chatterton taking a bowl of poison from the spirit of Despair* (reproduced by courtesy of the Trustees of the British Museum).

6 *Portrait of Chatterton*, engraving after an anonymous artist, frontispiece to John Dix, *The Life of Thomas Chatterton*, 1837 (by permission of the British Library).

7 D. Wilkie, *The Blind Fiddler* (The Tate Gallery, London).

8 J. M. W. Turner, *Life Boat and Manby Apparatus going off to a Stranded Vessel making Signal (Blue Lights) of Distress* (Victoria and Albert Museum, London).

9 J. Constable, *The Haywain* (reproduced by courtesy of the Trustees, The National Gallery, London).

10 W. Mulready, *The Butt* (Victoria and Albert Museum, London).

with Bristol but also with the Lake poets; Cottle was publisher of the first edition of Wordsworth's *Lyrical Ballads*. This is tantamount to a declaration of interest on the part of those poets in the young Chatterton.

Coleridge wrote his *Monody on the death of Chatterton* between 1790 and 1796; Wordsworth invoked the memory of 'the marvellous boy' in *Resolution and Independence* of 1802, and proceeded, as a result, to question the whole nature of a poet's existence. Keats who, because of his own untimely death, was often compared with Chatterton by editors and biographers, dedicated *Endymion* to the memory of Thomas Chatterton, which possibly might be said to compensate for the unfortunate couplets in his 1815 *Epistle to George Felton Mathew* which read:

> Yet this is vain – O Mathew lend thy aid
> To find a place where I may greet the maid –
> Where we may soft humanity put on,
> And sit, and rhyme, and think on Chatterton;

Browning, in an essay published in the *Westminster and Foreign Quarterly Review* in 1842,[22] was much concerned with what he saw as Chatterton's inner conflict, born of deceit, remorse and the loss of faith. Rossetti adopted a more common approach, viewing Chatterton as one in a line of poets (among whom he presumably included himself) who were the victims of philistine society:

> A city of sweet speech scorned, – on whose chill stone
> Keats withered, Coleridge pined, and Chatterton,
> Breadless, with poison froze the God-fired breath!
> (*Tiber, Nile and Thames*, lines 12–14)

In view of the enthusiastic response to English literature among artists in France, it is no surprise that the complete *Works* of Chatterton were translated into French in 1839. Chatterton was, however, already a familiar figure to French audiences through Alfred de Vigny's highly successful play of 1835, *Chatterton*. De Vigny presented Chatterton as representative of all those original minds which compulsively challenge authority, a youthful genius crushed by the forces of materialism and philistinism, the poet martyr. In his preface to the play, written at the end of June 1834, De Vigny spoke of his intentions:

I wanted to show spiritual man stifled by a materialistic society, in which the greedy calculator pitilessly exploits intelligence and labour. I have not in the least claimed justification for the desperate acts of unhappy people, but I have protested against the indifference which constrains them. Can this indifference which will not be aroused, this absence of mind which will not be arrested, be too strongly attacked? Is there any way in which society may be moved except by showing it the torture of its victims?

The poet was everything for me; Chatterton was no more than a man's name, and I have intentionally separated the exact facts of his life in order to take from his destiny only what makes of him for ever an example of a noble wretchedness.[23]

From the start, there was immense interest in Chatterton's physiognomy. Flaxman, during the 1780s, executed a washed drawing showing Chatterton taking a bowl of poison from the spirit of Despair (Plate 5). The starving poet drags his emaciated body from his bed to greet, with fevered eyes, the black female figure of Despair who, with an air of theatricality one associates with eighteenth-century illustrations to *Macbeth*, appears from the right holding out what looks like a large pudding basin in one hand. In the background, Genius speeds away into the distance in a horse-drawn chariot and the Muse spreads her hands in a gesture of abandonment. The drawing is a curious attempt to reconcile romantic subject matter with a traditional allegorical visual language.

One set of forgeries and its attendant controversy seem to have bred another. When John Dix published his popular *The Life of Thomas Chatterton* in 1837, it incorporated an engraved portrait of the poet with soulful eyes, innocent countenance and flowing locks (Plate 6). Some years later, a long article on an allegedly forged account of the inquest on Chatterton included the following statement from Dix on the subject of the portrait he had prefixed to his biography. It indicates not only the extraordinary response of nineteenth-century readers to Chatterton the man, a response based entirely on the assumption that the face could be 'read', but also the passion with which, totally unsuccessfully, people searched for an authentic portrait of the poet:

I may allude to another and (excepting to a few persons) hitherto unknown 'fabulous' Chattertonian matter. Prefixed to my Biography was a beautifully engraved portrait of C., from an oil painting. In a letter to Walter Savage Landor, published in Harper's edition of the Laureate's 'Life Correspondence' Southey refers to this painting, and after erroneously stating that it was discovered by me, goes on to say that he had no doubt of its genuineness, as he at once recognized in it a strong likeness to Mrs. Newton [Chatterton's sister]; – and it is somewhat amusing *now* to remember the opinions of some other eminent men to whom I presented proof impressions of this engraving. Ebenezer Elliot wrote to me – 'Poor child! it is a strange and striking countenance.' James Montgomery remarked: 'Just such a face as I imagined when I wrote the lines commencing – "A dying swan of Pindus sings."' Joanna Baillie wrote: 'The head and face are full of genius.' Dr. Wm. Cooke Taylor asserted that 'it was a portrait of genius and weakness'; and when I showed the painting itself to Walter Savage Landor, in my library at Bristol, he burst out with – 'It's the wickedest face I ever saw!' When I published the engraving I fully believed in its authenticity, as did also Mr. Breckenridge who owned the original painting, but years afterwards the truth came out. The likeness proved to be that of a lad, son of a poor painter of Bristol, who wrote 'Chatterton' on the back of it, and sold it for a mere song to a broker, in whose dingy shop a grubber among antiquities found it, and afterwards disposed of it to Mr. Breckenridge.[24]

Henry Wallis, artist of *The Death of Chatterton* (Plate 4), was born in 1830, when the flood of Chattertonism was in full spate. It is interesting to notice how he cultivated and also became a victim to the kind of tortuous literary and artistic relationships that were a feature of the poet's own short life and of the cult that developed after his death. William Michael Rossetti, recollecting his friendship with Wallis during the 1850s, wrote that he had always found him 'an agreeable companion, of solid character and open mind' and that Wallis was 'of some interest to me' as having known Thomas

Love Peacock, the friend of Shelley. 'He once gave me', Rossetti tells us, 'two hairs from Shelley's head which, to my shame, seem to have disappeared.'[25] *The Death of Chatterton* was to transform the young Wallis's life in an extraordinary way. Seeking the kind of authenticity that characterized the medievalism of the Pre-Raphaelite Brotherhood with which Wallis, though not a member, was closely associated, Wallis arranged to paint his picture of Chatterton in the Gray's Inn chambers of Austin Daniel, a friend of George Meredith, the novelist. Meredith is supposed to have posed for the dead poet, but, while the picture was being painted, Wallis and Meredith's wife were cultivating a common attraction that resulted in Mary Meredith bearing Wallis's child in 1858 and the eventual elopement of the couple.

The Death of Chatterton is a shocking image, all the more so because of the smallness of the painting (it measures only 80.2 × 108.7 cm) and its jewel-like brilliance which is reminiscent of a Van Eyck. It has been described as 'a secular pieta, the lonely single bed replacing the embrace of the Virgin Mother'.[26] Certainly the size of the painting and its format with curved top support that interpretation. But in viewing Wallis's presentation of Chatterton's lonely death, surrounded by burnt manuscripts and symbols of mortality (the burnt-out candle, the fragile flower which blossoms in its pot on the mean window sill) and of immortality (the open window through which St Paul's is visible and the dawn breaking over the city), it is important to bear in mind another pictorial tradition upon which Wallis subtly drew to render his interpretation all the more poignant. The implicit association between the suicide of a fraud and the death of Christ is powerful; equally effective in visual terms is the way in which Wallis exploited a long pictorial tradition of heroic death-bed scenes, which originated with the specifically Christian *Extreme Unction* of Poussin (1644, Duke of Sutherland) and was developed in England in the late eighteenth century as an antidote to the hedonistic pursuits of rococo artists through such works as Gavin Hamilton's *Achilles bewailing the Death of Patroclus* (1760–3, National Gallery of Scotland) and *Andromache bewailing the Death of Hector* (1761, engraved by Cunego in 1764), George Romney's drawing *Argia and Antigone with the dead body of Polynices* (c. 1775–80, Fitzwilliam Museum, Cambridge), Alexander Runciman's *The Death of Oscar* (1770–2, National

Gallery of Scotland) and countless tomb monuments from the end of the eighteenth and the beginning of the nineteenth centuries. The salient characteristic of all these depictions is that death was shown as a public event, the deceased or dying being universally and dramatically mourned. Gradually the hero or the warrior of these death-bed scenes was replaced by the artist or the writer, but the event remained essentially public. The earliest examples occurred in France with paintings like François Menageot's *Deathbed of Leonardo da Vinci* (Musée de l'Hôtel de Ville, Amboise) exhibited at the *Salon* in 1781. The type was developed in England and became very popular after Queen Victoria's accession. An interesting Victorian example of the genre is the constructed photograph (made from five negatives) *Fading Away*, taken in 1858 by Henry Peach Robinson.[27]

Wallis was able to exploit this well-known visual tradition on several levels. In the first place, the absence of the mourners whose presence is an essential and familiar part of the death-bed scene emphasizes the pathos of this youth's self-inflicted death. We are provoked to ask whether anyone will come to find him, whether there will be a single soul to mourn his death. In the second place, the visual association between the hero's death and the passing of the poet implies that the poet is equal in status to the hero of ancient Greece or the great artist of the Italian Renaissance. In the third place, by publicly exhibiting a painting representing a solitary death in a bare attic instead of the customary rhetorical death-bed scene, the artist demonstrates to the world the elegiac and devotional nature of his own creative act. He is, as it were, atoning for the neglect suffered by his brother artist during his lifetime and reminding the public of 1856 of its obligations towards poets and artists.

As an associate of the Pre-Raphaelite Brotherhood, Wallis was well qualified to place before the public a harsh reminder of the ultimate effects of genius neglected. It is, of course, important to remember that the Royal Academy's annual exhibition was virtually the only public arena for artists, and an event of greater significance for the press and the cultivated world generally than it is today. Only a few years before Wallis exhibited *The Death of Chatterton*, Millais's *Christ in the House of his Parents* (1849, Tate Gallery) had been savagely attacked in the press. The Pre-Raphaelite's challenge to academic authority, their criticism of the lack of serious and meaningful subject matter and sloshy techniques (they referred to the first president as Sir Sloshua Reynolds) are comparable to the rejection by neoclassical artists of the frivolities of rococo art in the late eighteenth century. Their attempt to capture intense moments of personal, emotional experience, their brave experiments with new modes of painting, their questioning of traditional patterns of art education and their enthusiasm for Romantic English literature (especially Keats) and for a medieval past ensure for the Pre-Raphaelites a central position in any discussion of Romanticism in the pictorial arts.

When his painting was exhibited at the Royal Academy, Wallis chose to append a quotation not from Chatterton's own work or from one of the many biographies of the artist, but from Marlowe's *Dr Faustus*, thus emphasizing the image of unfulfilled promise.

> Cut is the branch that might have grown full straight
> And burned is Apollo's laurel bough.[28]

Faust's story is that of a brazen challenger of authority, but it is also that of man's agonized exploration of the unknown. Later in this book, in chapter 4, Tamburlaine will be presented as a proto-Romantic. Perhaps Faustus, too, might be seen in that light. In 1856 Ruskin found the painting 'faultless and wonderful: a most noble example of the great school . . . it is one of the pictures which intend, and accomplish, the entire placing before your eyes of an actual fact – and that a solemn one'.[29] But we should, perhaps, give the last word to Holman Hunt:

> The cruelty of the world towards poor Chatterton, whose only offence was that he asked to be heard as a poet under a feigned name, will never henceforth be remembered without recognition of Henry Wallis, the painter who first so pathetically excited pity for his fate in his picture of the death of the hapless boy.[30]

Science and art

One of the most significant changes in English art between *c.* 1760 and *c.* 1860 took place in the classification of different kinds of painting. Reynolds had, in his *Discourses* (1769–1790), established a hierarchy which placed history painting in the great style (modelled

on antique art, Raphael and Michelangelo) at the top of the scale as
the only truly worthwhile pursuit of the artist. As Reynolds expressed a view of the comparative value of different genres in
painting that was so widely accepted as to be all but universal –
Blake was one of the very few dissenters – it is worth quoting him at
some length:

> If deceiving the eye were the only business of the art, there
> is no doubt, indeed, but the minute painter would be more
> apt to succeed: but it is not the eye, it is the mind, which
> the painter of genius desires to address; nor will he waste a
> moment upon those smaller objects, which only serve to
> catch the sense, to divide the attention, and to counteract
> his great design of speaking to the heart.
>
> This is the ambition which I wish to excite in your minds;
> and the object I have had in my view throughout this dis-
> course, is that one great idea, which gives to painting its
> true dignity, which entitles it to the name of a Liberal Art,
> and ranks it as a sister of poetry. . . .
>
> As for the various departments of painting, which do not
> presume to make such high pretensions, they are many.
> None of them are without their merit, though none enter
> into competition with this universal presiding idea of the
> art. The painters who have applied themselves more par-
> ticularly to low and vulgar characters, and who express with
> precision the various shades of passion, as they are ex-
> hibited by vulgar minds, (such as we see in the works of
> Hogarth,) deserve great praise; but as their genius has been
> employed on low and confined subjects, the praise we give
> must be as limited as its object. The merry-making, or
> quarrelling, of the Boors of Teniers; the same sort of pro-
> ductions of Brouwer, or Ostade, are excellent in their kind;
> and the excellence and its praise will be in proportion, as,
> in those limited subjects, and peculiar forms, they intro-
> duce more or less the expression of those passions, as they
> appear in general and more enlarged nature. This principle
> may be applied to the Battle-pieces of Bourgognone, the
> French Gallantries of Watteau, and even beyond the ex-
> hibition of animal life, to the Landscapes of Claude Lorrain,

and the Sea-Views of Vandervelde. All these painters have, in general, the same right, in different degrees, to the name of a painter, which a satirist, an epigrammatist, a sonneteer, a writer of pastorals, or descriptive poetry, has to that of a poet.[31]

During the early years of the nineteenth century, the lowly genres of painting to which Reynolds accords such reserved approbation, landscape and those paintings of ordinary people about their every-day business that are known, confusingly, as genre subjects, received new impetus and were radically reconsidered both by artists and by the public. Turner, whom everyone remembers as a 'landscape painter', practised all those 'departments of painting' frowned upon by Reynolds. He and Thomas Girtin transformed the traditional topographical, descriptive view of the estate, the gentle-man's seat or the site of antiquarian interest into a study of atmos-phere and mood through the rendering of light. Turner, arguably the most versatile of all British artists, tried his hand at every class of painting from the lyrical *fête-champêtre* (for example, *Richmond Hill*, *c*. 1825, Lady Lever Gallery, Port Sunlight) to the grand epic landscape or coastal scene (for example, *Ancient Rome; Agrippina landing with the ashes of Germanicus. The Triumphal Bridge and Palace of the Caesars restored*, Royal Academy 1839, Tate Gallery) and from localized genre (for example, *A Country Blacksmith dis-puting upon the Price charged to the Butcher for Shoeing his Poney* [*sic*], Royal Academy 1807, Tate Gallery) to the complex icono-graphical pastiche (as in *Rome from the Vatican. Raffaelle, accompanied by the Fornarina, preparing his Pictures for the Decoration of the Loggia*, Royal Academy 1820, Tate Gallery). The very titles indicate Turner's determined awareness of the manifold roles of landscape and genre painting in the nineteenth century and his consciousness of living in the age of Gibbon as well as in the age of Byron.

W. Vaughan has claimed of landscape that:

No mode of painting contributed more to the radical changes that took place in art in the succeeding century. For it was paradoxically through constant study before nature, the noting of effects of atmosphere and light, that artists gradually moved away from descriptive painting towards the communication of pure visual experiences – a development that culminated in the emergence of abstract art shortly before the First World War.

However, as Vaughan has also pointed out, the main issue for early nineteenth-century landscape artists was whether the representation of the forms of nature could in itself have the sort of significance hitherto accorded to the representation of ennobling events or ideas.[32] The terms in which John Constable passionately discussed his art are precisely those of universality and an appeal to the heart in which Reynolds couched his didactic message to his students on the merits of history painting. In a letter to his friend John Fisher about *A Boat Passing a Lock* (1824, Trustees of the Walter Morrison Pictures Settlement), which was on exhibition at the Royal Academy, Constable said that it

> forms a decided feature, and its light cannot be put out, because it is the light of nature, the mother of all that is valuable in poetry, painting or anything else where an appeal to the soul is required. The language of the heart is the only one that is universal; and Sterne says, he disregards all rules, but makes his way to the heart as he can.[33]

At the same time as Constable was seeking for naturalistic landscape painting the recognition accorded to history painting, artists like David Wilkie (1785–1841) and William Mulready (1786–1863) were establishing for themselves a respectable position in the English art world as painters of that other traditionally lowly form of art, the genre subject. Small-scale, intimate scenes like Wilkie's *The Blind Fiddler* (1807, Plate 7), commissioned by Sir George Beaumont, and Mulready's *The Rattle* (1808, Tate Gallery) possessed the moral strength of the classical history piece, but allied to it the close observation of human nature in particular and a narrative of human behaviour capable of capturing the emotions of the viewer. The first of these paintings shows a humble Scottish interior in which an itinerant fiddler is playing for the family which includes a babe in arms and a small boy naughtily aping the fiddler who, of course, cannot know that he is the subject of this imitation. The detail of the painting is memorable, ranging from an accumulation of toys and cooking utensils to an infantile drawing of a human figure pinned to the cupboard door. In *The Rattle* Mulready shows a similarly lowly interior in which a small boy entertains his baby brother or sister with a rattle. The two are seated on the floor in a shaft of sunlight that filters into the dark cottage down a stairway from a hay loft. Both paintings are isolated moments in time from the lives of ordinary people to which the artist has lent dignity, charm and a certain poignant nostalgia for the pleasures of child-hood.

Everyday life is presented by early nineteenth-century genre painters in England in an unusual aspect. Wilkie had arrived in London as a young, unknown, Scottish artist in 1805 and, like the poetry of Burns, his Scots subject matter possessed great appeal for an English audience. It might be said that rustic and humble life was chosen by Wilkie and Mulready for much the same reasons as expressed by Wordsworth in his Preface to the second edition of the *Lyrical Ballads*:

> because in that condition of life our elementary feelings coexist in a state of greater simplicity, and, consequently, may be more accurately contemplated, and more forcibly communicated; because the manners of rural life germin-ate from those elementary feelings, and, from the necessary character of rural occupations, are more easily compre-hended, and are more durable; and, lastly because in that condition the passions of men are incorporated with the beautiful and permanent forms of nature.[34]

It seems no accident that Constable, Wordsworth and Wilkie were all patronized by Sir George Beaumont, who, we are told by C. R. Leslie, had acquired Hogarth's mahl stick[35] and was deter-mined to keep it till a painter worthy to receive it should appear; he kept the stick till he saw Wilkie's *Village Politicians* (1806, Earl of Mansfield, Scone Palace).[36] Sir George entertained Constable, Wordsworth and Wilkie at Coleorton Hall in the early years of the century, and it was there that Constable painted *The Cenotaph* (1836), from the monument to Sir Joshua Reynolds that Sir George had had erected in his grounds. At the same time, Mulready and Wilkie were intimate friends, sharing accommodation, working habits and sketching excursions until the time of Wilkie's nervous breakdown and departure for the continent in 1825. C. R. Leslie,

Constable's friend and biographer and himself an able painter of genre scenes, said in 1855 that forty years' observation of the art world had convinced him that nothing had contributed more 'to retard the advancement of Painting than the well-meant, but often thoughtless and mistaken talk' about High Art.[37] Leslie went on to say that pretension and false sentiment were often found in High Art or, as the term was then more generally used, in religious art, the subjects of which were taken from the Bible or the legends of the church. Leslie was ideally placed to defend the position of landscape and genre painters:

> It is clear to me, that had any of the early Christian painters descended to subjects of familiar life, their treatment would not, in principle or in execution, have differed from that in their religious pictures, for in their portraits it did not. I think, therefore, that the attaching of more importance, than they deserve, to such definitions as *religious art*, and *religious painters*, is calculated to blind us to many of the beauties of Nature, and to lead us to suppose that because, by the early masters, some of her grandest and most charming qualities were unperceived, they are inconsistent with religious feeling; and that there must be a marked difference between religious men, women and children, and the rest of the world; and that even skies, trees, fields, rivers and mountains may become religious and therefore sublime, by their unlikeness to Nature.[38]

By the time F. G. Stephens came to write his biography of William Mulready in 1864 there was no problem about placing Mulready in the worthy ranks of the painters of history, for, after all, paintings like *The Wolf and the Lamb* (1820, Royal Collection), the subject of which is a bully threatening a mother's pet, clearly were able to be interpreted as moralizing expositions of universal characteristics of human nature:

> Mulready's biography presents more than a record of works produced, honours won, and wealth acquired. One of the best-known artists of this age, independent and thoroughly English, a master in painting, a humourist without malice, an indefatigable student – he, whether with touching

pathos or gaiety, imparted to numerous *genre* subjects that
artistic completeness we seek in historical painting, and, by
the truthfulness of all he did, ennobled them in the process.
It was no small thing to have, with a newer purpose, carried
onwards in art that which Wilkie began, and in doing so,
rounded a long life with half-unconscious heroism.[39]

As we shall see in chapter 4 in greater detail taste and beauty no
longer satisfied the Romantic as a basis for art (see, in particular,
pp. 177–86). Knowledge and imagination were seen to play equally
important roles in the creation of what became the characteristically
modern idea of 'the work of art'. Art was separated from craft, and
the artist had become a highly self-conscious creator, assessing and
questioning his position in relation to his own artwork and to
society.

For the pictorial artist, and especially for the painter of landscape
and genre scenes, the enquiry into the relationship between
knowledge and imagination is one that brought him most closely
into contact with the natural sciences. Advances made during the
nineteenth century in geology, botany, astronomy and meteorology
could scarcely be ignored by artists preoccupied with their relationship to the environment. For the genre painter phrenology,
physiognomical studies, psychology and various branches of pseudo-
science were of considerable interest, whilst the landscape painter
became increasingly concerned with understanding causes as well as
observing effects.

From the end of the eighteenth century, art and science were
regarded as the natural sisterhood that painting and poetry had
been since the seventeenth century. Prince Hoare, in 1810, edited a
journal called *The Artist* with the manifest aim of demonstrating
how the arts and sciences were unified in the search for knowledge:

> It is the design of *The Artist* to seek professional informa-
> tion on the subject of the liberal arts in the most dis-
> tinguished sources of his country, and to present their
> recondite stores in a familiar garb to his readers. With these
> offerings he proposes to connect accounts of the modern
> improvements in science, and such observations on them as
> experience and equally appropriate study can best supply.
> With this view, he regards every adept of Art or Science

under the general description of an Artist, or the *active
student* of Nature and Science; for the practice which
renders science useful to life, what is it but Art.[40]

The connexion between the aims and methods of the scientist and
those of the artist was invoked frequently in the nineteenth century,
not always in the most expected places. Samuel Palmer, an artist we
associate more with mysticism than with naturalism, recalled
William Mulready's saying: 'We cannot proceed a step without
anatomy; and in landscape what is analogous to it. We cannot
rightly see or imitate what is before us without understanding
structure.'[41] F. G. Stephens, writing in 1850 in the short-lived Pre-
Raphaelite journal *The Germ*, suggested that modern artists should
emulate the geologist or the chemist in exactness when they studied
and attempted to represent natural forms.[42] By this time, however,
the desire for 'truth' in pictorial representation had reached obsessive proportions; and when Mrs Jameson, writing in 1868, spoke of
'a scientific class of art as of books', hers was the voice of the critic in
search of illustration, far removed from a discussion of the creative
artist's enquiring after knowledge.[43]

The visual impact of industrial technology was considerable at the
end of the eighteenth century. Coal mines and furnaces provided
the sort of ingredients in a landscape which Edmund Burke had
prescribed in his essay on the sublime. Nevertheless it is by and large
futile to look for pictures treating subjects drawn directly from the
natural sciences. Joseph Wright's *An Experiment with an Air Pump*
(1768, Tate Gallery) is an exceptional subject, arising from the particular social and intellectual climate of Derby during the second
half of the eighteenth century. However, it demonstrates more convincingly the artist's predilection for the combination of artificial
lighting and moonlight – which fascinated Wright, just as it was to
intrigue Turner in some of his early sea-pieces – and the varied
emotional responses of the observers than his interest in science *per
se*. It might be argued that Turner's painting of 1831, *Life Boat and
Manby Apparatus going off to a Stranded Vessel making Signal
(Blue Lights) of Distress* (Plate 8), reveals an interest in the
technological advances of George William Manby, who was made a
Fellow of the Royal Society in 1831 for the invention of the lifeline
rocket-flare system. But the picture is striking for the splendid

atmospheric effects of the stormy beach scene, only one small part of which is the distant blue light of Manby's rocket. Turner's fascination with natural and mechanical sciences is indisputable, but it is most accurately reflected in the experimental nature of much of his own painting and in the way in which he read, absorbed and re-interpreted Goethe's answer to Newton's analysis of the spectrum. *Zur Farbenlehre*, first published in 1810, was translated into English by C. L. Eastlake and published in 1840 as the *Theory of Colours*. It was the first of a long series of treatises on the physiological and psychological effects of light and colour avidly read and tested by artists and leading ultimately to the painting of Seurat and Signac in France at the end of the century.

Precisely how the Romantic artist was affected by the principles of scientific knowledge, how he balanced these with his own view of the role of the imagination, can best be demonstrated by looking closely at select works by two artists we have already mentioned, the landscape painter, John Constable (1776–1837), and the genre painter, William Mulready (1786–1863). Neither had any pre-tensions to intellectualism or erudition. Constable's father was a prosperous corn merchant. He was brought up with all the advantages of a well-to-do family, and inherited from his parents a mistrust of political reform and religious dissent, as well as a pious and honest approach to life. William Mulready, on the other hand, was the son of an Irish leather-breeches-maker who had settled in London in the very early years of the nineteenth century. He knew poverty and hardship, and so greatly impressed William Godwin with his self-sufficiency at the age of sixteen that Godwin made his life the subject of an exemplary tale for children called *The Looking Glass*, published in 1805 under the pseudonym Theophilus Marcliffe. Neither artist mixed socially with contemporary great men of science. At best they can have been aware only very generally of scientific developments in their own day. Admittedly Constable in 1833 was reading William Phillips's *Outlines of Mineralogy and Geology* (1815), but this was scarcely a progressive work, and much of his knowledge of botany was acquired from Gilbert White's *Natural History of Selborne*. Mulready was conversant with discussions on pigments, colour and light. He had read George Field's *Chromatography* of 1835, but there is no evidence that he possessed or had read anything one would recognize as a scientific text.

Yet clearly both men were keenly aware of something distinctive called scientific method, and were ready and able to exploit the reverberations of science in their own art. They were, in an important way, typical of their generation.

In an often quoted statement of *c.* 1836, Constable said:

> In such an age as this, painting should be *understood*, not looked on with blind wonder, nor considered only as poetic aspiration, but as a pursuit, *legitimate, scientific and mechanical*.[44]

Recourse to the *Oxford English Dictionary* is a help in explaining what Constable meant by these words. 'Legitimate', in its most familiar usage, means of lawful descent or authoritative. But an obsolete meaning gives us 'legitimate' as genuine or real as opposed to spurious, and it is in this sense, I believe, that Constable used the word, thereby setting up painting as a genuine pursuit as opposed to a decorative, dilettante's and connoisseur's amusement. When Constable called painting a 'mechanical' pursuit, he did not in any way mean that it is connected with machine-like procedures. His usage of the word 'mechanical' is, again, an obsolete form used in the sense of 'skilled in the application of an art', as opposed to 'speculative'. 'Scientific' is used by Constable in its ancient sense of referring to knowledge as opposed to practice, thus implying that painting is not merely a craft or an art that produces something to please the senses but a genuine means of discourse and the communication of knowledge.

Constable's belief in the imagination is greatly at odds with, say, that of Blake. Nonetheless the alliance of knowledge and imagination which is fundamental to his art is just as much a part of Romanticism as is Blake's insistence on the irrational. We can more fully appreciate Constable's position by looking at the opening lines of his lecture to the Royal Institution on 26 May 1836 in which he is anxious to establish the status of the landscape painter through analogy with the practice of the scientist:

> I am here on behalf of my own profession, and I trust it is with no intrusive spirit that I now stand before you; but I am anxious that the world should be inclined to look to painters for information on painting. I hope to show that

ours is a regularly taught profession; that it is *scientific* as well as *poetic*; that imagination alone never did, and never can, produce works that are to stand by a comparison with *realities*; and to show, by tracing the connecting links in the history of landscape painting, that no great painter was ever self-taught.[45]

Constable applied this statement to painting *in his own age*; he was making a plea for the complete reappraisal of the foundations, intentions and assumptions of landscape art in an age which he felt to be different in important ways from previous ages. Constable is often seen primarily as an artist of sentiment, a painter who recorded vividly and energetically for posterity his own emotional response to scenes that were familiar and dear to him. No one would argue about the personal content, the subjective element in Constable's art. After all, the evidence of the memorable scenes in the area of the Stour Valley and Hampstead that he knew so well is clear enough, and it is supported by many remarks and statements by the artist, the best known of which is his comment: 'Painting is with me but another word for feeling.'[46] But it is essential to an understanding of Constable as a Romantic artist that we appreciate not only the subjective aspects of his art but also what he believed to be the role and the right concern of the landscape painter in the early years of the nineteenth century.

There is no doubt that Constable saw himself as an innovator, but he also acknowledged his debt to Claude, Ruisdael and many other landscape painters of the past. Like Wordsworth, he was aware of his own position in relation to tradition whilst being much concerned with new ways of seeing and modes of expression in landscape:

In Art as in Literature . . . there are two modes by which men endeavour to attain the same end, and seek distinction. In the one, the Artist, intent only on the study of departed excellence, or on what others have accomplished, becomes the imitator of their works, or he selects and combines their various beauties; in the other he seeks perfection at its PRIMITIVE SOURCE, NATURE.[47]

Nor did Constable merely use words in his attempt to master the causes. Instructing his engraver Lucas on how the Stour Valley should be depicted, Constable made a diagrammatic study which can be identified with some accuracy from the 1805 Ordnance Survey map. Lucas inscribed on the back:

> This drawing was made by John Constable July 1830 to illustrate the general characters of the valleys of England particularly that which divides the counties of Essex and Suffolk. Telling me of the great attachment of the villagers to the place where they were born relating the story of a farm laborer [*sic*] who after crossing the valley on to the Essex side being about to descend the rising ground looking back said 'Goodbye old England perhaps I may never see you any more'.[48]

About thirty years ago, the German writer, Kurt Badt, suggested that the unusual cloud studies that Constable executed in Hampstead mainly between 1821 and 1822, and which frequently include detailed citations of the prevailing weather conditions, the directions of the wind and the immediate prospects for change, were inspired by Constable's reading of *The Climate of London* by Luke Howard, published 1818–20.[49] But it is typical of Constable that he should have been more deeply affected by his own observation and by his knowledge of the work of his predecessors in the visual arts than by any single text. The coincidence of dates is not significant as recently cloud studies by Constable dating from long before 1821 have come to light.[50] Moreover, Constable was a miller's son, accustomed from his earliest years to keep an eye on the weather, and in 1821 he had just moved from Suffolk to live in Hampstead, which commands impressive views and where the observer is conscious of perpetually changing skies.

The systematic study of clouds had, as Constable was certainly aware, been undertaken by other English artists. Alexander Cozens (1717–86) had been much concerned with observing and classifying natural phenomena including cloud formations and trees. In 1771 he published a collection of analytical studies entitled *The Shape, Skeleton and Foliage of Thirty Two Species of Trees for the use of Painting and Drawing*. A companion volume had the title *The Various species of Composition in Nature: Sixteen Subjects in four plates, with Observations and Instructions*. Unfortunately no complete copy of either work has survived, though some engraved illustrations to the works are extant. More interesting is the fact that a set of very close copies by John Constable after Alexander Cozen's studies are still extant. Constable, the landscape artist, who, when Blake said of one of his drawings, 'Why, this is not a drawing, but *inspiration*,' replied, 'I never knew it before; I meant it for a drawing,'[51] laboriously and methodically built on the experience of the past and the evidence of his eye. The resulting paintings were, however, in no way dehumanized or lacking in feeling.

A landscape like *The Haywain* (Plate 9) often appears to be the epitome of the English Romantic painting. It is indeed, yet what sort of a picture is it, how was it made and what sort of questions should we ask about it? To begin with, it was painted in 1821, by which time Constable was no longer living in Suffolk. He signed the painting 'John Constable pinxit, London 1821', using the time-honoured formula of the painter in the great tradition. The picture is not an on-the-spot record; the subject is one that Constable knew and loved, but he painted it from a distance in a measured and considered way, writing to ask a Suffolk friend, Johnny Dunthorne, for details when he was unable to remember the exact appearance of the local hay cart that he wished to incorporate into his painting. *The Haywain*, like many Romantic works, does not exhibit the sort of frenzied self-expression that has traditionally been regarded as one of the characteristics of Romanticism. In order to paint it Constable distanced himself in place and in time (the genesis of all the large Stour scenes lies in the sketches done on holiday in Suffolk), and he also placed himself at one remove emotionally from the picture by a completely innovative procedure. Paint was, for Constable, a highly expressive medium. His oil sketches are bold and spontaneous, often with a violence of handling and a degree of impasto unprecedented in European painting at the time. When painting the large Stour scenes of the mid-1820s ('the six-footers', as they are often called) Constable was in a calculated way challenging by the scale of his canvases and the method of his operation the establishment art world. In order to do this, it was imperative that *The Haywain* should, without losing any of the freshness and immediacy that Constable knew to be his strength, possess a degree of monumentality and composure which would win for it the sort of consideration accorded to the history piece. Constable therefore devised the full-scale oil sketch (now in the Victoria and Albert Museum), and there, outside the finished and exhibited canvas, worked out much of the violence and emotion in his response to the subject. Even so, when *The Haywain* was exhibited at the *Salon* in Paris in 1824, even though it was admired, it was regarded as a sketch. In subsequent paintings like *The Leaping Horse*, Constable found it increasingly difficult to relinquish the full-scale sketch, and he worked on both canvases alongside each other, delaying the decision about which should be the finished work for as long as possible.

The Haywain offers all the typical paradoxes of the Romantic work of art. It is, in a sense, a manifesto for an undervalued genre of painting. It incorporates the results of an intensive study of the natural world – the weather, for example, is uncertain, and squalls are sure to come before the afternoon is out; the swallows are skimming the water; and the fisherman at the right is taking advantage of the conditions in which fish rise to the surface – yet that study is not an end in itself. When the painting was exhibited at the Royal Academy, the title given was simply 'Landscape Noon'. It is subsequent generations who have picked out the moment of narrative as significant and endowed the painting with its present title. For Constable the subject is a landscape at a particular time of day; no detail carries the weight of an event in the painting for the landscape is itself the event. It is for this reason that the weather is so precisely observed, that the young woman by the cottage does her washing before the water is stirred up by the imminent rain, that the hay-makers in distant fields labour, that the fisherman throws his line. The landscape and our response to it is what is important, and Constable has calculated this to the last degree, distancing us from the scene by the elliptical curve of the bank in the foreground, painting out the figure on horseback that is prominent in the oil sketch as a point of contact between us and the distant view and whose ghostly form is still faintly discernible in the original painting, and highlighting the distant meadow with sunlight. For if we identify too closely with any of the many incidents of the painting then we lose the event that is the landscape. It is ironic that the haywain on its apparently pointless journey – this is clearly not a ford and the river is deep in the direction the cart is moving – should have become the focal point of the picture for generations of spectators reared on anecdotal pictorial art.

To sum up, Constable classified, analysed and made immensely detailed studies of fragments of nature directly observed. He was keenly aware of his own art as a methodical labour in which he built on the accumulated experience of others just as the scientist does. He believed that landscape painting had the same power to inspire the intellect and the emotions as had always been thought to be the reserve of history painting. But Constable's paintings are neither polemical nor didactic, nor even scientifically accurate in the way that, for example, Ruskin's drawings are. For Constable, a study of the same areas of nature that were occupying the attentions of natural scientists could result in a new understanding of the phenomena observed. This led to a new sort of pictorial structure, which discarded the old-fashioned schematic landscape composition built up of receding horizontals, stabilizing verticals and figures carefully placed to lead the eye into the distance (a form of composition which Constable himself knew well how to exploit). The order and structure of Constable's art is, therefore, a 'natural' one, mimetic of structures observed in the external world, not imposed on visual experience by means of artifice. Classification and understanding of the relationship of parts to the whole lead to the creation of a work of art which possesses its own unity, emulative of that which could be observed scientifically in nature.

John Constable and William Mulready were contemporaries and acquaintances, but no more. Indeed, Constable regarded Mulready's work with deep suspicion and, with the single-mindedness of the true innovator, refused to consider seriously the art of a man whose interests were parallel but dissimilar. Mulready grew up in the London house of John and Cornelius Varley, and married their sister, Elizabeth, from whom he very quickly became estranged. John Varley was an astrologer, and Cornelius was an inventor and 'scientist'. Their circle included William Godwin, Blake and Shelley, a radically-minded group many of whom were to some degree interested in science. John and Cornelius Varley were both watercolourists of no mean reputation, earning their living by teaching, by the publication of treatises on landscape drawing for the benefit of amateurs and by the sale of their own paintings. Of the two, Cornelius is the more interesting, though few of his pictures or drawings survive. His studies around Kensington and Bayswater from the early years of the century and his watercolours of Wales are characterized by a sensitivity to light and an ability to view nature with a literal and unsentimental eye. In their own day both men were as well, or better known for their activities outside the field of landscape art as for their landscape paintings. In the *Philosophical Magazine* Cornelius Varley published many papers on subjects such as atmospheric electricity, live boxes for animalculae, cages for keeping animals and plants alive for several days to watch their development and progress, and the phial microscope for the continuous observation of *chara vulgaris* and *nitella*. He was also a specialist in optical instruments and the inventor of the graphic telescope, a device for making accurate portraits of objects. John Varley's son, Cromwell, was a pioneer in the study of electricity, and his grandson became famous in phrenology and theosophy.

It was at John Varley's behest that William Blake drew his celebrated visionary head, from which he later painted *The Ghost of a Flea* (Tate Gallery) – a tempera version. It is typical of the intellectual ambience of this circle that this image, for all the well-authenticated visionary circumstances in which it was produced, bears a strong resemblance to an engraving of a flea in Robert Hooke's *Micrographia*[52] and to an image in Lavater's influential book on physiognomy, the English edition of which had been edited by his friend, Fuseli, in 1800. The young Mulready eventually came to possess the Blake–Varley sketch-book containing the drawing of the ghost of the flea and Varley's account of how, one afternoon, Blake observed the apparition walking into the room, carrying its bowl of blood. Mulready's own portrait featured as one of the illustrations in John Varley's *A Treatise on Zodiacal Physiognomy* of 1828, a work which took the sort of physiognomical study made popular in the eighteenth century by Lavater and allied to it Varley's own speciality, astrology. Zodiacal physiognomy, Varley insisted, was 'properly a branch of natural philosophy'.

William Mulready did not wholeheartedly embrace the Varleys' enthusiasms, but they made a profound impression on him. The study of physiognomy, especially of profile, in relation to psychology is apparent in paintings like *The Butt* of 1848 (Plate 10), in which the enacted drama and narrative are conveyed to the spectator through facial expression. The event is simple and unimportant – a moment of play in a rural environment – it is the human response to the event that is significant and worthy of record. Here are no caricatured or stereotyped expressions such as we find in Gillray or

Rowlandson and no sentimental clichés that we expect to see in the anecdotal country scenes of Wheatley or Morland. The practice of recording and classifying observed material which Mulready learned in his youth from a circle of men interested in science and art never left him, and formed the foundation of the pictorial and thematic unity of a painting like *The Butt*. Between a buttress of trees, one boy prepares to shoot a cherry into the mouth of a second boy while two girls await the result. The boy on the left has his mouth tightly shut, lips pursed, muscles flexed ready to project the cherry into his friend's mouth. The tense curves of his body as he concentrates on the act are reiterated in the curve of the jar on which he has laid his ammunition. The other boy has eyes and mouth wide open, back straight and elbow drawn in. He is almost the exact reverse image of his opposite number. Both boys are seen in profile, tightly expressive. In the centre are two girls whose eyes and hands are relaxed and who convey enjoyment. The group is remarkably tightly knit. The two girls look at the butt but the dog looks at the boy who is aiming his cherry, thus maintaining the balance.

Formal unity is, of course, something one would expect to find in almost any painting of interest executed between 1400 and 1900. But there is much evidence that Mulready thought deeply about conceptual unity – the unity of ideas through images – which can be something different. Pages of notes recording every sort of phenomenon and grouping and classifying characteristics and events are to be found among Mulready's notebooks from *c.* 1812 until the late 1840s. Here is one example:

> The fishermen and watermen wear Red, Blue and Dark and Light green jackets. A few wear brown. Blacksmith and grocer is [*sic*] distinguished from the working Baker by leathern apron and the colour of his *shirt*, a shoemaker or cobbler differs little in general from smiths – the cobbler wears a waistcoat & often a nightcap. Paviours and their labour men are very like the above in dress but generally are not always without the apron.
>
> They carry no very obvious character about with them.
> . . . The working navigator is also the same kind of fellow but his dirt is redder – more clayey daub. The brick maker is like but still redder & he wears the dark cloth apron.

All other fellows are distinguished by the colour of the Dirt.[53]

The sense of balance between the individual and the group as well as the coherence of theme and composition in Mulready's work are the result of the same sort of rigorous discipline and empirical observation to which Constable was committed, but in a different area of subject-matter. In a notebook Mulready recorded fragments of thought about his art:

A *Well Ordered Multitude*, one, divided, subdivided and further divisible upon further research Phenomena, Choice, The Multitude, the group, the man, the face, the eye, the hand, the fingers, The Forest, the clump, the tree, the branch, the leaf, as there is a time so there is a distance for all things. The distance which shows the parts of larger things, show the whole [?] smaller things.[54]

Whether or not one would agree with the notion that Romantic man is a recognizable type, there is no doubt that artists of the Romantic period like Constable and Mulready were consciously endeavouring to encompass the universe in their art, and to discern in external nature, in the broadest sense of the words, a structure that was endemic and that owed nothing to the divinely ordered concept of the universe that their predecessors had endorsed.

Romanticism in the visual arts has no single identity, no overriding single characteristic. If Romantic artists shared one thing, it was their consciousness of being innovators, of creating, within a cultural experience broad enough to contain both literal and intuitive concepts of knowledge, works of art that exploited the interdependence of human experience. There is, about many Romantic works of art, a quality of the manifesto, a determination to challenge. Alongside the introspective and even obsessive exploration of interior worlds and private tragedies is a strong adherence to experience that is universal and by which both the past and the present may be measured.

Notes

1 The drawing, previously in the collection of the Countess of Guildford, bears a false signature 'W. Blake' and is now in the Kunsthaus, Zurich.

2 James Barry, Lecture II to the Royal Academy, 'On design', in R. Wornum (ed.), *Lectures on Painting by Royal Academicians*, London, 1848, 91.

3 Anon. review of Cowper's *Homer, Analytical Review* (Jan. 1793), in Eudo C. Mason (ed.), *The Mind of Henry Fuseli*, London, 1951, 323.

4 J. Sherwood and N. Pevsner, *The Buildings of England, Oxfordshire*, Harmondsworth, 1974, 111.

5 H. Walpole, 'Anecdotes of painting in England', *Works*, London, 1798, III, 94.

6 J. W. Goethe, *On German Architecture*, D. M. Ervini a Steinbach, 1773, trans. from Goethe's *Werke*, Weimar, 1896; reprinted in Lorenz Eitner (ed.), *Neoclassicism and Romanticism*, London, 1971, 76.

7 H. Walpole, *A Description of the Villa of Mr. Horace Walpole*, 2nd edn, London, 1784, iv (1st edn, 1774).

8 Wilmarth Sheldon Lewis, *Horace Walpole*, London, 1961, 102.

9 H. Walpole to Horace Mann, 12 June 1753, quoted in Lewis, *Horace Walpole*, 102.

10 J. H. Fuseli, aphorism 105, *Aphorisms on Art*, quoted in Eitner, *Neoclassicism and Romanticism*, 93.

11 S. Johnson, 'Preface to Shakespeare', in Mona Wilson (ed.), *Dr Johnson, Prose and Poetry*, London, 1963, 497.

12 *Destruction of a Church in the Gothic style, by Means of Fire*, Explication des ouvrages de peinture et dessins . . . exposés au Musée Central des Arts, no. 516, Paris, 1800, in Eitner, *Neoclassicism and Romanticism*, 142.

13 British Library, Add. MSS 39780; quoted in D. Irwin, *English Neo-Classical Art*, London, 1966, 89.

14 W. Hayley, *Memoirs*, London, 1823, I, 309, in Irwin, *English Art*, 88.

15 Alexis François Rio, *The Poetry of Christian Art*, trans. anon., London, 1854, 123–4.

16 M. R. D. Foot (ed.), *The Gladstone Diaries*, Oxford University Press, 1968, II, 390; and S. G. Checkland, *The Gladstones: A Family Biography, 1764–1851*, Cambridge University Press, 1971, 254.

17 N. Wiseman to W. Dyce, 1 September, 1834, unpublished MS, Aberdeen Art Gallery, Dyce Papers, ch. 1.

18 Geoffrey Keynes (ed.), *The Complete Writings of William Blake*, Oxford University Press, 1957, 569.

19 David Bindman, *Blake as an Artist*, London, 1977, 159–60.

20 A. C. Coxhead, *Thomas Stothard, R. A. His Life and Work*, London, 1909.

21 Mrs Bray (Anna Eliza Stothard), *Life of Thomas Stothard, R. A.*, London, 1851, 107–8.

22 Roma A. King, Jr *et al.* (eds), *The Complete Works of Robert Browning, with Variant Readings & Annotations*, Athens, Ohio, 1971, III, 364–5.

23 Alfred De Vigny, 'Dernière nuit de travail du 29 au 30 juin 1834', in A. H. Diverres (ed.), *Chatterton*, London, 1967, 58-9. In the original:

> J'ai voulu montrer l'homme spiritualiste étouffé par une société matérialiste, ou le calculateur avare exploite sans pitié l'intélligence et le travail. Je n'ai point prétendu justifier les actes déspérés des malheureux, mais protester contre l'indifférence qui les y contraint. Peut-on frapper trop fort sur l'indifférence si difficile à éveiller, sur la distraction si difficile à fixer? Y a-t-il un autre moyen de toucher la société que de lui montrer la torture de ses victimes?
>
> Le poète était tout pour moi; Chatterton n'était qu'un nom d'homme, et je viens d'écarter à dessein des faits exacts de sa vie pour ne prendre de sa destinée que ce qui la rend un example à jamais déplorable d'une noble misère.

24 J. Dix, 'The inquest on Chatterton', *Athenaeum*, 1578 (23 January 1858), 114-15.
25 W. M. Rossetti, *Reminiscences*, London, 1906, I, 158.
26 Tim Hilton, *The Pre-Raphaelites*, London, 1970, 122.
27 Royal Photographic Society of Great Britain, illustrated in J. Maas, *Victorian Painters*, Barrie & Jenkins, 1969, 202.
28 C. Marlowe, *Doctor Faustus* (1604), *The Plays of Christopher Marlowe*, Oxford University Press, 1961, 197.
29 J. Ruskin, 'Royal Academy notes' (1856), *The Works of John Ruskin*, Library edn, XIV, 60.
30 W. Holman Hunt, *Pre-Raphaelitism and the Pre-Raphaelite Brotherhood*, London, 1905, II, 417.
31 Sir Joshua Reynolds, Discourse III, delivered to students of the Royal Academy, 14 December 1770, in R. Wark (ed.), *Discourses on Art*, Yale University Press, 1975, 50-2.
32 W. Vaughan, *Romantic Art*, London, 1978, 132-7.
33 J. Constable to J. Fisher, 8 May 1824, in C. R. Leslie, *Memoirs of the Life of John Constable*, London, 1951, 121 (1st edn, 1843).
34 W. Wordsworth, Preface to 2nd edn of the *Lyrical Ballads* (1802), in R. L. Brett and A. R. Jones (eds), *Lyrical Ballads*, revised impression, Methuen, 1965, 245.
35 A stick with a pad at one end which an artist uses to steady his hand.
36 C. R. Leslie, *A Handbook for Young Painters*, London, 1855, 146.
37 ibid., 55-6, 59-60.
38 ibid., 60-1.
39 F. G. Stephens, *Memorials of William Mulready*, revised edn, London, 1879, 1 (1st edn, 1867).
40 *The Artist*, collected papers 1807-10, London, 1810, I, 11.
41 S. Palmer to L. R. Valpy, May 1875, in R. Lister (ed.), *The Letters of Samuel Palmer*, Oxford University Press, 1975, II, 912.

42   Laura Savage (pseud. F. G. Stephens) in *The Germ, being a facsimile reprint of the literary organ of the Pre-Raphaelite Brotherhood, published in 1850, with an introduction by W. M. Rossetti*, London, 1901, 171.

43   Mrs Jameson, *Memoirs of Early Italian Painters*, London, 1868, xvi (1st edn, 1845).

44   R. B. Beckett (ed.), *John Constable's Discourses*, Ipswich, 1970, 69 (note found by C. R. Leslie attached to lecture IV). My italics.

45   ibid., 39.

46   R. B. Beckett (ed.), *John Constable's Correspondence*, 6 vols, Ipswich, 1962–8, VI, 78.

47   Constable, 'Various subjects of landscape, characteristic of English scenery . . .' (1833), in Beckett, *Constable's Discourses*, 10.

48   Reg. Gadney, *John Constable 1776–1837, A Catalogue of Drawings & Watercolours . . . in the Fitzwilliam Museum, Cambridge*, Arts Council, 1976, cat. no. 30.

49   Kurt Badt, *John Constable's Clouds*, London, 1950.

50   Louis Hawes, 'Constable's sky sketches', *Journal of the Warburg and Courtauld Institutes*, XXXII (1969), 344–65.

51   Leslie, *Memoirs of Constable*, 280.

52   Robert Hooke, *Micrographia*, new edn with explanation of plates, London, 1745 (1st edn, 1665).

53   William Mulready, unpublished notes and drawings, D.121.1895, Whitworth Art Gallery, University of Manchester.

54   William Mulready, Notebook (unpublished), Victoria and Albert Museum Library, quoted in A. Rorimer, *Drawings by William Mulready*, London, Victoria and Albert Museum, 1972, 10.

Further reading

Honour, Hugh, *Romanticism*, London, 1979.

Rosenblum, Robert, *Modern Painting and the Northern Romantic Tradition*, London, 1975.

Rosenblum, Robert, *Transformations in Late Eighteenth Century Art*, Princeton, 1967.

Vaughan, William, *Romantic Art*, London, 1978.

3 The religious context

STEPHEN PRICKETT

Organized religion

Contemporary descriptions of the state of the Church of England at
the end of the eighteenth century vary in detail, but little in their
overall verdict. In the words of one such account in the *Edinburgh
Review*:

> The thermometer of the Church of England sank to its
> lowest point in the first thirty years of George III. Un-
> believing bishops and a slothful clergy, had succeeded in
> driving from the Church the faith and zeal of Methodism
> which Wesley had organized within her pale. The spirit was
> expelled, and the dregs remained. That was the age when
> jobbery and corruption, long supreme in the State, had
> triumphed over the virtue of the Church; when the money-
> changers not only entered the temple, but drove out the
> worshippers; when ecclesiastical revenues were monopol-
> ized by wealthy pluralists; when the name of curate lost its
> legal meaning, and, instead of denoting the incumbent of
> a living, came to signify the deputy of an absentee.[1]

Granted, the *Edinburgh Review* was not by disposition inclined to
be friendly to a church sometimes aptly described as 'the Tory party
at prayer', but other sources, inclined to be pro-Anglican, give a surprisingly similar picture. The poet Crabbe, himself a country

clergyman in Suffolk, describes in *The Village* (1783) the pleasure-seeking parson:

> A jovial youth, who thinks his Sunday's task,
> As much as GOD or Man can fairly ask;
> The rest he gives to Loves and Labours light,
> To Fields the morning and to Feasts the night;
> None better skill'd the noisy Pack to guide,
> To urge their chace, to cheer them or to chide;
> A Sportsman keen, he shoots through half the day,
> And skill'd at Whist, devotes the night to play;
> Then, while such honours bloom around his head,
> Shall he sit sadly by the Sick Man's bed,
> To raise the hope he feels not, or with zeal
> To combat fears that ev'n the pious feel?
>
> (lines 306–17)

Nor was the spiritual vacuum confined to rural areas. On Easter Day 1800, for example, there were a mere six communicants at St Paul's Cathedral in London. Thomas Mozley, a generation later, writing his *Reminiscences* in his old age cast his mind back to the early years of the nineteenth century when 'thousands of livings were without parsonages, and with incomes so small as not to admit of building or even renting'. As a result 'non-residence was almost the rule in some districts, and . . . even the pastoral duties of which all clergymen are capable and which are always welcome, were discharged intermittingly and cursorily'. 'Church fabrics fell into disorder and even decay . . . bishops and dignitaries made fortunes, and used their patronage for private purposes.' [2] Mozley was no less scathing about the spiritual state of the Church, and of the nation at large:

> Forty years ago the negative side of the Church of England . . . was rapidly increasing. The state of things just as they were did not seem a sufficient basis for defence against the general dissolution of faith threatening the Church. . . . This growing indifference was the great fact of that day. It was a public fact, a social fact, an academic fact, a domestic fact. A man might avow any phase of unbelief, and any contempt of religion, without loss of character, in the

service of the state, in society, at Oxford, and at home. It was
expected of every young man in 'the world'. . . . For everything short of fanatical and intolerant atheism, there was
not only condonance, but a certain degree of admiration.[3]

Modern impressions confirm this contemporary feeling of
spiritual and physical decay. Over and over again one notices in
parishes where there is a medieval church that the vicarage beside it
is nineteenth century. The chances are that it will be the *original*
vicarage.[4] In other words, before the nineteenth century there
simply was no resident parson in that parish – even though someone living miles away might be drawing a substantial stipend for the
office. In 1807 (the first year for which we have any figures) out of
some 10,000 odd benefices, no fewer than 6145 clergy (61 per cent,
or nearly two-thirds) were non-resident. When Sydney Smith was
finally given his first living at Foston-le-Clay in Yorkshire in 1806,
he went to thank his patron, who happened to be the Lord
Chancellor. 'Oh, don't thank *me*, Mr. Smith,' said Erskine, 'I gave
you the living because Lady Holland insisted on my doing so; and if
she had desired me to give it to the devil, *he* must have had it.'[5]
Smith's joy was in any case short-lived. Arriving at Foston he found
there was nowhere at all for him to live. Under the terms of the
Residence Bill of 1808 he was forced to build a parsonage at his own
expense: a crippling imposition for someone who had only just
moved into the parish and had no private fortune.

In many places a pluralist incumbent, drawing the stipends of
several parishes, would employ a curate to deputize for him, at a
fraction of the salary he was drawing for supposedly doing that job.
As might be expected, such curates were rarely men of the moral
stature of Mr Crawley, perpetual curate of Hogglestock in Trollope's
The Last Chronicle of Barset. The Wordsworths' curate at Grasmere,
for instance, was frequently drunk. Wordsworth declared to a rather
startled Dorothy in 1812 that he would gladly 'shed his blood' for
the Church of England, but confessed he did not know when he had
last been inside his local church: 'All our ministers are such vile
creatures.'[6] Only a few years before, in 1800, Coleridge, who had
ostensibly just returned to the fold of Anglicanism, wrote to his
friend Godwin about his doubts at having his sons Hartley and
Derwent baptized:

> Shall I suffer the Toad of Priesthood to spurt out his foul
> juice in this Babe's face? Shall I suffer him to see grave
> countenances and hear grave accents, while his face is
> sprinkled, and while the fat paw of a Parson crosses his
> Forehead? [7]

If this language seems to be trimmed to suit its audience – Godwin
was, after all, an extreme radical and armchair revolutionary – the
same cannot be said for another entry in a private notebook as late as
1828, at a time when Coleridge is often supposed to have been a
pillar of the establishment:

> A very useful article might be written on the History and
> Progress of the Vice of Lying on the Christian Church. . . .
> Can a man of mind, for whom *the Truth* on *all* subjects, &
> philosophic Freedom in the pursuit of it, are *good* per se
> . . . adopt the Church for a Profession? [8]

While Blake had no higher opinion of the clergy than Wordsworth or Coleridge, he was not disposed to think them unique in
their capacity for lying and deception. In the work now entitled *An
Island in the Moon* (1784) he satirized a whole collection of fashionable cultural attitudes, including those towards the churches:

> "Ha, ha!" said Inflammable Gass. "What! don't you like
> to go church?"
>
> "No," said Mrs. Nannicantipot. I think a person may be as
> good at home."
>
> "If I had not a place of profit that forces me to go to
> Church," said Inflammable Gass, "I'd see the parsons all
> hang'd, – a parcel of lying – "
>
> "Oh!" said Mrs. Sistagatist. "If it was not for churches and
> chapels I should not have liv'd so long. There was I, up in a
> Morning at four o'clock, when I was a Girl. I would run like
> the dickens till I was all in a heat. I would stand till I was
> ready to sink into the earth. Ah, Mr. Huffcap would kick
> the bottom of the pulpit out with Passion – would tear off
> the sleeve of his Gown & set his wig on fire & throw it at the
> people. He'd cry & stamp & kick & sweat, and all for the
> good of their souls."

"I'm sure he must be a wicked villain," said Mrs. Nannicantipot, "a passionate wretch. If I was a man I'd wait at
the bottom of the pulpit stairs & knock him down & run
away!"

"You would, you Ignorant jade? I wish I could see you hit
any of the ministers! You deserve to have your ears boxed,
you do."

"I'm sure this is not religion," answers the other.

Inflammable Gass (a conflation of several prominent scientists of the
day) is, we notice, quite as much of a hypocrite as the parsons he
attacks. Similarly, though Mrs Nannicantipot echoes the conventional distaste for religious enthusiasm, her own conversation is
hardly a model of reason and restraint. Her final retort to Mrs
Sistagatist is a crowning irony.

Though they enjoyed a much higher sense of community among
their own membership, the state of the Old Dissenters – the
Presbyterians, Baptists and Independents (as the Congregationals
were then called) – was little better than that of the Church of
England. All were more or less Calvinistic in their beliefs, ranging
from a fierce and narrow sectarianism to that kind of vague contradiction in terms, 'moderate Calvinism', later to be described so contemptuously by Mark Rutherford.[9] Though the dissenting clergy
were often marked by a much higher standard of learning, biblical
scholarship and even general culture than their opposite numbers in
the Established Church,[10] it is remarkable how small a contribution
they were to make to the development and growth of Romanticism.

The Unitarians, however, were a different matter. Though
numerically a tiny sect at the end of the eighteenth century, they,
rather than the other branches of Old Dissent, were the true heirs of
Milton and the Puritans of the seventeenth century, and constituted
a kind of intellectual élite amongst Nonconformity. Donald Davie
concludes that: 'It could be argued, and with justice, that the
Unitarians have, in proportion to their numbers and their relatively
brief history, made a greater contribution to English culture than all
the other dissenting sects put together.'[11] The Wedgwoods and the
Darwins, for instance, were among the great Unitarian families of
the West Midlands. At the Unitarian 'university', the Warrington
Academy, which by the 1790s was probably academically superior to

either Oxford or Cambridge, were such leading intellectuals as Joseph Priestley and Richard Price. Moreover, the Unitarians were about the only religious body to give equal education to women. Mrs Barbauld, a celebrated poet of her day and friend of Coleridge, was the daughter of John Aikin, a doctor, author and literary critic, whose house in London was the resort of many leading thinkers of the day. In the next generation Harriet Martineau (1802–76) was nearly as well known a writer as her brother, James, and Mrs Gaskell (1810–65) was to become one of the most important of the mid-Victorian novelists. As another eminent Unitarian woman, Elizabeth Haldane, remarked, 'the sect was small but extraordinarily intellectual and efficient, and if born within it, it was impossible not to gaze at the world from rather a superior angle'.[12] It was to the Unitarians, rather than to the more orthodox Christian dissenters, that the young and rebellious Coleridge was to turn in the 1790s under the influence of William Frend, who was himself later to be expelled from his fellowship in Cambridge for his anti-trinitarian views. Even F. D. Maurice, by most reckoning the greatest Anglican theologian of the Victorian age, and certainly one of the leading Coleridgeans, was brought up as a Unitarian. Yet the very references to Coleridge and Maurice prove another point: if Unitarianism was so often to be important in the growth of a Romantic's religion, it was in a *negative* sense. The dry and optimistic logic of Hartley and Priestley that was to dominate Unitarian thought was in the end totally alien to the religious sensibility of the new generation of poets caught up in the excitement and disillusion of the French Revolution. 'The Unitarianism which formed so large an element in the religious sentiments of the eighteenth century was', said Maurice, looking back, 'essentially *impersonal*.'[13] Priestley, for instance, wrote in his *History of the Corruptions of Christianity* (1782) that 'the great object of the mission and death of Christ' was 'to give the fullest proof of a future life of retribution, in order to supply the strongest motives to virtue'.[14] Wordsworth was to remark to his friend, Crabb Robinson, that he could not feel with the Unitarians in any way. Their religion allowed no room for the imagination, and satisfied none of the cravings of the soul. 'I can feel more sympathy with the orthodox believer who needs a redeemer.'[15] An intellectual élite, however 'superior' its viewpoint, does not of itself constitute a thriving church. A religion of

Reason that positively discouraged emotion or devotional piety was never likely to be popular or have much institutional hold on its members, and in fact throughout the Romantic period the Unitarians declined in numbers.

But it is always dangerous to work in generalizations and stereotypes, and doubly dangerous in an area so inward and complex as that of religious belief. What we learn from contemporary accounts may not necessarily be the 'actual' state of religion (a matter beyond the competence of the historian!) but what many contemporaries *believed* was its state. Now this raises an interesting and relevant paradox. The more such diverse observers as Sydney Smith, George Crabbe, William Blake, Samuel Taylor Coleridge or William Wordsworth denounced the appalling state of the contemporary Church, the more we become aware not merely of the abuses that so disturbed them, but also of the concern and high moral expectations of the observers themselves. Though the church had critics enough from outside, all those I have listed were 'Christians' of one kind or another; all but Blake ended up as loyal members of the Church of England. Desperate as the state of the English Church undoubtedly was under George III and his son, the Prince Regent, it still represented a religion that could capture and hold the imaginations of Smith, Crabbe, Coleridge, Wordsworth and even, tenuously, Blake, as well as a host of others – among them the finest and most sensitive spirits of the age. In a peculiar kind of way, Romanticism is rooted in the felt tension between moribund religious institutions and the reaction of *believers* against them.

It was a paradox the Romantics themselves were not blind to. The notion of the church as permanently failing and permanently under judgement from its own best ideals lay at the heart of Coleridge's idea of 'the Clerisy' in *Church and State*, published in 1830. For Coleridge, the relationship of Church and State was essentially a *dialectical* one. The two forces within the nation were to be seen as polar opposites, standing for entirely different things, yet each implying the existence of the other merely by its own existence – just as the opposite poles of a magnet cannot exist without each other. Furthermore, each of these two 'poles' or, rather, dynamic forces within the nation is itself the product of a similar dialectical tension. The 'State' contains within itself two opposite principles, which Coleridge calls the 'Permanent' and the 'Progressive'. The former was to be identified with the landowning interest, the latter with the manufacturing and commercial. Thus, he implies, the two traditional political parties, Tories and Whigs, are not just warring, self-seeking factions, but do actually represent real conflicts and tensions within the country's political life. More surprisingly, Coleridge goes on to claim that the 'Church' is *also* composed of polar opposites: the 'National Church' and the 'Church of Christ'. There is nothing inherently Christian, he points out, about a 'National Church'. It is rather the repository and guardian of the spiritual values of the nation – even of the national mythology, that peculiar moral sense of communal identity that differentiates one country from another, that makes the Scots, for instance, feel themselves collectively distinct from the English. A good modern example of such a National Church which is non-Christian and even non-religious, at least in its rhetoric, is the Communist Party in Soviet Russia or post-revolutionary China, but, lacking such apposite examples, Coleridge was forced to find his non-Christian examples of a National Church rather less convincingly in the Levites of Old Testament Israel or the Druids of Celtic Britain. To the English National Church belongs what he calls 'the Clerisy'. This is his collective term for its guardians, both clerical and lay. It includes not merely the clergy of the Church of England, but also those he calls 'the learned of all denominations', such as the teachers in universities and the great schools. He sees them as the defenders and upholders not just of religion, but of culture in its broadest sense, the parson and the schoolmaster providing in effect a representative of civilization and learning in every parish in the kingdom. When we remember the actual state of the clergy at the time Coleridge was writing, and recall that in many cases the state of the universities and schools was little better, either morally or academically, it is easy to see the argument as being either disingenuous or hopelessly naive. Those Victorians who, like Matthew Arnold, attempted to defend the privileges of what was at its worst simply a class interest, by means of reference to Coleridge's clerisy as a kind of endowed secular clergy, were open to immediate attack on grounds of truth. As Edward Miall, a prominent Nonconformist member of parliament and leading advocate of Disestablishment of the Church of England, said in 1871:

I wish to say something of the rural parishes of the kingdom. In each of these, we are told, the clergyman, maintained by national endowment, is a living link between the highest and the lowliest of the parishioners – is a cultivated gentleman, located just where there is, if not the greatest need, at any rate the best opportunity, for diffusing both 'sweetness and light' – is the fixed centre in the parish of civilization, of education, of charity, of piety – and I am told that I propose to abolish him and leave the people to fall back again into ignorance and Paganism . . . These rural parishes have been in the undisturbed spiritual occupation of the clergy of the Church of England for generations past . . . Well, what, on a large scale, has been the result? What are the most conspicuous characteristics of our labouring agricultural population? Do they include 'sweetness and light'? Do they include fairly-developed intelligence? Do they include a high state of morality? Do they include affectionate veneration for religion? Are these the most prominent features by which the character of our agricultural population is distinguished, and in respect of which they bear away the palm from the inmates of towns? And the discouraging and painful answers to these queries – are they not to be found in blue-books, verified as they may be by minute personal observation?[16]

Though Miall's target in this instance is Arnold rather than Coleridge (hence the references to 'sweetness and light'), the argument demolishes both. As a description of the actual state of affairs, Coleridge's position was never tenable for a moment. But, in fact, Coleridge had already met this obvious weakness and turned it into one of its greatest strengths. As we have already seen, he had no higher opinion of the *actual* state of the rural parishes or their clergy than Miall himself. For unlike his Victorian 'clerisical' successors, Arnold and Mill, Coleridge himself never envisaged the clerisy of the National Church standing alone as a primarily cultural institution. In *Church and State* the National Church is set against its polar opposite, the 'Church of Christ', which *is* Christian in the fullest, most unworldly and idealistic sense. The two ideas are entirely separate and distinct, yet, by a 'blessed accident', they coexist within and animate the same institution.

As the olive tree is said in its growth to fertilize the surrounding soil, to invigorate the roots of the vines in its immediate neighbourhood, and to improve the strength and
flavour of the wines; such is the relationship of the
Christian and the National Church. But as the olive is not
the same plant with the vine . . . even so is Christianity
. . . no essential part of the being of the National Church,
however conducive or even indispensable it may be to its
well being. And even so a National Church might exist,
and has existed, without . . . the Christian Church.[17]

But though other countries and ages might have had their 'National
Churches' unmodified by Christianity, it is impossible to think of
the clerisy in this way. The National Church and the Christian
Church in England coexist in a single organic unity in exactly the
same way that Jesus himself could be described as both 'wholly Man'
and 'wholly God':

two distinct functions do not necessarily imply or require
two different functionaries: nay, the perfection of each may
require the union of both in the same person. And in the
instance now in question, great and grievous errors have
arisen from confounding the functions; and fearfully great
and grievous will be the evils from the success of an attempt
to separate them.[18]

In short, as Coleridge envisaged it, the clerisy is not something that
can exist by itself. It is one pole of an institution under tension,
whose opposite pole is *real* Christianity. It can no more exist by itself
(as Arnold or Mill wanted it to) than the negative pole of a magnet
can exist without the positive. The clerisy, as Coleridge thought of
it, can exist only *under judgement* from Christ. The very existence of
a church and its parson (with or without a vicarage) in every parish
and village throughout the land bears witness to those eternal
principles against which the institutional Church will one day be
weighed in the balance and found wanting. As Coleridge, like
Blake, saw very clearly, when we condemn the corruptions and vices
of Christianity, it is by reference to Christian principles.

In this sense, perhaps, the paradox of Romanticism as a reassertion of spiritual values arising from the very degeneracy of the

contemporary Church is not so much a special phenomenon, peculiar to eighteenth-century England, as a normal condition of any religious revival. What *was* peculiar to this period was the form that revival took and its close association with other contemporary movements, both philosophical and aesthetic. Coleridge's *Church and State* grew out of a unique moment of self-awareness when political, religious, sociological and philosophic ideas could not merely be viewed intellectually as a unity, but could be experienced as such. Behind it lies a new psychological appreciation of human complexity. The advent of Romanticism in the 1780s and 1790s was closely associated with sharp changes both in ways of understanding the human mind, and therefore knowledge itself, and in ways of understanding art; the unifying factor in all these new ideas is to be found in a quite fundamental shift in the climate of *feeling*, and in attitudes towards emotion. And that change, for all its later development in the sentimental novel, was in origin a religious one.

The roots of this climactic change in emotional climate lie in a strand of eighteenth-century religious sensibility very different from either the Established Church or Old Dissent: a strand which we associate above all with Methodism. Methodism is unique among the English Protestant sects in that its theology never differed significantly from that of the Anglicanism out of which it grew. John Wesley, the founder of the movement, claimed to the end of his life to be a priest of the Church of England – as indeed he was, of high church and Tory persuasions to boot. Where Methodism differed sharply from its parent was in its Presbyterian (and therefore in some senses at least, democratic) organization, and, more importantly from our point of view, in its fervid emotionalism. In place of the calm and pious rationality admired and preached (if not always practised) by the Church of England, Methodism grew from a renewed sense of the drama of the human condition revealed in the Bible. Man was seen to be stretched between terror of damnation and joy at Christ's free gift of salvation – neither earned by his merits nor predestined by a God who was an omniscient stage manager. Wordsworth's description of himself in *The Prelude* at the end of the century as 'fostered alike by beauty and by fear' is a secularized epigraph to the whole growth of Methodism. The movement traditionally saw its own beginnings in the day when, in 1738, John Wesley had 'felt his heart strangely warmed' in the course of a service in a little chapel in Aldersgate Street in London. Significantly, it was not a 'conversion' of intellectual conviction (Wesley was already a clergyman) but of emotional acceptance. In the violent emotional scenes that accompanied Wesley's preaching, and in his and his brother Charles's poetry, there was rediscovered a whole lost dimension of religious experience.

'Joy', for the Wesleys, was not so much a human emotion as a divine one, attributed to God in the act of Creation. Creation was the spontaneous overflow of God's joy and power, and human joy was an echo of this moment 'when the morning stars sang together, and all the sons of God shouted for joy' (Job 38.7). John Wesley took up this close association of joy with creativity:

> Father of all! whose powerful voice
> Called forth this universal frame;
> Whose mercies over all rejoice,
> Through endless ages still the same.[19]

Charles Wesley paraphrased a text from Zephaniah (3.17), 'He will save, he will rejoice over thee with joy, he will joy over thee with singing', like this:

> Thy gracious Lord shall soon for thee
> His whole omnipotence employ,
> Delight in thy prosperity,
> And condescend to sing for joy;
> Thy God well pleas'd and satisfied
> Shall view his image in thy breast,
> Shall glory o'er his spotless bride,
> And in his love for ever rest.[20]

God's joy comes from his recognition of his own image in man. But man is no longer represented by Adam, made according to Genesis by God in his own image, but by Jesus, the 'second Adam'. His 'spotless bride' is, of course, the church, 'the bride of Christ'. God's discovery of himself in man offers a kind of theological paradigm for man's later discovery of himself in nature. Once again we find, as so often, that in Wordsworth the supernatural doctrines of the eighteenth century have been secularized and naturalized. An even more striking example of this process can be found in Charles

Wesley's verse paraphrase of John 1.14 ('The Word was made flesh, and dwelt among us . . .'):

> Transform'd by the extatic sight,
> Our souls o'erflow with pure delight,
>   And every moment own
> The Lord our whole perfection is,
> The Lord is our immortal bliss,
> And Christ and heaven are one.[21]

Here the 'spontaneous overflow of powerful feelings' is man's response to God, but its *form* is poetry. By experiencing joy, 'transform'd' man was partaking of an essentially divine activity touching the mystery of creation. Creativity begins in overwhelming emotion.

Charles Wesley's hymns were known to millions by the end of the century. Not merely was he one of the best-known poets of his day, he was also one of the best. Familiarity with such carols as *Hark the Herald Angels Sing* or *Let Earth and Heaven Combine* can easily blur our appreciation of a poetic subtlety and compression that lifts him far above most of his contemporaries, and puts him, at his best, in the same class as Herbert or Newman – both of whom had a much smaller range. A single couplet from *Let Earth and Heaven Combine* makes the point:

> Our God contracted to a span,
> Incomprehensibly made man.

God becomes man; the boundless is reduced to a quantifiable phenomenon. But what exactly does that word 'span' mean in context? The primary meaning, of course, is a period of time – traditionally the length of a human life. Infinity is compressed into time. But the original meaning is a unit of linear measurement: an outstretched hand from thumb to little finger. It might be the length of a very tiny new-born baby or the measurement of God's outstretched hand to man – either way, a unit of measurement by which all other things are to be judged. But 'span' has other meanings also. It is a bridge – the leaping arch which incomprehensibly joins earth to heaven; it can also be the rope or cable by which a ship is made fast, echoing the rope and cable images so frequent in Herbert's poetry (which Wesley knew well). Suddenly we see the second meaning of 'contracted': not merely made small, but 'under contract' of the divine Covenant itself. No wonder, then, that the making of God-man is 'incomprensible', both in its modern sense of 'not to be understood' and in its older senses of 'not to be grasped' (physically) and 'not to be contained within limits'. The original meaning of 'span', the verb, is to 'grasp', physically, in an exactly corresponding sense, while the idea of 'comprehend' as 'containing' or 'grasping' echoes too the first chapter of John, where, speaking of the Incarnation, John writes 'the light shineth in the darkness; and the darkness comprehended it not'. Christ made man is the shining of the light that could not be extinguished. The syntax of that second line of the couplet has now become very ambiguous indeed. For instance, is 'made' active or passive? Is God merely allowing himself to be made into man, and by that 'contract' through obedience making true man for the first time – the doctrine of the second Adam – or is he by that act to be seen as 'making' man afresh as an active agent?

The whole couplet is an echo of a stanza from *The Pulley* by Herbert:

> When God at first made man,
> Having a glass of blessing standing by,
> 'Let us,' said he, 'pour on him all we can:
> Let the world's riches, which dispersed lie,
> Contract into a span.'

For Herbert's riches of the world, Wesley has substituted, at man's 'second creation' in the Incarnation, the riches of God himself. The theme of *The Pulley* is that man's inward need will eventually make him turn to God; Wesley's theme is God turning into man. Deliberately similar to Herbert as he so often is, in his stress on the joyful paradox of God's gift to man Wesley displays a quite different kind of sensibility.

Because of a modern tendency to separate 'hymns' from 'poetry' Wesley's influence on the Romantic poets is often overlooked. Yet, as is suggested even in the few quotations above, that influence is not just in a similar attitude towards emotion, but in a whole aesthetic theory. The proclamation of 'joy' as being at the heart of creativity, though it begins with God, rapidly comes to have answering resonances at every level of human experience. The 'overflow of pure delight' that Wesley discovered in St John's account of the Incarnation had a direct counterpart, as we shall see, in the revival of interest in the poetry of the Bible as *poetry* that was inaugurated by Robert Lowth's *Lectures on the Sacred Poetry of the Hebrews* in the 1740s. The new poetic and critical aesthetics alike found their inspiration in the scriptures, and it is entirely in keeping with this tradition that Wordsworth should, in *Tintern Abbey*, invoke the 'deep power of joy' to 'see into the life of things', or that Coleridge, in *Dejection*, should resolve his crisis over the loss of poetic creativity in a hymn to joy of almost Wesleyan devotional intensity:

> Joy lift her spirit, joy attune her voice;
> To her may all things live, from pole to pole,
> Their life the eddying of her living soul!
>   O simple spirit, guided from above,
> Dear Lady! friend devoutest of my choice,
> Thus mayest thou ever, evermore rejoice.

Writing just over a decade after Coleridge's death, F. D. Maurice was under no doubt about the importance of the Methodists in transforming the climate of feeling in England during the eighteenth century, and so preparing the way for the Romanticism of which they themselves never really partook:

> The Methodists, however, led other men into a belief which they did not entertain themselves; they were the unconscious and unacknowledged, but not the least powerful instruments of a great change in the views of philosophers. . . . It does not consist in any dry, tame acknowledgement that man has an immortal part or property which may survive the dissolution of his animal frame; it amounts to nothing less than a distinct affirmation, that those powers and properties which he has within him, of which the senses can take no account, and which are not reducible under any mechanical conditions, are what constitute him a man. . . . A dynamical philosophy has gradually superseded a mechanical one.[22]

What began, with the Methodists, as a reassertion of man as a spiritual being, was transformed by the following generation of philosophers and artists into an assertion of organic unity. But if, on the one hand, Methodism pointed the way implicitly towards the development of anti-empiricist philosophies, it was no less influential in its latent aesthetics. Maurice linked the influence of the Methodists with a change in the attitude to nature in a way that seems to refer us directly to such passages from *Tintern Abbey* and *Dejection* as those we have just quoted. 'Above all,' he declared, 'nature itself has been, to a very great extent, conquered from the natural philosopher.' In other words, man is no longer to be seen as a detached observer; he is inseparable from his environment.

> Sympathies have been discovered between the beholder and the objects which are presented to him, and attempts to express these sympathies or investigate the conditions and laws under which they exist, have become the favourite, are threatening to become the exclusive, occupation of the more thoughtful and abstracted men in this time.[23]

For Maurice, the connections between this religious and philosophic shift of climate and the poetry of the period were clear:

> From about the middle of the last century, we may trace the commencement of a poetry which had a much more direct and substantive reference to the outward universe than that of earlier periods. The doings of men, as well as the songs in which they were celebrated, had become artificial and conventional: those whom domestic habits had inspired with a dislike of the hollowness of general society, or whom their early cultivation had taught to desire something more living and permanent than the modes of a particular generation, took refuge in nature.[24]

It is also clear in the development of Maurice's argument that he is not thinking just of Wordsworth. Though he does not mention any of them by name, he distinguishes by implication between the poetry of Scott, Byron, Wordsworth and Coleridge. The impact of the French Revolution was like that of 'an earthquake' which loosened and dissolved the existing conventions, 'snapt assunder' the old links and released 'passions which had been smothered or icebound by the rules of ettiquette'. Men rediscovered their common humanity. 'The admiration and love of nature became strangely connected with all these movements of the human heart and will, and different forms of poetry appeared to illustrate and exhibit the connection.' Each made a special contribution to the new view of man and nature as an inseparable unity. It is not merely a philosophic or aesthetic truth, but a *religious* one to assert that 'the law of the imagination is a law of fellowship or intercommunion with nature'.

Partly because they possessed at least one major and several minor poets among their number, Methodists were clearly a major influence on this shift in emotional climate. But in spite of the importance attributed to them by Maurice, it would be a mistake to see them as an isolated phenomenon in eighteenth-century religion. They formed merely the largest, best organized and most conspicuous example of a much more widespread religious trend. Indeed, in spite of the strong discipline exerted by John Wesley himself on his followers, which checked some of the natural development of splinter groups which seems to accompany any new spiritual revival, Methodism can hardly be said to have been a single movement. One of the earliest divisions was with George Whitefield over Calvinism. Whitefield had gained the support of the Countess of Huntingdon, and some of their adherents eventually became known as the Countess of Huntingdon's New Connexion – a sect which still has chapels in many parts of the country. Others passed into the main stream of Anglican evangelicalism. Still other groups of what would now be described as of a 'charismatic' or 'pentecostalist' character flourished and withered on the wilder millenarian shores of Methodism.

In 1788 the followers of the Swedish scientist, philosopher and mystic, Emmanuel Swedenborg (1688–1772) met together in Eastcheap to form the New Jerusalem Church, and in April of the following year there was held a general conference of British Swedenborgians. Those attending signed a document accepting the authenticity of Swedenborg's revelations, which were codified into thirty-two propositions. Among the signatories were William Blake and his wife, Catherine. Though Swedenborg had never attempted to found a new sect himself, his teachings were apocalyptic and revolutionary in character. He taught that the Second Coming had already begun in 1757 (significantly, the year of Blake's birth, and also that of Richard Brothers – of whom more in a minute). It involved the complete destruction of the old church, whose doctrine of the Trinity was misconceived and contradictory, and the creation of a new doctrine based on the 'Divine Humanity', Jesus Christ. There was much debate about free love and the interpretation of Swedenborg's *Chaste Delights of Conjugal Love: after which follow the Pleasures of Insanity and Scortatory Love*. Those who took concubines were expelled. Others aspects of his thought were, however, more unusual for an apocalyptic creed. Swedenborg had been also a distinguished scientist and engineer. He had held a Chair of mathematics, and made important contributions to geology, chemistry, physiology and mining technology. Many of his conclusions, such as the idea that space and time are mental constructs, anticipate uncannily those of Kant, though his process of reaching them seems to have been more a matter of mystical assertion rather than of philosophical reasoning. Kant, however, was certainly aware of Swedenborg's work, and it seems probable that he was influenced by him. Whatever their exact relationship, the net result was that something very like Kantian notions were, via the Swedenborgians, beginning to percolate into the religious circles of which Blake was a part at least a decade before Coleridge first encountered Kant's thought on his visit to Germany in 1800.

Blake was also in contact with some of the various Antinomian sects that had survived in small numbers in London ever since the time of Cromwell and the Commonwealth. Pushing to its logical limits the Calvinist doctrine of Election, the Antinomians argued that since they were totally justified by God they could do no wrong. The moral law was therefore to be swept away in its entirety by faith, and the elect could live in perfect liberty and love. Earlier in the century (22 March 1746) John Wesley had recorded in his *Journal* a debate with an Antinomian:

> "Do you believe you have nothing to do with the law of God?"
> "I have not; I am not under the law; I live by faith."
> "Have you, as living by faith, a right to everything in the world?"
> "I have. All is mine since Christ is mine."
> "May you then take any thing you will, any where, (suppose out of a shop,) without the consent or knowledge of the owner?"

"I may, if I want it; for it is mine; only I will not give
offence."
"Have you also a right to all the women in the world?"
"Yes, if they consent."
"And is that not a sin?"
"Yes, to him that thinks it is a sin; but not to those whose
hearts are free."[25]

It is this confidence in justification – even for murder – that James
Hogg made the psychological lynchpin of his brilliant metaphysical
thriller, *The Private Confessions of a Justified Sinner*, in 1822.

There were in Blake's London various Antinomian groupings,
among them Ranters, Shakers and Muggletonians. The last-named
had been founded in the mid-seventeenth century by one Muggleton, a tailor, and William Reeves, a cobbler, who claimed to
be the two Witnesses of Revelation. They continued a millenarian
tradition (going as far back as Joachim of Fiore) that there had been
three ages – redefined by them as those of Moses, Jesus and
Muggleton (water, blood and spirit respectively). William Hurd, in
his magnificently named *New Universal History of the Religions,
Rites, Ceremonies, and Customs of the Whole World* (1811), tells
us that:

> Their followers of the present age, still retain that notion
> (that the Witnesses will return); and they believe that these
> two apostles, or witnesses, will meet them when they are
> assembled together. They meet in the evenings of Sundays,
> at obscure public houses in the outparts of London, and
> converse about those of their sect who have gone before
> them. They have very little serious discourse, but are ex-
> tremely free, sometimes going home drunk. . . . There
> must be still a considerable number of these people in dif-
> ferent parts of England; for only a few years ago a new
> edition in three volumes quarto was printed, of the
> rhapsodies of Muggleton Reeves, and had there not been
> people to purchase them they would not have been
> printed.[26]

How closely Blake was associated with such groups is a matter for con-
jecture. Some historians, such as Hobsbawm[27] and E. P. Thompson,[28]
have stressed their importance not as religious movements so much as

a form of social protest at a time when the natural language of egalitarianism was still theological and apocalyptic. Lindsay, for instance, argues that:

> Blake cannot be understood unless there is seen in him the re-emergence of the submerged revolutionary traditions that had carried on mainly among the craftsmen and small tradesmen of the towns. Enriched, the Ranter tradition burst out to meet the new situation in which total revolutionary change seemed at last again possible.[29]

As might be expected, the French Revolution gave a new impetus to such movements, and from the 1790s onwards there were a whole series of millenarian outbreaks. Even as late as the 1820s London was stirred by the Irvingites – the followers of a Scottish divine, Edward Irving. In his early days he had been a conventional Presbyterian minister (who had been in love with Jane Welsh, later Carlyle's wife). In 1832, after a decade in London of increasingly apocalyptic preaching based on his interpretation of the Book of Revelation, he founded the Holy Catholic Apostolic Church. In addition to the familiar Pentecostal stress on faith-healing, prophecy and the gift of tongues they were, interestingly, also influenced by some of Coleridge's more obscure metaphysics.

The two most important millenarian movements of the period, however, were those of Richard Brothers (1757–1824) and Joanna Southcott (1750–1814). Brothers was a half-pay naval officer who, in 1792, began to prophesy against the impending war with France, on the grounds that it was the one 'alluded to by St. John, in the nineteenth chapter of Revelation, which God called a war against himself'. He proceeded to petition the King, the Prime Minister, Pitt, and other ministers, and in 1794 he published *A Revealed Knowledge of the Prophecies and Times* in which he predicted the conquest of England and the destruction of the empire. This was too much for a government already alarmed by fears of a revolutionary fifth column at home, and in March 1795 he was arrested. After examination before the Privy Council he was declared insane and shut up in a lunatic asylum in Islington for the next eleven years. In the asylum he continued to receive visits both from disciples and from revolutionary sympathizers, and he was able to issue further publications, including a very detailed *Description of* [the New]

Jerusalem (1801). There are a number of striking parallels between his prophecies and those of Blake, who was exactly the same age, but whereas Blake used the language of apocalypse figuratively and symbolically in his verse, Brothers remained a simple literalist who saw in contemporary events clear signs of the end of the world.[30]

Joanna Southcott was a Devonshire farmer's daughter who had spent some time as a domestic servant. She had herself been a Methodist. In 1792, however, she announced her supernatural gifts to the world and began writing and dictating her prophecies in verse. A delegation of Brothers's followers came to see her at Exeter and were won over. She was, she claimed, the woman referred to in Revelation 12.1 'clothed with the sun, with the moon under her feet, and on her head a crown of twelve stars' who, in one of the most apocalyptic passages in the Bible, was destined to bring forth a man-child who was 'to rule all the nations with a rod of iron' (12.5). Coming to London in the early 1800s she began to 'seal' those who wished to secure a place among the 144,000 predestined elect. Among the wide range of her followers were half-a-dozen Anglican clergy, several army officers and an engraver, William Sharp, who was an acquaintance of Blake. In 1814, when she was over sixty, Joanna Southcott announced that she would be delivered of Shiloh – the miraculous son somewhat obscurely predicted in Genesis 49.10, and linked by her with the man-child of Revelation. She was examined by doctors, some of whom believed she was indeed pregnant. When, in November, Shiloh failed to appear, it was given out that she was in a trance, but in fact she was already dying – possibly of her hysterical pregnancy. She died on 27 December. During her life she had published sixty-five works, mostly in doggerel verse. Her most famous bequest, however, was her 'box'. This enormous and mysterious object apparently contained her writings and other things, and weighed 165 pounds. It was kept locked and preserved by her followers, who were under instructions that it was to be opened at a time of national crisis by all the bishops assembled together.

The significance of Brothers and Southcott is that they were the most visible tip of a widespread but submerged popular millenarian culture in England.[31] The fact that Joanna Southcott was widely believed to have raised nearly 100,000 followers (in fact the number was probably much smaller) out of a population of about ten million is remarkable enough, and indicates the extraordinary spiritual hunger of those years immediately following the French Revolution. No less important, from the point of view of the contemporary Romantics like Wordsworth and Coleridge, is the way in which their activities served to give mysticism a bad name.

From our point of view, the mystical religious elements in both Wordsworth and Coleridge seem obvious. Both *Tintern Abbey* and *Kubla Khan*, for instance, hint at paranormal states of consciousness (whether or not connected with opium in the latter case is immaterial). Similarly, Blake, in *The Marriage of Heaven and Hell*, declared, 'If the doors of perception were cleansed every thing would appear to man as it is, infinite.' [32] But both Wordsworth and Coleridge in fact went out of their way to avoid the charge of mysticism, and Coleridge, in a famous attack on private inspiration, seems to have the examples of Brothers and Southcott very much in mind:

> When a man refers to *inward feelings* and *experiences*, of which mankind at large are not conscious, as evidences of the truth of any opinion – such a Man I call A MYSTIC: and the grounding of any theory or belief on accidents and anomalies of individual sensations or fancies, and the use of peculiar terms invented or perverted from their ordinary signification, for the purposes of expressing these idiosyncracies, and pretended facts of interior consciousness, I name MYSTICISM.[33]

But it would be a mistake to assume that religious fervour was only to be found among extreme fanatics and millenarian sects. Even in the mid-eighteenth century there were within the Established Church profound counter-currents to the surface rationalism. Dr Johnson's gloomy and neurotic terrors of damnation, for instance, if devoid of any corresponding 'joy', at least bear witness to the strength and seriousness of his own religious convictions. Nor should it be forgotten, merely because it came at a time when Boswell was not in his usual close attendance, that Johnson was an admirer and, for a period, quite a close friend of John Wesley.

By the end of the eighteenth century the renewed stress on personal religion, with its feeling for the responsibility of the individual before God, had blossomed into an organized movement quite as influential as, and perhaps more so than, Methodism. The Evangelical Revival, as it is called, was peculiar if not unique among religious movements in that though it was often as highly organized as any Methodist Society it was never denominationally based. Though the members of its most influential group, the so-called Clapham Sect, were mostly members of the Church of England, many of its adherents and supporters were drawn from the ranks of the dissenting churches though there usually remained a class distinction between Anglican and Nonconformist Evangelicals. Though the Evangelicals all laid great stress upon the experience of personal conversion, they included among their ranks both Arminians (who held that salvation was potentially open to all who were willing to accept it) and Calvinists. Calvinism, at least in its strict form, held that because of the inherent sinfulness of mankind it was constitutionally impossible for us to understand the 'justice' and 'mercy' of a righteous God who, because of his infinite wisdom and omniscience, predestined some to salvation, others to damnation, in a way that could only seem arbitrary to our debased intelligences. It was this that had so terrified many of the more serious minded eighteenth-century figures – Johnson and Cowper among them. In practice, however, among the Evangelicals in the early years of the nineteenth century the apparent contradiction between Arminianism and Calvinism had become blurred in the common desire to save souls. Many were less concerned with the causes than the fruits, and when sinners turned to God and gave the glory to Him, they were not disposed to ask whether it was the work of predestination or free will. Evangelicalism was more a way of life and a vocabulary than a philosophical movement. It never had any elaborate theology. As Newman, himself an Evangelical 'convert' in the early years of the century, was later to put it:

> Evangelicalism, in its origin, was a reaction against the High-Church 'evidences'; the insurrection of the heart and conscience of man against an arid orthodoxy. It insisted on a 'vital Christianity', as against the Christianity of books. Its instinct was from the first against intelligence. No text found more favour with it than 'Not many wise, not many learned'.[34]

Perhaps hardly surprisingly, it was from the first as much a lay as a clerical movement. The membership of the Clapham Sect tells its own story. At its centre was Henry Thornton, a wealthy banker and member of parliament. William Wilberforce and Lord Shaftsbury were both members of the group, as were two other prominent bankers, the brothers Samuel and Abel Smith; Charles Grant was an East India merchant; James Stephen a Chancery lawyer; Zachary Macaulay, a company secretary; and T. F. Buxton, a brewer. Associated with this central group were such clergymen as Edward Bickersteth, Charles Simeon and Henry Venn, but from the first the real power of the movement lay in its political and financial muscle rather than in its ecclesiastical connexions. Hannah More, a writer, was also linked with the group, whose literary onslaught upon the nation ranged from More's novels down through a host of tracts and improving booklets designed to appeal to every class and section of society. Though numerically the Evangelicals were relatively insignificant even within the church, their cohesiveness, sense of purpose and amazing powers of political lobbying and organization gave them an influence out of all proportion to their size. Charles Simeon (1759–1836), for instance, though a Cambridge don, was also a nationally known figure. In 1844 T. M. Macaulay, the son of Zachary Macaulay, said of Simeon: 'If you knew what his authority and influence were, and how they extended from Cambridge to the most remote corners of England, you would allow that his real sway was greater than any primate.' [35]

The effects of the Evangelical Revival were enormous. A recent book on the Evangelicals quotes from Harold Perkin's *The Origins of Modern English Society* the comment that:

> between 1780 and 1850 the English ceased to be one of the most aggressive, brutal, rowdy, outspoken, riotous, cruel and bloodthirsty nations in the world and became one of the most inhibited, polite, orderly, tender-minded, prudish and hypocritical.[36]

The book argues that this 'profound change . . . in the morals and habits of the English people' was primarily due to Evangelical influence. Other historians might be more cautious about both the initial generalization and the assessment of the Evangelicals' role, but there is no question that the Evangelicals did play a key part in a sweeping change of both public and private attitudes during the opening years of the nineteenth century. They worked through a series of organized religious pressure groups of pervasive and unremittingly high-minded purposefulness. Many are familiar names to us even today: the Anti-Slavery Society, the British and Foreign Bible Society, The Lord's Day Observance Society, The Royal Society for the Prevention of Cruelty to Animals, the YMCA; others, such as the Religious Tract Society (one of many) or the Bettering Society, were no less important in their own day. Wilkie Collins's British Ladies' Servants' Sunday Sweethearts Supervision Society in *The Moonstone* is scarcely improbable. Altogether there were hundreds of Evangelical associations for transforming the nation (and ultimately the world) by means of personal godliness, hard work and ceaseless political lobbying. They aimed to evangelize the country, revitalize the Church of England, stamp out vice of all kinds, convert the heathen overseas and the Jews at home. Organization was the key. Though these multitudinous religious and philanthropic groups were nominally independent, there was a wide overlap of membership; and a handful of leading figures like Wilberforce and Shaftsbury, with the other members of the Clapham Sect, belonged to, patronized and chaired a superhuman number of them.

An Evangelical household carried its religion into every part of its daily life. 'Seriousness' was the word which they chose to describe the tone of their lives. It did not exclude gaiety and even boisterous practical joking, but it implied the underlying sense of purpose and discipline that characterized the Evangelical approach to life. Central to family life were family prayers, which involved every member of the household in an act of patriarchal collective piety. This is a description of the Wilberforce family at prayer in July 1806:

> About a quarter before 10 o'clock, the family assembled to prayers, which were read by Wilberforce in the dining-room. As we passed from the drawing-room I saw all the servants standing in regular order, the woemen [*sic*] ranged in a line against the wall and the men the same. There were 7 woemen and 6 men. When the whole were collected in the dining-room, all knelt down against a chair or a sopha, and Wilberforce knelt at a table in the middle of the room, and after a little pause began to read a prayer, which he did

very slowly in a low, solemnly awful voice. This was
followed by 2 other prayers and the grace. It occupied
about 10 minutes, and had the best effect as to the manner
of it.

After prayers were over, a long table covered with cold
meat, tarts, etc. was drawn to a sopha on which sat Mrs.
Wilberforce and Miss Hewit. Wilberforce had boiled milk
and bread, and tasted a little brandy and water which at
night He said agrees better with Him than wine.[37]

The tone of Evangelical piety was surprisingly pervasive, extend-
ing not merely to such non-Evangelicals as Crabbe, Wordsworth or
Coleridge, but even into circles where it would be difficult for a
modern observer to expect any trace of 'seriousness'. Indeed the
Romantic period was one of stark contrasts and strange overlappings
at every level of society. The world of Wordsworth and Coleridge
was also that of Jane Austen, the Prince Regent, William Pitt, the
Duke of Wellington and of William Wilberforce and Evangelical
prayer meetings. These worlds, moreover, far from being separate
circles, intermingled in the most extraordinary ways. Wilberforce
was a member of parliament, rubbing shoulders with Regency bucks
and dandies in public, if not in social life. Only after 1812 did
Wilberforce abandon his parliamentary seat to devote more time to
his family. Wordsworth himself reflects something of the Evangelical zeal for reform in his sonnet of 1807:

> Milton! thou shouldst be living at this hour:
> England hath need of thee; she is a fen
> Of stagnant waters; altar, sword, and pen,
> Fireside, the heroic wealth of hall and bower,
> Have forfeited their ancient English dower
> Of inward happiness . . .

Lady Bessborough was an even less likely candidate for Evangelical
'seriousness'. The witty and talented wife of an Anglo-Irish peer,
she was a close friend of Charles James Fox. She and her sister, the
Duchess of Devonshire, both had illegitimate children by their
lovers without quarrelling with or parting from their husbands. Lady
Bessborough had two children by Lord Granville Leveson Gower
(1773–1846), and her sister, the Duchess, one by Charles Grey

(later Lord Grey, the Prime Minister responsible for the Reform Bill). For some years the Duchess, the Duke and the Duke's mistress, Lady Elizabeth Foster, all lived amicably together under one roof. Lady Bessborough's (legitimate) daughter, Lady Caroline, married William Lamb, the future Lord Melbourne and the future Prime Minister (rumoured to be the son of Lord Egremont), and had a tempestuous and notorious love affair with Lord Byron. Nevertheless, Lady Bessborough could pause in a letter to her lover to pen her thoughts on Sabbath observance:

> There are several places in the New Testament where our Saviour evidently reproves the Austerity of the Jews on the Sabbath; but, still, the 4th commandment is very strong, and none of the other Jewish institutions, tho' strongly recommended in Leviticus, &c., are mentioned in the Commandments. There is somewhere in a Sermon of Porteous a very fine passage I always liked, but a little in Paley's sense of it – that with the Heathen months, years, life passed with their wretched slaves without one day of rest, till death gave what man denied them; and that the Sabbath is, or ought to be, one day in every sense a solemn pause throughout the whole Christian world, giving rest to man and beast, and in which at the same moment thousands of hearts and voices are lifted up to the throne of God in Prayer and thanksgiving.[38]

It is very hard indeed to grasp the moral tone of late Regency or early Victorian England without understanding that the country was in the throes of one of the greatest and most drastic periods of reform any complex industrial society has ever undergone short of actual physical revolution. For many, the primness we associate with Victorian religiosity (or 'seriousness') seemed a small price to pay for the clean-up of public and private life that the Evangelicals fought for and often achieved. Many of their societies, such as the RSPCA, have left a permanent mark on the life of the nation; others, like the YMCA have become worldwide.

Of course there was another side to the Evangelicals. Though 'seriousness' was one of their favourite words, they did not have a monopoly of it; it was a characteristic of the age, shared by Christians and non-Christians alike. Many high-churchmen felt that

Evangelical piety was one-sided and hollow. Thomas Mozley, a high-church clergyman, had nothing but contempt for the reforming zeal of the typical Evangelical parson, complaining that all too often the zeal was a sham.

> The great mass of the people committed to his care he assumed to be utterly bad or hopelessly good, that is hopelessly trusting to good works; or perhaps waiting for the day and hour when the divine call was to reach them. Anyhow, he could discard them altogether from his consideration. He had delivered his message and that was enough, for him at least. He could thus reserve his attention for a few, and would naturally consult his tastes and preferences in the selection. Relieved thus from the dull reiteration of house to house work, and from close parochial duty generally, he became mobilised. He preached and heard preaching; he spoke from platforms and heard speeches; he came across missionaries, philanthropists, and the flying staff of societies. He saw something of the higher, richer, and more educated classes. He was in the world, and he daily acquired more and more of that knowledge and of those manners that in the world make the chief difference between one man and another. The Evangelical preacher very soon discovered that his vocation was not in cottages or hovels, or in farm-houses, or in garrets and cellars far up or down, in dirty lanes and courts. Very soon, too, did he discover his own great spiritual superiority to the rank and file of the Church, consigned to the only drudgery they were capable of.
>
> These clergymen were known, while the others were unknown. Evangelical preachers were announced and paraded. The corners of the streets and the newspapers proclaimed their appointments and invited listeners from all quarters. They sought the most capacious and best situated churches, and long before the Oxford movement rich partisans were fast buying up the most important pulpits for them.[39]

A biased view, perhaps, but Trollope's mid-Victorian portrait of Mr Slope in *Barchester Towers* implies much the same motivation.

But accusations of hypocrisy are the stock-in-trade of religious controversy. What is clear is that their stress on individual feeling and exalted ideals, as well as their tendency to describe every aspect of life in a special pious vocabulary that found the hand of God behind every chance event, could leave the Evangelicals more than usually exposed if people noted that (as is commonly the case) there was a gap between the ideal and the reality.

Prophet and poet

Though both Methodism and Evangelicalism were for many of their critics interchangeable terms,[40] and both contributed to a general and growing protest against the laxity and emotional tepidness of the English church, neither displayed that particular union of the emotional, intellectual and aesthetic powers that is so typical of the religious sensibility of Blake, Wordsworth or Coleridge, and provides such close parallels with contemporary German Romanticism.[41] For evidence that Romanticism in both countries was primarily a religious phenomenon we need to look not merely at contemporary changes in the emotional climate but also at the transformation of the whole way of understanding religious belief that underlay those changes.

In Book XII of *The Prelude* (1805 version) Wordsworth makes the astonishing assertion

> That Poets, even as Prophets, each with each
> Connected in a mighty scheme of truth,
> Have each for his peculiar dower, a sense
> By which he is enabled to perceive
> Something unseen before.   (lines 301–5)

It is not an isolated claim. As we have seen in the case of Joanna Southcott, there was already an established millenarian tradition of prophetic verse. In *All Religions are One* (1788), Blake's 'Voice of one crying in the wilderness' proclaimed that 'The Religions of all Nations are derived from each Nation's different reception of the Poetic Genius, which is everywhere call'd the Spirit of Prophecy.' Two years later, in *The Marriage of Heaven and Hell*, he elaborated this statement in more concrete terms:

The prophets Isaiah and Ezekiel dined with me, and I asked them how they dared so roundly to assert that God spoke to them; and whether they did not think at the time that they would be misunderstood, & so be the cause of imposition.

Isaiah answer'd: "I saw no God, nor heard any, in a finite organical perception; but my senses discover'd the infinite in every thing, and as I was then perswaded, & remain confirm'd, that the voice of honest indignation is the voice of God, I cared not for consequences, but wrote."

Then I asked: "does a firm perswasion that a thing is so, make it so?"

He replied: "All poets believe that it does, & in ages of imagination this firm perswasion removed mountains; but many are not capable of a firm perswasion of any thing."

Then Ezekiel said: ". . . we of Israel taught that the Poetic Genius (as you now call it) was the first principle and all the others merely derivative, which was the cause of our despising the Priests & Philosophers of other countries, and prophecying that all Gods would at last be proved to originate in ours & to be the tributaries of the Poetic Genius."[42]

Similar identifications can be found in Coleridge and even in Shelley. Indeed, so typical is this Romantic claim for the prophetic status of poetry that we can easily lose sight of just how extraordinary it would have seemed to an earlier generation for whom the two things would have seemed self-evidently distinct.

To find the origins of this new revelatory status attributed to poetry we must turn back to the middle of the eighteenth century to the publication of a book that was to transform biblical studies in England and Germany alike, and was to do more than any other single work to make the biblical tradition, rather than the classical one, the central poetic tradition of the Romantics: Bishop Robert Lowth's *Lectures on the Sacred Poetry of the Hebrews*. Delivered first as the Oxford Poetry Lectures in 1741, it was published first in Latin in 1753, and achieved much wider circulation with its English translation in 1787. In Germany the biblical scholar Johann David Michaelis brought out an annotated Latin edition in 1758 (volume 2,

1761) and various continental translations followed. The *Lectures* were to be a major influence on the new generation of biblical critics and historians such as Herder, Eichhorn and Gesenius.

Robert Lowth (1710–87) was not merely one of the most distinguished theologians of his day, he was also an outstanding Orientalist. After a highly successful Oxford career (he was only thirty-one when he became Professor of Poetry), he became successively Bishop of St David's (1766), Oxford (1766) and finally London (1777). To Lowth we owe the rediscovery of the Bible as a work of literature within the specific context of ancient Hebrew life. Hitherto, it had been read almost exclusively in terms of allegory and typology as a timeless compendium of divinely inspired revelation. One popular mid-eighteenth-century commentary on the Old Testament, for instance, explained that the story of Elijah on Horeb, confronted by the earthquake, the wind and the fire, followed by the 'still small voice' (I Kings 19. 8–12) is a pre-figuring of the way in which 'the soft and gentle persuasions' of Jesus in the New Testament were to follow 'the storms, thunders, lightnings and earthquakes which attended the promulgation of the law' in the Old.[43] The event itself was lost entirely in its 'typological' meaning, whereby the significance of an event in the Old Testament was held to pre-figure and even to 'explain' events in the New. In extreme cases the Bible was taken to hold authoritative answers to every problem of contemporary life. Lowth, in contrast, argued that

> He who would perceive the particular and interior elegancies of the Hebrew poetry, must imagine himself exactly situated as the persons for whom it was written, or even as the writers themselves; he is to feel them as a Hebrew . . . nor is it enough to be acquainted with the language of this people, their manners, discipline, rites and ceremonies; we must even investigate their inmost sentiments, the manner and connexion of their thoughts; in one word, we must see all things with their eyes, estimate all things by their opinions: we must endeavour as much as possible to read Hebrew as the Hebrews would have read it.[44]

Common-sense as this might seem to us today, Lowth was, in effect, insisting on a quite new and even revolutionary kind of scholarship. The clue to the relationship between the prophecy and poetry of the

Bible, for instance, he pointed out, must lie in a detailed study of the social setting from which they arose:

> It is evident from many parts of the Sacred History, that even from the earliest times of the Hebrew Republic, there existed certain colleges of prophets, in which the candidates for the prophetic office, removed altogether from an intercourse with the world, devoted themselves entirely to the exercises and study of religion.[45]

The Hebrew word 'Nabi', explained Lowth, was used in an ambiguous sense denoting equally 'a Prophet, a Poet, or a Musician, under the influence of divine inspiration'.[46] Solomon, for instance, 'twice makes use of the word, which, in its ordinary sense, means prophecy, strictly so called, to denote the language of poetry'.[47]

> From all these testimonies it is sufficiently evident, that the prophetic office had a most strict connexion with the poetic art. They had one common name, one common origin, one common author, the Holy Spirit. Those in particular were called to the exercise of the prophetic office, who were previously conversant with the sacred poetry. It was equally part of their duty to compose verses for the service of the church, and to declare the oracles of God.[48]

Lowth also pointed out that one of the words commonly used for a poem is also the word translated in the New Testament as 'parable'.[49] In other words, Jesus's parables were not an innovation but merely an extension (by the greatest of the biblical 'poets') of the basic mode of Hebrew thought as it had been handed down by the Old Testament.[50]

In spite of being frequently of humble background, like David, who was a shepherd boy, the prophets of Israel were not rustics but men whose religious training had included an elaborate grounding in aesthetics, in particular, in the arts of music and verse. In short, the prophets were the inheritors of a highly sophisticated aesthetic and intellectual tradition. Though Lowth's *Lectures* were to lead directly to a revival of primitivism in English poetry during the later part of the eighteenth century, there was no suggestion that the poet (or poets) of Isaiah or the Psalms were themselves primitives, any more than were those they inspired, like Smart, Blake, Cowper or Wordsworth. In his humble origins, Jesus was also quite in keeping with the Old Testament poetic tradition. Unlike European poets, the Hebrew poets had never been part of a courtly circle, but remained, often in opposition to the political establishment of the day, in close touch with the rural and pastoral life of the ordinary people, using in their verse (or parables) the homely metaphors of agriculture and everyday life.[51] This very simplicity and directness, claimed Lowth, gave Hebrew poetic language its unmatched, 'almost ineffable sublimity'.

Lowth's capacity to anticipate, and in many cases, originate, critical principles that were only to come to fruition with Romanticism is everywhere extraordinary. Even his repeated stress on 'sublimity' as the ultimate criterion of greatness in art actually anticipates Burke's own *Enquiry into the Sublime and the Beautiful* by several years.[52] Foreshadowing Wordsworth's preface to the *Lyrical Ballads* he described the language of poetry as the product of 'enthusiasm', 'springing from mental emotion'.[53] Even more similar to Wordsworth were Lowth's rejection of the conventions of Augustan diction and his praise for the 'simple and unadorned' language of Hebrew verse, that gained its sublimity not from elevated diction but from the depth and universality of its subject-matter. It is hardly surprising that through Lowth's influence the Bible was to become for the Romantics not merely a model of sublimity, but also a source of style and a touchstone of true feeling.

To Lowth we owe, above all, the rediscovery of Hebrew prosody: that is, the technique of its construction. It had always been clear, of course, that a great deal of the Bible was 'poetic', and writers like Addison had laid great stress on the poetic qualities of the scriptures, but even in the Psalms (which were known to be songs) it was perplexingly difficult to find any trace of either rhyme or regular metre in the original Hebrew. Even among the Jews the traditional arts of Hebrew verse had been lost completely. Scholars, such as Bishop Hare, had made valiant attempts to discover scansion and rhyme-schemes in the Psalms, but their results looked distinctly unconvincing. Lowth demonstrated, with impressively detailed evidence, that Hebrew poetry had never depended on the normal conventions of European verse at all, but was constructed instead on a quite different principle which he called 'parallelism'.

> The correspondence of one verse, or line, with another, I
> call *parallelism*. When a proposition is delivered, and a
> second subjoined to it, or drawn under it, equivalent, or
> contrasted with it in sense; or similar to it in the form of
> grammatical construction; these I call parallel lines; and
> the words or phrases, answering one to another in the
> corresponding lines, parallel terms.[54]

This 'correspondence of one verse, or line, with another', Lowth
argued, was the basic principle of Hebrew metre. Its origins lay in
the antiphonal chants and choruses we find mentioned in various
places in the Old Testament. He cited, for example, I Samuel 29:
when David returned victorious from battle with the Philistines the
Hebrew women greeted him with the chant of 'Saul hath smote his
thousands', and were answered by a second chorus with the words
'And David his ten thousands'.[55] This simple, rhythmic, antiphonal
structure of statement and counter-statement, offering either
repetition or contrast as desired, gave the Hebrew psalmists and
prophets a basic pattern of extraordinary flexibility. Lowth himself
distinguished no fewer than eight different types of parallelism.
From the simplest form of repetition and echo it could provide endless variation, comparison, contrast (as between David and Saul, for
instance, in the example above), antithesis and even dialectic. Form
helped to shape content in a way almost unknown in European
poetry. Furthermore, this extraordinary coincidence of style and
content had another, apparently providential, consequence for
European readers of the Bible. It was only in the wake of Lowth's
pioneering work that it could be appreciated how *little* of Hebrew
poetry was actually lost through the normal linguistic problems of
translation. Whereas contemporary European poetry, which relied
heavily on essentially untranslatable effects of alliteration, asson-
ance, rhyme and metre, was extremely difficult to render in another
language with any real equivalence of tone and feeling, Hebrew
poetry was almost all translatable.

> A poem translated literally from the Hebrew into the prose
> of any other language, whilst the same form of the
> sentences remain, will still retain, even as far as relates to
> versification, much of its native dignity, and a fair
> appearance of versification.[56]

Translated into Greek or Latin, however, with a different word order 'and having the conformation of the sentences accommodated to the idiom of a foreign language' it 'will appear confused and mutilated'. This point of Lowth's was eagerly taken up by succeeding critics, who noticed also the corollary that Hebrew poetry was better translated into *prose* than into verse. As Hugh Blair, a Scottish admirer of Lowth put it:

> It is owing, in a great measure, to this form of composition, that our version, though in prose, retains so much of a poetical cast. For the version being strictly word for word after the original, the form and order of the original sentence are preserved; which by this artificial structure, this regular alternation and correspondence of parts, makes the ear sensible of a departure from the common style and tone of prose.[57]

Though Lowth could hardly have foreseen the consequences of his work, its effect was nothing less than a critical revolution. Not merely did the Bible now give authority for the prophetic status of the poet as the transformer of society and the mediator of divine truth, but it was also taken as a model both of sublimity and naturalness – with the added assurance that its precious content was almost providentially preserved in the rich prose of the English Authorized Version.

Yet if Lowth, and his critical successors such as Blair, helped to revitalize the understanding of the poetic nature of the scriptures, that very word was elsewhere acquiring connotations of a very different character. For all the interpretative brilliance of his scholarship, Lowth was never a historian in the modern sense of the word. He accepted the biblical narrative at its face value and never questioned the textual history of the material he was dealing with – no more would he have questioned the miracles or the chronology of Genesis. For him, as for his forebears, the Bible was the inspired Word of God. For all the emphasis on its context in the life of its day, Hebrew poetry was still regarded as having 'one common author' in the person of the Holy Spirit. Lowth was certain that the Books of Jonah and Daniel, for instance, were 'the bare recital of fact', and the nearest he went to speculation about authorship was when he discussed whether Moses or Elihu (one of the characters

involved) wrote the Book of Job. In Germany, however, by the end
of the eighteenth century critics and historians were beginning to
take a quite different view of the poetic nature of the Bible.

For Lowth, the Bible was a book that was simply different *in kind*
from any other. It was not a historical document in the sense that the
ancient Greek and Roman histories by Herodotus or Livy were; since
it was divinely inspired by God himself, it provided the yardstick by
which the authenticity of other histories might be judged. As Mrs
Trimmer succinctly put it in her *Help to the Unlearned in the Study
of the Holy Scriptures* (1805):

> The Histories they contain differ from all other histories
> that ever were written, for they give an account of the *ways
> of* GOD; and explain *why* GOD *protected and rewarded*
> some persons and nations, and *why* he *punished* others;
> also, *what led* particular persons mentioned in Scripture to
> *do* certain things for which they were approved or con-
> demned; whereas writers who compose histories in a
> common way, without being *inspired of God*, can only
> form guesses and conjectures concerning God's dealings
> with mankind, neither can they know what passed in the
> hearts of those they write about; such knowledge as this,
> belongs to *God* alone, whose ways are *unsearchable and
> past finding out*, and *to whom all hearts are open, all
> desires known*!

But, without guessing it, Lowth and his successor critics had
helped to strike a death-blow to this certainty. Once Lowth had
begun to see the scriptures in the context of their own time, as the
literature of a primitive nomadic and then agricultural Near-Eastern
tribe, it was inevitable that their 'history' should also be viewed in
the same way. It was clear, for instance, that there are many levels of
sophistication in the Bible; many miracles seem to reflect primitive
taboos rather than the actions of the loving father proclaimed by
Jesus in the New Testament. Indeed, to put it bluntly (and Hume,
for instance, had put it very bluntly in the 1750s), miracles themselves belonged to a pre-scientific mental set that interpreted impersonal natural forces in terms of the direct intervention of a
personal God with human characteristics and emotions. To take a
fairly minor example: if the sun had *really* stood still in the sky for

Joshua (*Joshua* 10.12–14), the rotation of the earth would have been suspended – an event so catastrophic that all life on earth would probably have been extinguished. In another – non-biblical – context such a story would be seen as a mere hyperbole, or rhetorical exaggeration, or even, if it were in a particularly important or dramatic setting, as a 'pious fraud' to impress and strengthen the faith of the tribe. Stories of this nature have to be seen as part of a world-picture which took miracles as a matter of course – and even saw military victories in terms of miracles.

In his *Introduction to the Old Testament* published between 1780 and 1783, the German biblical critic, Eichhorn, used just such a 'historicist' case to oppose the even more extreme deist argument that the Old Testament prophets were dishonest. So, far from being deliberately fraudulent, the prophets, according to Eichhorn, were simply men of their age, credulous in their approach to natural phenomena. (There is, in any case, no word in Hebrew for 'nature': everything is the direct action of God.)[58] As the Victorian novelist, Mrs Humphry Ward, was to put it in 1890, in what is still one of the best English accounts of the German method of 'higher criticism':

Testimony like every other human product has *developed*. Man's power of apprehending and recording what he sees and hears has grown from less to more, from weaker to stronger, like any other of his faculties, just as the reasoning powers of the cave-dweller have developed into the reasoning powers of a Kant. . . .

To plunge into the Christian period without having first cleared the mind as to what is meant in history and literature by 'the critical method' which in history may be defined as the 'science of what is credible' and in literature as 'the science of what is rational' is to invite fiasco. The theologian in such a state sees no obstacle to accepting an arbitrary list of documents with all the strange stuff they may contain, and declaring them to be sound historical material, while he applies to all the strange stuff of a similar kind surrounding them the most rigorous principles of modern science. Or he has to make believe that the reasoning processes exhibited in the speeches of the Acts, or in certain passages of St. Paul's Epistles, or in the Old

Testament quotations in the Gospels, have a validity for
the mind of the nineteenth century, when in truth they are
the imperfect, half-childish products of the mind of the
first century, of quite insignificant or indirect value to the
historian of fact, of enormous value to the historian of
testimony and its varieties.[59]

Though this attempt to see the literature of the Bible in the context
of its time is essentially the same as Lowth's, the *tone* is very
different. Whereas Lowth's study of Hebrew aesthetics led him into
an increasing admiration for the technical skills and sophistication of
the prophets, Mrs Ward's interest in the modern value of their testimony leads her towards a much more critical and patronizing
approach. As we shall see, this was a split that had already begun by
the end of the eighteenth century, a split that was to drive poets and
biblical scholars further and further apart in the nineteenth century.

Mrs Ward was certainly a formidable scholar in her own right. She
was the grand-daughter of the great Dr Arnold of Rugby (immortal-
ized by Thomas Hughes in *Tom Brown's Schooldays*), and niece of
Matthew Arnold, the poet, whose attempt to popularize the
German higher criticism in *Literature and Dogma* had, as late as
1873, scandalized pious English opinion. Its reception illustrates
how relatively unknown, even in mid-Victorian times, historical
criticism was in Britain. Though by the 1790s the work of Eichhorn,
Herder and Lessing had begun to filter into intellectual circles in
Britain, chiefly through Unitarian channels, and though there were
even home-grown critics and scholars of international standing (such
as Alexander Geddes, a Scottish Roman Catholic priest), it proved a
false start for the new wave of biblical scholarship. The popular
reaction against the French Revolution by 1793 meant that
Unitarianism, with its dangerous intellectual and radical associations, was itself suspect. As part of a witch-hunt against suspected
Unitarians and radicals, William Frend was expelled from his
Fellowship at Cambridge and Thomas Beddoes from Oxford. The
higher criticism was not merely felt to be un-Christian, it was also
considered unpatriotic and politically dangerous. For a whole
generation it was virtually ignored in a Britain isolated as ever by the
appalling quality of modern language teaching in her schools and
universities, and, moreover, engaged in the long wars with Napoleon.

It was not until the 1820s that the intellectual climate was again favourable to the German historical critics, but when, in 1823, Edward Bouverie Pusey, shortly to become a leading figure in the Oxford Movement, became interested in the new ideas he could find only two men in the whole University of Oxford capable of reading German.[60]

Yet there *were* a few, mostly outside the universities, who could read German and who had studied the Germans. Coleridge was one. Frend had been a Fellow of Jesus College while Coleridge was an undergraduate there, and had been a big influence on Coleridge's intellectual and religious development. It was Beddoes who had persuaded Coleridge to go to the University of Göttingen when he was in Germany in 1798 to read Eichhorn and attend his lectures. We know more than we otherwise might about this period because Coleridge was an indefatigable scribbler in the margins of the books he read. On the whole he seems to have approved of Eichhorn's approach and, as we can see from his later notebooks, he was heavily influenced by him in his own biblical studies; but he was by no means uncritical. Eichhorn was generally in agreement with Lowth that the prophets were also the poets of Israel – but this time there was a sting in the tail. If, for instance, Ezekiel was the greatest 'artist' among the prophets, he was, argued Eichhorn, to that degree the least authentic visionary among them, for to be an artist involves the notion of deliberate creation, fabrication and, in this case, therefore, deceit. 'ALL these raptures and visions', declared Eichhorn uncompromisingly, 'are in my judgement mere cover-up, mere poetical fancies.'[61] 'Poetical', we notice, is now no longer a term of praise from aesthetics, but implies something that is historically untrue. The word has come full circle from Lowth: from praise to abuse. Coleridge rejected this 'cold-blooded' division between artist and visionary, and the down-grading of 'poetic' in his brilliant reply to Eichhorn's argument that Ezekiel's visions were 'so magnificent, varied, and great that the presentation can hardly be an impromptu, but must have been planned and worked out with much art':

> It perplexes me to understand how a man of Eichhorn's
> Sense, Learning, and Acquaintance with Psychology could
> form, or attach belief to, so cold-blooded an hypothesis.
> That in Ezekiel's Visions Ideas or Spiritual Entities are

presented in visual Symbols, I never doubted; but as little
can I doubt that such Symbols did present themselves to
Ezekiel in Visions – and by a Law closely connected with,
if not contained in, that by which Sensations are organized
into Images and mental Sounds in our ordinary sleep.[62]

Coleridge's criticism of Eichhorn was not over the analogy between
the Bible and a work of art, but over the status of a work of art itself.
Whereas for Eichhorn a work of art was a conscious artifact, for
Coleridge it was an expression of man's deepest powers, which involved both conscious and unconscious minds, and was capable of
saying more than its author intended or knew. Their disagreement
focuses the new dilemma that was to haunt the biblical critics of the
nineteenth century. If the Bible, with its pre-scientific world-picture
of miraculous intervention in the natural order, was no longer
acceptable as history, was it then to be discarded as valueless superstition? For some, the rigid certainties of Newtonian science and the
confident materialism of an age that did not believe in psychic
phenomena or faith-healing made the apparent conflict between
science and religion much more clear-cut and uncompromising than
it would appear today. For most of the Romantics, however, even
those opposed to established churches (like Blake) or even atheists
like Shelley, the answer was still an emphatic 'No!' To them the
Bible showed poets not as mere decorators of truth, but as *prophets*,
'the makers and shakers of things' and the 'unacknowledged legislators of mankind'. It was the repository of the most profound
spiritual truths known. Liberated from the need to defend it as a
record of unerring historical fact, for many the Bible assumed,
paradoxically, a new and enhanced status. Romantic literature is
steeped in biblical images and references in a way that even
Augustan literature is not. The scriptures, said Coleridge, are
nothing less than 'the living educts of the Imagination', conveying
their meaning in 'a system of symbols'. Their contents 'present to us
the stream of time continuous as Life and a symbol of Eternity,
inasmuch as the Past and the Future are virtually contained in the
Present'.[63] Coleridge clarified this by explaining what he meant by a
symbol. It is characterized 'above all by the translucence of the
Eternal in and through the Temporal. It always partakes of the
Reality which it renders intelligible; and while it enunciates the

whole, abides itself as a living part in that Unity, of which it is the representative.'[64] In other words, it both particularizes and focuses a general principle in a particular example, while at the same time bearing an organic relationship to that general principle. The Bible is full of such 'symbols', whether it be Elijah denouncing Ahab for taking Naboth's vineyard in the Old Testament, proclaiming that even the King is not above the law, or the 'acted parables' of Jesus's 'miracles' in the New, which particularize the divine compassion.

Nor would Blake have disagreed with this new 'symbolic' status of the scriptures. Though we do not have the same kind of firm evidence for his reading that we have for Coleridge, there is every reason to believe from internal evidence (in, for instance, *The Marriage of Heaven and Hell*) that he too was acquainted with the higher criticism. Certainly he was moving in circles during the 1790s where the ideas of the German critics were known and discussed. He too, for instance, knew William Frend. He also belonged to a circle that met regularly at the house of Joseph Johnson, a radical bookseller and publisher, in St Paul's Churchyard. Other members of the group included William Godwin, Tom Paine, Mary Wollstonecraft, Joseph Priestley, Dr Price and Thomas Holcroft.

Yet the new stress on the scriptures as poetic, commanding our assent as works of art not by any outward objective historical authority, but by an inward and subjective appeal, did not remove the difficulty of verification but actually enhanced it. If, on the one hand, this progressive 'internalization' of religious experience during the Romantic period intensified and deepened the belief of many, others were quick to point out that such a subjective conviction of truth was even harder to accept than the old external 'proofs' of God. These still flourished. William Paley, a Cambridge don and (non-resident) Archdeacon of Carlisle, had made his name with a best-seller in 1794 called *A View of the Evidences of Christianity*. It opened with a sturdy defence 'of the Direct Historical Evidence of Christianity; and wherein it is distinguished from the Evidence Alledged for other Miracles'. In a sense, Paley was forward-looking. He was conscious of the new kinds of question being asked, and his opening was a direct attempt to face and refute the arguments used by Hume in his highly sceptical *Essay on Miracles*. But Paley's defence of Christianity against its critics in *A View of the Evidences of Christianity*, and in a later and even more popular book, *Natural Theology* (1802), were to draw Coleridge's attack from the opposite flank, in *Aids to Reflection*:

> I more than fear, the prevailing taste for Books of Natural Theology, Physico-Theology, Demonstrations of God from Nature, Evidences of Christianity, &c., &c. *Evidences* of Christianity! I am weary of the Word. Make a man feel the *want* of it; rouse him, if you can, to the self-knowledge of his *need* of it; and you may safely trust it to *his* own Evidence.[65]

Paley's evidences were based upon an outmoded idea of history – the very sort that Mrs Humphry Ward was to attack so effectively in *Robert Elsmere*; his natural theology was based on a concept of nature that was fixed, immutable and dissectible. For outward evidence Coleridge insisted that we should substitute inward need; for *natura naturata*, 'nature natured', and laid out upon a slab for our pious post-mortem, Coleridge insisted upon *natura naturans*, 'nature naturing', in a living organic process of change and flux from which man is not a separable and detached observer, but a participant. We are existentially involved. The idea that there *could* be 'objective' proofs for something as inward and personal as religious belief was itself a fallacy.

But the new analogy between the Bible and a work of art, so ironically and unintentionally foreshadowed by Lowth, though it may have been an improvement upon the other analogy with science, still presented its problems. A work of art demands only a 'willing suspension of disbelief'. We can accept, for instance, that Shakespeare consciously altered the known 'facts' of English history in order to show his audiences the truth of the historical process; we do not therefore have to commit our lives on his version or believe that the Tudor monarchy was right and inevitable. But Christianity *does* demand just such a commitment by its adherents if they are to enter into its world. As Coleridge put it, again in *Aids to Reflection*: 'Christianity is not a Theory, or a Speculation, but a *Life*. Not a *Philosophy* of Life, but a Life and a Living Process. . . . TRY IT.'[66]

Yet is existential commitment enough? What, for instance, of Joanna Southcott and her followers? Mere belief or sincerity is evidently not by itself a guarantee of truth. For Coleridge, personally, it seems clear that this problem was not a central one;

his vision of the poetic imagination was apparently in some way self-authenticating. In this, as so often, he was not unlike Blake (see above, p. 144):

> Then I asked: "does a firm perswasion that a thing is so, make it so?"
> He replied: "All poets believe that it does & in ages of imagination this firm perswasion removed mountains; but many are not capable of a firm perswasion of any thing."

It was left to John Henry Newman, perhaps the last and certainly one of the greatest of the Romantic religious thinkers, in the *Grammar of Assent* (1869) to spell out the implications of Coleridge's ideas and to carry them to their logical conclusion.[67] Newman's argument looks back to a work that had also been a great influence on the development of Coleridge's thinking: Bishop Butler's famous *Analogy of Religion* (1736). Certainty, argued Butler, is rarely, if ever, given to man. We act not upon certainties but upon accumulations of probability. Newman had read not only Butler but Hume, and knew well the uncertain foundations of all human reasoning. We possess, he concluded, what he called an 'illative' sense, by which we are enabled to make an imaginative leap from scattered and disparate parts to an intuition of the whole, and by which we convert probabilities and inferences into practical certainties upon which we act with complete assurance. This is not just a question of *religious* certainty (which is of a kind with any other), but affects every part of our lives from the simplest and most basic forms of sense perception through to the most complex metaphysical propositions. As Hume had demonstrated so powerfully, the empiricist theory of mind had, paradoxically, destroyed all objective certainty: even our household surroundings and everyday acts involve complex acts of inference and assent from unreliable and questionable evidence. Yet, for practical purposes, we are content to call this unconscious illative process 'certainty', and to trust our lives to it every day. Thus it is not, Newman argued, that our religious assent demands a peculiar *kind* of existential leap, but that it represents the most extreme, and therefore the most clearly visible, example of a process that is constantly going on at every level of our lives. From being a doubtful borderline area of our experience, religious belief is suddenly transformed into the paradigmatic example of the whole epistemological problem: the problem, that is, of how we can *know* anything at all. It becomes the touchstone by which we interpret everything else.

As we have seen, such an argument draws together many of the interwoven strands of Romantic thought into what was, perhaps, the most comprehensive and successful Romantic restatement of the necessity of belief. For the true Romantics at the end of the eighteenth century such a conclusion was still in the future, latent rather than explicit within the new religious vision that was emerging from the shattered shell of ecclesiastical formalism. If, as we have also seen, religious belief was central to the intellectual and emotional evolution of Romanticism, it is also true that Romanticism was to prove central to the evolution of religious belief. It was to Coleridge and his followers, men like Julius Hare, F. D. Maurice and even Newman, more than to any other group, that the survival of Christianity in nineteenth-century England was to depend. Yet Victorian Christianity, for all its many qualities, was somehow a weaker, thinner, narrower affair than the vision of Blake or Coleridge.

We might perhaps sum up the argument in this essay in the following manner. For a brief period, round about 1800, a number of great poets, who were also great theologians, were able to hold together in a single world-picture two different traditions of thought which have since become separated. On the one hand there were the biblical critics and textual scholars who, in their efforts to accommodate the essence of Christianity to what was then conceived of as 'scientific' and 'historical' truth, tended to see the Bible as a multi-layered collective work, the creation of a tradition rather than of individual writers, and belonging to a mental set that was both childish and credulous in its belief in miracles and divine intervention. On the other hand were the defenders of biblical inspiration – most of them of Evangelical origin – for whom the actual words of the Bible retained paramount importance and who came to insist on the literal truth of every line. *Both* attitudes, we notice, were essentially modern. Neither would have been intelligible to, say, a sixteenth-century Christian for whom the Bible was interpreted by means of typology and allegory. The former group, feeling acutely the distance between themselves and the biblical writers, came increasingly in the nineteenth century to interpret the

Bible according to their own ideas of myth, anthropology and primitive religion, and to lose any sense of the actual text as poetry or even as relevant communication. The latter group, desperately defending themselves by theories of literal inspiration, were doubly vulnerable to the attacks of geologists and Darwinians upon the historicity of the Book of Genesis. Maurice and Newman, well aware of the controversies surrounding both groups, remained curiously untroubled by the dilemmas posed by either. In their different ways, they remained in touch with the older sensibility of the Romantics who had assimilated the work of Eichhorn while yet retaining a sense of the symbolic and poetic power of the actual text before them. The cultural breadth that enabled Coleridge, standing in the tradition of Lowth and Blair, to move freely from discussions of Hebrew customs to questions of cross-cultural influence via an investigation of prosody and aesthetics was all but lost by the middle of the nineteenth century. Questions of the influence of Isaiah on Virgil's fourth *Eclogue*, or of Genesis on the influential Roman critic, Longinus, which had fascinated earlier critics, concerned as they were with the interaction of the classical and biblical worlds, tended to become lost in discussions of comparative anthropology. With them, too, was lost the sense of the poet as prophet; the belief that scholarship went hand in hand with a social and moral message; and the conviction that the artist was uniquely privileged to speak to the whole human soul. As Coleridge himself recorded in one of his late notebooks, the gifts required for that kind of biblical critic were at once too broad and too demanding for the later generation of specialists:

> Great and wide Erudition, with curious research; a philo-
> sophic imagination quick to seize hold of analogies; an
> emancipation from prejudice, and a servile subjection to
> the prejudices of great names; a faith that shutteth out fear;
> a freedom from the superstition which assumed an absolute
> *sui generis* in every word of the O. and N. Testaments, and
> is for ever craving after the supernatural; a sound and pro-
> found Psychology – these are the principal requisites.[68]

Notes

1 Anon. Cited by Lady Holland, *Memoir of the Rev. Sydney Smith*, London, 1855, I, 61–2.

2 Thomas Mozley, *Reminiscences: Chiefly of Oriel College and the Oxford Movement*, London, 1882, I, 184.

3 ibid., II, 384–5.

4 In post-Reformation times. Where there had been accommodation for a medieval priest, even if it had survived, it was often quite unsuitable for married clergy with families.

5 Hesketh Pearson, *The Smith of Smiths*, Penguin, 1948, 154.

6 Mary Moorman, *William Wordsworth: The Later Years*, Oxford University Press, 1965, 104–5.

7 E. L. Griggs (ed.), *Letters of Samuel Taylor Coleridge*, Oxford University Press, 1956, I, 352.

8 Samuel Taylor Coleridge, Notebook no. 39 (unpublished), British Library, MS 47534, p. 52.

9 W. Stone, *Religion and the Art of William Hale White*, New York, AMS Press, 1967, 21.

10 Donald Davie, *A Gathered Church: The Literature of the English Dissenting Interest, 1700–1930*, Routledge & Kegan Paul, 1970, 56.

11 ibid., 67.

12 ibid.

13 F. D. Maurice, *The Kingdom of Christ*, 4th edn, Macmillan, 1891, I, 150.

14 Cited by Basil Willey, *The Eighteenth Century Background*, Peregrine, 1962, 182.

15 Cited in Edith Morley (ed.), *Henry Crabb Robinson on Books and their Writers*, Dent, 1938, I, 87.

16 Davie, *A Gathered Church*, 78.

17 Samuel Taylor Coleridge, *Church and State*, H. N. Coleridge (ed.), 2nd edn, London, 1839, 60.

18 ibid., 61.

19 *The Methodist Hymn Book*, London, 1933, hymn no. 47.

20 *Short Hymns on Select Passages of the Holy Scriptures*, London, 1796, II, 82.

21 ibid., 202.

22 Maurice, *The Kingdom of Christ*, I, 171, 172–3.

23 ibid., 177.

24 ibid., 177–8.

25 Cited by Jack Lindsay, *William Blake*, Constable, 1978, 278.

26 Cited by Lindsay, *William Blake*, 48–9.

27 E. J. E. Hobsbawm, *Primitive Rebels: Studies in Archaic Forms of Social Movement in the 19th and 20th Centuries*, Manchester University Press, 1959.

28 E. P. Thompson, *The Making of the English Working Class*, Gollancz, 1963.

29 Lindsay, *William Blake*, 48.

30 See Morton D. Paley, 'Wiliam Blake, the prince of the Hebrews, and

the woman clothed with the sun', in Morton D. Paley and Michael Phillips (eds), *William Blake: Essays in Honour of Sir Geoffrey Keynes*, Clarendon Press, 1973.

31 See J. F. C. Harrison, *The Second Coming: Popular Millenarianism 1780–1850*, Routledge & Kegan Paul, 1979.

32 Geoffrey Keynes (ed.), *The Complete Writings of William Blake*, 2nd edn, Oxford University Press, 1966, 154.

33 Samuel Taylor Coleridge, *Aids to Reflection*, Thomas Fenby (ed.), Edinburgh, 1905, 349.

34 Cardinal Newman, 'Learning in the Church of England' (1863), in H. Nettleship (ed.), *Essays*, Oxford University Press, 1889, II, 268.

35 Cited by Alec Vidler, *The Church in an Age of Revolution: 1789 to the Present Day*, Pelican History of the Church, Penguin, 1961, V, 36.

36 Cited by Ian Bradley, *The Call to Seriousness*, Jonathan Cape, 1976, 106.

37 David Newsome, *The Parting of Friends: A Study of the Wilberforces and Henry Manning*, John Murray, 1966, 33.

38 Castalia, Countess Granville (ed.), *Private Correspondence of Lord Granville Leveson Gower*, John Murray, 1916, II, 358–9.

39 Mozley, *Reminiscences*, I, 185–6.

40 Bradley, *Call to Seriousness*, 16.

41 See M. H. Abrams, *Natural Supernaturalism*, Oxford University Press, 1971.

42 Keynes, *Complete Writings of Blake*, 135.

43 *The Royal Bible*, with a commentary by Leonard Howard, London, 1761.

44 Robert Lowth, *Lectures on the Sacred Poetry of the Hebrews*, trans. G. Gregory, London, 1787, I, 114, 113.

45 ibid., II, 12.

46 ibid., II, 13.

47 ibid., II, 12.

48 ibid., II, 18.

49 ibid., I, 76–8.

50 ibid., I, 224.

51 ibid., I, 123, 311.

52 ibid., I, 169.

53 ibid., I, 336.

54 ibid., II, 32.

55 ibid., II, 53.

56 ibid., I, 71–2.

57 Hugh Blair, *Lectures on Rhetoric and Belles Lettres*, Edinburgh, 1820, II, 270–1 (1st edn, 1783).

58 See H. Wheeler Robinson, *Inspiration and Revelation in the Old Testament*, Oxford University Press, 1962, 34.

59 Mrs Humphry Ward, *Robert Elsmere*, London, 1890, 317.

60 See Newsome, *Parting of Friends*, 78.
61 Cited by E. S. Shaffer, *'Kubla Khan' and 'The Fall of Jerusalem'*, Cambridge University Press, 1975, 88.
62 ibid., 89.
63 Samuel Taylor Coleridge, 'The statesmen's manual', in R. J. White (ed.), *Lay Sermons*, Routledge & Kegan Paul, 1972, 28–30.
64 ibid., 30.
65 Coleridge, *Aids to Reflection*, 60.
66 ibid., 178.
67 See Stephen Prickett, *Romanticism and Religion*, Cambridge University Press, 1976, ch. 7.
68 Samuel Taylor Coleridge, Notebook no. 41 (unpublished), British Library MS 47536, pp. 34–5.

Further reading

Abrams, M. H., *Natural Supernaturalism: Tradition and Revolution in Romantic Literature*, Oxford University Press, 1971.

Barth, Robert, *The Symbolic Imagination: Coleridge and the Romantic Tradition*, Princeton University Press, 1977.

Bradley, Ian, *The Call to Seriousness*, Jonathan Cape, 1976.

Brantley, Richard, E., *Wordsworth's 'Natural Methodism'*, Yale University Press, 1975.

Butler, Marilyn, *Jane Austen and the War of Ideas*, Oxford University Press, 1975.

Currie, Robert (Alan Gilbert and Lee Horsley), *Churches and Churchgoers: Patterns of Church Growth in the British Isles Since 1700*, Clarendon Press, 1977.

Davie, Donald, *A Gathered Church: The Literature of the English Dissenting Interest 1700–1930*, Routledge & Kegan Paul, 1978.

Feuerbach, Ludwig, *The Essence of Christianity*, trans. George Eliot, introduction by Karl Barth, Harper & Rowe, 1957.

Harrison, J. F. C., *The Second Coming: Popular Millenarianism 1780–1850*, Routledge & Kegan Paul, 1979.

McFarland, Thomas, *Coleridge and the Pantheist Tradition*, Clarendon Press, 1969.

Prickett, Stephen, *Romanticism and Religion: The Tradition of Coleridge and Wordsworth in the Victorian Church*, Cambridge University Press, 1976.

Pym, David, *The Religious Thought of Samuel Taylor Coleridge*, Colin Smythe, 1978.

Roston, Murray, *Prophet and Poet: The Bible and the Growth of Romanticism*, Faber & Faber, 1965.

Shaffer, E. S., *'Kubla Khan' and 'The Fall of Jerusalem': The Mythological School in Biblical Criticism and Secular Literature 1770–1880*,

Cambridge University Press, 1975.

Storr, V. F., *The Development of English Theology in the Nineteenth Century, 1800–1860*, Longman, 1913.

Vidler, Alec, *The Church in an Age of Revolution: 1789 to the Present Day*, Pelican History of the Church, Vol. 5, Penguin, 1961.

Willey, Basil, *Samuel Taylor Coleridge*, Chatto & Windus, 1972.

4 The roots of imagination: the philosophical context

T. J. DIFFEY

Nature that fram'd us of four elements,
Warring within our breasts for regiment,
Doth teach us all to have aspiring minds:
Our souls, whose faculties can comprehend
The wondrous Architecture of the world:
And measure every wand'ring planet's course,
Still climbing after knowledge infinite,
And always moving as the restless Spheres,
Will us to wear ourselves and never rest,
Until we reach the ripest fruit of all,
That perfect bliss and sole felicity,
The sweet fruition of an earthly crown.

So speaks Tamburlaine in the play by Christopher Marlowe first
staged about 1587. Later Tamburlaine soliloquizes:

What is beauty saith my sufferings, then?
If all the pens that ever poets held
Had fed the feeling of their masters' thoughts,
And every sweetness that inspir'd their hearts,
Their minds, and muses on admired themes:
If all the heavenly quintessence they still
From their immortal flowers of Poesy,
Wherein as in a mirror we perceive
The highest reaches of a human wit;

If these had made one poem's period,
And all combin'd in beauty's worthiness,
Yet should there hover in their restless heads
One thought, one grace, one wonder at the least,
Which into words no virtue can digest.

About a hundred years after these speeches had been composed for Tamburlaine, there appeared in 1690 the first edition of the great *Essay Concerning Human Understanding* by the philosopher John Locke (1632–1704). By now the four elements had gone, to be replaced by a world of colourless, odourless, tasteless particles of matter in motion. How the mind or soul comprehends the wondrous architecture of the world and what sort of place it really was had now become problematic. Tamburlaine's pride in climbing after knowledge infinite had yielded to a cautious reasonableness, for Locke had found that 'it was necessary to examine our own abilities and see what objects our understandings were, or were not, fitted to deal with'.[1] Contrary to the aspirations expressed by Tamburlaine, God, so Locke believed, had placed us on earth in a 'state of mediocrity and probationership' where we are daily checked by our tendency to fall into error.[2] 'The busy mind of man', Locke warned, must 'be more cautious in meddling with things exceeding its comprehension.' Rather, we must analyse the powers of human understanding with a view to discovering their limits. This done, we should 'sit down in a quiet ignorance of those things which upon examination are found to be beyond the reach of our capacities'.[3]

We can safely conclude that for Locke the ripest fruit of all was not an earthly crown, but the knowledge of those things which concern the conduct of us all. It is evident from his political writings that Locke had no patience with kingly aspirations. His interest was far more in such questions as what a king's duties to his subjects were, and by what right he ruled, always assuming that the sovereign power took the form of monarchy.

Locke's *Essay* dominated the intellectual history of the century that followed its publication. Locke himself scarcely considered Tamburlaine's question 'What is beauty?' beyond remarking that beauty consists in 'a certain composition of colour and figure, causing delight in the beholder'.[4] After Locke, however, all manner of writers, and not merely philosophers in any narrow sense of the term, did pursue the question with some eagerness, though their inquiries were conducted more in the spirit of Locke's reasonableness than of Marlowe's anguish.

Locke's philosophy and the Romantics

To place Romantic imagination in a philosophical context means, so far as English poetry and the native philosophical tradition are concerned, beginning with a consideration of some aspects of empiricism. This in turn means beginning with aspects of Locke's philosophy, which are central both to empiricism and to an understanding of the imagination, ideas about which in the writing of the Romantic poets and in their thinking about imagination break out of the limits imposed by empiricism.

Essentially Lockean empiricism and English Romanticism are at issue over two main questions: the nature of perception, and the nature of language and meaning, though as we shall see in the next section, philosophers, particularly writers on aesthetics but men of letters generally, in what was little more than a century between the publication of Locke's *Essay* and, say, the birth of Keats, were to narrow the divisions between Lockean empiricism and Romantic thought.

Locke denied that we bring into the world with us 'primary notions' already imprinted upon our minds. His view was that the mind, in its original state, is to be thought of as 'white paper void of all characters'.[5] Locke had more than one image for the mind in its pristine state: it is an empty cabinet,[6] a mirror that cannot refuse the images offered to it in perception,[7] a presence-room served by the organs of sense,[8] a dark room or a closet wholly shut from light.[9]

William Blake was particularly hostile to the rejection of innate ideas. In his copy of the *Discourses on Art* by Sir Joshua Reynolds (1723–92), the painter and thinker who had diligently absorbed Locke's philosophy, Blake noted: 'Reynolds Thinks that Man Learns all that he knows. I say on the Contrary that Man Brings All that he has or can have Into the World with him. Man is Born Like a Garden ready Planted & Sown. This World is too poor to produce one Seed.'[10]

However, Locke and the Romantic poets were even more at odds, perhaps, over what importance to attach to Locke's belief that 'the objects of our senses . . . obtrude their particular *ideas* upon our minds whether we will or no'. Locke introduced this observation with the remark: 'In this part the *understanding* is merely *passive*.' [11] Since this is no more than the common sense for which Locke is famous, it is difficult to see how anybody might wish to criticize it. And of course Wordsworth and Coleridge recognized the passivity of sense-perception. It is admitted on all sides that something is given in experience – in Wordsworth's version:

> The eye – it cannot choose but see;
> We cannot bid the ear be still;
> Our bodies feel, where'er they be,
> Against or with our will.
>
> (*Expostulation and Reply*, 1798)

And in Locke's: 'Men that have senses cannot choose but receive some *ideas* by them.' [12]

Yet to regard perception as essentially passive in character is to take an incomplete view of it. For the poets recognized what they called 'the despotism of the eye', and believed that this, like all tyrannies, should be resisted. In these lines from Book XI of *The Prelude* (1805), Wordsworth is characterizing a phase of experience and therefore not that which must be the foundation of all experience:

> The state to which I now allude was one
> In which the eye was master of the heart,
> When that which is in every stage of life
> The most despotic of our senses gained
> Such strength in me as often held my mind
> In absolute dominion.   (lines 171–6)

According to Locke, our minds, originally blank, become furnished with ideas by means of the senses. Locke used the word 'idea' in a much broader sense than we do, to mean 'whatsoever is the object of the understanding when a man thinks'. [13] It could include anything from what is expressed by the words 'whiteness', 'hardness', 'sweetness', to what is expressed by 'drunkenness', 'man', 'army', 'elephant', 'thinking' or 'motion'. In Locke's view, there are two fountains of knowledge 'from whence all the *ideas* we have . . . do spring'.[14] These are sensation and reflection. Reflection is the mind taking notice of its own operations. These operations could not occur without there being the materials of sensation to work with.

To experience a piece of wax, for example, is to be aware simultaneously of various qualities: softness, warmth, colour, etc. Yet although there is a blending of qualities in our experience, ideas produced in the mind, Locke insisted 'enter by the senses simple and unmixed'.[15] The suggestion is that we can analyse our perceptions of things into constituent elements of sense according to the various senses by which we perceive them. If this means that for any given perceptual experience we can distinguish distinctly, say, the several colours in our visual field, the various sounds that we can hear, and so on, it seems harmless, though in fact it is sheer dogmatism. Moreover, this, which we might call the atomistic approach to perception, so easily leads to a conclusion which many philosophers nowadays hold to be pernicious: namely that the world is nothing but patches of colour, noises, etc.

Evidence deriving from the scientific study of optics has sometimes appeared to reinforce this conclusion. If seeing involves the formation of images on the retina, it is tempting to infer that we don't 'really' see things, but only the images of them, somewhat as an image of a sandcastle on photographic film is to be distinguished from the sandcastle itself on the beach. Seeing then becomes looking, not at the world, but at images of it. This offends common sense, is philosophically controversial, and, as A. D. Nuttall has argued, is a catastrophic philosophy which has had considerable consequences for literature.[16]

Locke sometimes wrote as if physiological and philosophical analyses of perception were one and the same. In any case, what interested him are not people as individuals but people as they represent types or belong to kinds. Thus he made allowance for exceptional cases such as deafness. Indeed Locke was fascinated by the fact that if we are disabled in one sense then we must lack the simple ideas which only that sense can furnish. Conversely, for all we know, there may be creatures who possess senses not numbered within our five (or whatever the number of our senses is).

Locke assumed what the Romantic poets challenged: that under standard conditions and given similar nervous systems we will 'see the same thing', 'experience similar ideas'. But if perception is the active experience of each of us and not the passive fate of all then, as Blake said, everyone is responsible for the world he experiences. 'Every Eye sees differently. As the Eye, Such the Object.' [17] 'I see Every thing I paint In This World, but Every body does not see alike . . . The tree which moves some to tears of joy is in the Eyes of others only a Green thing that stands in the way . . . As a man is, So he Sees.' [18]

Locke's view that we perceive ideas prompts the question: how do we know that the images or ideas which we are conscious of represent or resemble the real world? Locke believed that some ideas do resemble the things which cause them and others do not. In some cases, objects will produce in us simple ideas which also belong to them. For example, weight, shape and generally the properties which interest the physicist are regarded as belonging to the object itself and not merely to the mind which perceives it. On the other hand, many of the qualities which often contribute to an object's human interest do not belong to the object itself: for example, its colour, taste, smell, the sound it may make. Of course these are ideas in our experience, no less than the primary qualities of weight, figure, etc. However, properly understood, they are not properties objectively belonging to things but sensations produced in us by the physical characteristics – bulk, figure, texture, motion – of things. A quality is the power to produce an idea in the mind. Primary qualities resemble characteristics that belong to objects themselves, whereas there is 'nothing like' the ideas of secondary qualities (colours, tastes, etc.) 'existing in the bodies themselves'.[19]

The distinction between primary and secondary qualities did not originate with Locke, who apologized to his reader for this 'little excursion into natural philosophy'. We also have had to undertake the excursion because, as the philosopher Alfred North White-head[20] and others have pointed out, one consequence of the doctrine of primary and secondary qualities is that it reduces what most gives savour to human experience to a sort of illusion or unreality. Correlatively, reality is reduced to a world of colourless, lifeless, material particles, silently in motion. This is the world that I began by describing as in stark contrast to that of Marlowe's Tamburlaine. No room is found for poetry in this scheme of things; nor is a place found for an adequate account of it in Locke's *Essay*.

In his discussion of Galileo's formulation of the doctrine of primary and secondary qualities, E. A. Burtt observed: 'Its effects in modern thought have been of incalculable importance. It is a fundamental step toward that banishing of man from the great world of nature.'[21] Man, Burtt said, is read out of the primary realm. 'His was a life of colours and sounds, of pleasures, of griefs, of passionate loves, of ambitions, and striving'[22] – the life, one might say, of Tamburlaine. Henceforth, 'the real world must be the real world outside man'.[23]

This was the philosophy which Locke was affably to adopt, and against which Keats's Lamia, and not only she, was to prove helpless:

> Do not all charms fly
> At the mere touch of cold philosophy?
> There was an awful rainbow once in heaven:
> We know her woof, her texture; she is given
> In the dull catalogue of common things.
> Philosophy will clip an Angel's wings,
> Conquer all mysteries by rule and line,
> Empty the haunted air and gnomed mine –
> Unweave a rainbow . . .
>
> (*Lamia*, Part II, lines 229–37)

In so far as we are inclined to identify knowledge with the sciences, we are faced with the problem which first became acute for the Romantic poets, in whose time it assumed a recognizably modern form: namely, how to account for poetry or, more broadly, how to account for the life of the imagination in a universe which, it seems, can be known only by the methods of science.

Locke did not give imagination the sustained attention he gave to perception. When I speak therefore of his theory of imagination, or of the empiricist theory of imagination, I am referring to a theory that has to be reconstructed from Locke's *Essay* rather than to what can be directly quoted from it. I am speaking of what Locke's theory of the imagination would have been if he had thought imagination worthy of a theory. With these provisos, it can be asserted that there is sufficient material in Locke's *Essay* to warrant the following view of imagination.

Locke distinguished between real and fantastical ideas.[24] Real ideas conform to the existence of things whereas fantastical ideas have no foundation in nature. A chimera, which is a monster with a lion's head, a goat's body, and a serpent's tail, is a typical example of a fantastical idea, of what the imagination imagines, or of what is the object of imagination. Such fantastical ideas are made up of simple ideas which the mind has collected together from experiences that were originally separate and distinct. They are never united or found together in any substance.[25]

In a similar vein David Hume (1711–76), the greatest philosopher of the eighteenth century and, for that matter, one of the greatest of any age, observed in his *Treatise of Human Nature* (1739): '*the liberty of the imagination* [is] *to transpose and change its ideas* . . . Nature [in fables] . . . is totally confounded, and nothing mentioned but winged horses, fiery dragons, and monstrous giants.'[26]

However, fictitious objects compounded out of remembered sense-perceptions are not typical of literature, Hume's remarks notwithstanding. The theory of imagination proposed by empiricist philosophies such as Locke's and Hume's is therefore woefully inadequate to serve as an account of the nature of poetic imagination. Given these singularly unpromising accounts, there is a problem in philosophically understanding the place of imagination in Romantic poetry.

Locke may be regarded as, in effect, distinguishing between perception as the source of knowledge and imagination as something which is in principle dispensable, for it is the fanciful fabrication of fictitious objects.

Locke's theory of language is no more propitious to poetry. We use words, he thought, to stand as the outward marks of our internal ideas.[27] The end of language is 'to mark or communicate men's thoughts to one another with all the dispatch that may be'.[28] The purposes of discourse are chiefly to make known one man's thoughts or ideas to another, as easily and as quickly as possible, and with a view to conveying the knowledge of things.

Locke was the champion of plain speech and the enemy of conceits, euphuisms and the elaborate rhetoric which so delighted the Elizabethans. He attacked ambiguity, which nowadays is often seen as a source of strength in poetry. But if it were eliminated, Locke said, 'many of the philosophers' . . . as well as poets' works might be contained in a nutshell'.[29] For philosophy, the fate may be a desirable one, but, so reduced, poetry would altogether be destroyed.

The theory of language which Locke advocated maintains that words name or stand not for things but for ideas in our minds. Of course he did not hold the theory in so crude a form since he saw as clearly as anybody that many kinds of words are not by themselves names of ideas – conjunctions for example. Our interest in the theory is that it is inimical to poetry. To understand the nature of poetic meaning we need to break free from the notion that meaning is the naming of mental states or ideas.

What is remarkable in the thought of the Romantic poets is not merely the importance which they attached to imagination but that they could regard imagination as so important a force in human life given the inferior character imagination must have in the kind of empiricist philosophy we have so far considered. Therefore we now need to examine claims made for the imagination by the poets, claims which themselves involve new ways of thinking about imagination.

Romantic imagination

Phrases such as 'the poetic imagination' or 'Romantic imagination' are dangerous if they suggest that there is some single phenomenon to be explained or analysed. They are to be taken here merely as shorthand references to the poetry of the English Romantic poets such as Blake, Wordsworth, Coleridge, Shelley and Keats, and to their ideas about imagination.

We can discuss some ideas that the phrase 'Romantic imagination' characterizes if we do not press too hard. For example, it is quite commonly supposed that the Romantic poets regarded the imagination as a peculiar faculty of the mind for the apprehension of that kind of truth which is beyond the power of reason, the senses or common experience to apprehend. The poet leads the reader into a world which in character is profound, religious, ultimate, and which, but for the poet's imagination, must have remained inaccessible. According to this view, the imagination yields insight into a world that is transcendental or supersensible in its nature. The implication is that there are two worlds, the one available to ordinary people in possession of the usual senses, and the other open only to those who have the imagination or genius to see it. Of course, it is not difficult to find support in Romantic poetry for this view of imagination.

Thus it has been said that the dominant factor in Romanticism is the transfiguring imagination.[30] Such a phrase, however, is better understood by reference to perception than to metaphysics. For, besides the Romantic theme of imagination as a transcending agency, there is also the idea of imagination as the capacity to *see* – to see more deeply into the life of things. Thus Blake, whose poetry lends support for the transcendental interpretation of imagination, speaks of cleansing the doors of perception, not of shutting them in the interests of a less distracted contemplation of a higher reality.

There are, then, at least two views of imagination implicit in Romanticism: one emphasizes the powers of mind in perception, the other addresses itself to the nature of what is imagined. In one interpretation of Romantic imagination, what is imagined is a higher reality beyond the reach of the senses; in another, imagination is the power to perceive more adequately the universe in which we already live rather than some alien, supersensible reality.

Of course, when thinking about imagination as perception, a richer conception of perception is required than what is permitted by the classical empiricism of Locke. According to this way of thinking about imagination – that is, in terms of perception – imagination should be seen not as rejecting experience in favour of some higher, or transcendental reality, but as widening the limits of experience as described by the empiricist philosophers. Indeed, as we shall see in the next section, Locke's successors, without abandoning empiricism, had themselves already begun to chafe at the limits of experience set by his philosophy.

For all his evident concern with the transcendental, Blake was more interested in exploring the capacities of perception than in distinguishing between that reality which is ordinarily perceived and another which is extraordinarily imagined. Blake challenged the empiricist belief that perception can be distinguished atomistically into the several senses, sight, hearing, etc., each with its own kind of object, such as colour patches or sounds. In *There is No Natural Religion* Blake wrote: 'Man's perceptions are not bounded by organs of perception; he perceives more than sense (tho' ever so acute) can discover.'[31] And in *The Marriage of Heaven and Hell*: 'Isaiah answer'd: "I *saw* no God, nor *heard* any, in a finite organical perception; but *my senses discover'd* the infinite in every thing"' (my italics).[32]

In *The Marriage of Heaven and Hell*, Blake's Voice of the Devil (appropriately) is particularly clever, for it castigates the distinction the French philosopher René Descartes drew between mind and body, a distinction which was imported by Locke. To this doctrine, 'That Man has two real existing principles: Viz: a Body & a Soul', the Devil poses the contrary: 'Man has no Body distinct from his Soul; for that call'd Body is a portion of Soul discern'd by the five Senses, the chief inlets of Soul *in this age.*' (my italics).[33] The Devil is playing Locke at his own game; that is to say, Blake's most important words here are the last three and the least obvious: 'in this age'. For Locke had described his philosophical method as historical, which implies that his account of the human mind should be of what the mind happened to be like in his time. But Locke and his successors, being philosophers, naturally overlooked the possibility that what is historically inquired into is subject to change, and interpreted the findings presented in the *Essay* universal or timeless truths about the human mind.

Locke, for all his apparently reasonable modesty, spoke of human nature *as such*, that is to say, in universal terms, whereas the Romantic poets, Blake and Wordsworth conspicuous among them, were aware of human individuality and of the dependence which even apparently universal truths have on the historical circumstances in which they are formulated.

Blake reported that the Revd Dr Trusler had said to him: '*Your Fancy* . . . seems to be in the other world, or the World of Spirits.'[34] Blake's reply to this accusation of transcendentalism is of considerable interest for our argument, which stresses the perceptual character of imagination: 'I feel that a Man may be happy in This World. And I know that *This World* Is a World of imagination & Vision.'[35]

No confident distinction, then, between what is seen and what is (merely) imagined can survive a reading of Blake, for what his poetry shows is not that there are two worlds, one ordinary and the other transcendental, but that, depending upon the person who sees, there are many ways of seeing, some more stupid than others, some more alive, some less so.

Consider Blake's description of Felpham, the village in Sussex, to which he moved from London:

> Felpham is a sweet place for Study, because it is more Spiritual than London. Heaven opens here on all sides her

Golden Gates; her windows are not obstructed by vapours; voices of Celestial inhabitants are more distinctly heard, & their forms more distinctly seen; & my Cottage is also a Shadow of their houses. . . .[36]

The Villagers of Felpham are not mere Rustics; they are polite & modest. Meat is cheaper than in London, but the sweet air & the voices of winds, trees & birds, & the odours of the happy ground, makes it a dwelling for immortals. Work will go on here with God speed.[37]

Consider now this description taken from a good modern guide-book:

FELPHAM, once an attractive village, but now a suburb of Bognor. The church, a little south of the main road, shows work of the 13th–15th centuries and has a Norman font and a good 13th-century chest. It is the burial-place of William Hayley. . . . In Vicarage Lane, close to the old rectory south of the church, is the charming thatched cottage where the poet-visionary, William Blake, lived under the patronage of Hayley from 1801–1804 . . . he would find it [Felpham] much changed to-day, a con-glomeration of villas and bungalows.[38]

Blake's account certainly includes transcendental references: heaven, celestial inhabitants, golden gates. But it cannot be said that there are two villages: Blake's, which is transcendental, and Mr Banks's, which is on earth. Rather, setting aside the complication that 150 years separate Blake's Felpham from Mr Banks's, the des-criptions by the two writers are descriptions of the same place. Blake responded imaginatively to his new home; the guidebook, with its more abstract and restrained terminology, admirably serves its purpose of directing the visitor. Both descriptions are appropriate in their places. If they were switched so that Blake's words were passed off for a guidebook and Mr Banks's for a letter, the result would be an unusable guidebook and a dull, unimaginative letter. My sugges-tion, then, is that there are not two Felphams, an earthly village to be visited by the tourist, and an other-worldly village only to be seen in the imagination of a poet. There is one place but many ways of responding to it. Imagination is the name for some of these ways.

The argument, of course, does not depend on the example used, but is the perfectly general claim that there are not two realms, only one of which is the object of the poet's imagination.

Wordsworth's poetry suggests more obviously than Blake's that what the poet perceives is not some other-worldly realm, but is something which has lain unacknowledged and undiscovered in our world. Poets, like prophets,

> Have each for his peculiar dower, a sense
> By which he is enabled to perceive
> Something unseen before.[39]
> > (*The Prelude*, 1805, lines 303–5)

Poetry may give some *intimation* of a transcendental or super-sensible reality. But intimation is not realization. This point will be of some importance when we come to discuss Kant.

Imagination, then, is not some special mental capacity distinct from all others with its own access to a peculiar kind of truth, but is another name for quickened faculties of mind:

> Imagination, which, in truth,
> Is but another name for absolute strength
> And clearest insight, amplitude of mind,
> And Reason in her most exalted mood.
> > (*The Prelude*, 1805, lines 167–70)

As virtually any passage from his poetry will show, Wordsworth is not trying to create illusions or to fabricate fictitious entities. One gets the sense, rather, that he is faithfully reporting his experiences. Wordsworth, so A. D. Nuttall has argued, is a poet of the figural imagination.[40] The figural poet describes literally what he encounters in real life and feels to be quite objectively significant. The reality described by the imagination is won by a mind open to experience which is broader and richer than that experience which the categories of philosophy or common sense can analyse.

The Romantics emphasize the workings of the mind in imagining, whereas the Lockean theory of imagination is concerned more with the object of imagination, preferring dragons, centaurs and the like, as typical cases of those objects. Romanticism, as is well brought out by Coleridge in his *Biographia Literaria*, centres upon the activities of mind brought into play by imagination, whatever the imagined object may be. The reader of poetry, Coleridge said, 'should be carried forward . . . by the pleasureable activity of mind excited by the attractions of the journey itself'.[41] 'The poet . . . brings the whole soul of man into activity.'[42] Thus Mary Warnock is fully justified in saying: 'We must beware, then, of trying to be too specific about *what* the imaginative object was, and attempt to concentrate on the *manner* in which the imagination sought its object.'[43]

Aesthetic philosophy from Locke to the Romantics

We shall now explore changes in the idea of imagination in the period between Locke and the Romantics, particularly in order to see how the writers on poetry and art, who were thinking about the imagination before the Romantic poets, were already often dissatisfied with the rather narrow limits attributed to imagination by the classical empiricism of Locke. We shall have, of course, to be selective since a complete or even adequate treatment of the topic here is impossible.

Perception and imagination   Joseph Addison (1672–1719), Whig politician and man of letters, published his essays on the 'Pleasures of the Imagination' in the *Spectator* in 1712. The undertaking was entirely new, he said;[44] so it filled a lacuna in Locke's system. Given the well-known fact that Coleridge distinguished between imagination and fancy, it is worth noting that Addison made a point of saying that he was using the terms synonymously, or 'promiscuously' as he put it.[45]

Whether imagination and fancy *are* distinct was a live issue in the eighteenth century. James Beattie (1735–1803), professor of moral philosophy and minor poet, thought that they differed in degree. In 1783, in his *Dissertations Moral and Critical*, he wrote: 'According to the common use of words, Imagination and Fancy are not perfectly synonomous. They are, indeed, names for the same faculty; but the former sense seems to be applied to the more solemn, and the latter to the more trivial exertions of it.'[46]

The philosopher Dugald Stewart (1753–1828) explained in *Elements of the Philosophy of the Human Mind* (1792) why 'fancy' and 'imagination' are used synonymously, and argued how they should be distinguished. The tendency of the human mind to associate its thoughts, though intimately related to the imagination, should not, Stewart argued, be identified with it. The best writers seem to be referring to habits of association when they make use of the word 'fancy'.[47] Fancy is the 'ground-work of poetical genius'. Its task is to collect materials for the imagination, so imagination presupposes fancy but fancy is possible without imagination.[48] Imagination, or that which will be a source of pleasure to others, requires other powers of mind too, 'particularly the powers of taste and of judgment'.[49]

Two further comments are in order before we return to Addison. Stewart used the phrase so common with us: 'creative imagination'. But he was not, as one might suppose, the earliest writer to do so. The *Oxford English Dictionary* cites Cudworth, 1678, Thompson, 1745 and Shenstone, *c.* 1750 as using the term, and these are all of course uses before Stewart's in 1792. Stewart said that the creative imagination implies fancy, or the power 'of summoning up, at pleasure, a particular class of ideas' (in Locke's sense).[50] But, as we have seen, the power of fancy though necessary to imagination is not sufficient.

Dugald Stewart also observed that the faculty of association is very strong in childhood and early youth, so that early memories have a more permanent hold upon the mind than subsequent ones.[51] Supposing this to be true, it is tempting to speculate whether this might not have some bearing on Wordsworth's failure to complete the grand design of *The Recluse*, to which *The Prelude* was intended to be what its title implies.

To return to Addison's argument in the 'Pleasures of the Imagination': it is sight, he thought, which as 'the most perfect and most delightful of all our senses . . . furnishes the imagination with its ideas'.[52] In the spirit of Locke, Addison explained that ideas of visible objects are what arise in our minds from them when we have them in view or when such ideas are called to mind by paintings, statues or descriptions. From these examples it follows that for Addison what a work of art depicts is what we can see for ourselves if we visit the scene the painter or poet render in their art.

Addison then sketched in the main premise of the Lockean theory of imagination, namely that we cannot 'have a single image in the fancy that did not make its first entrance through the sight'.[53]

Later in the century, in 1769, Sir Joshua Reynolds expressed essentially the same claim in the second of his *Discourses*: 'Invention, strictly speaking, is little more than a new combination of those images which have been previously gathered and deposited in the memory: nothing can come of nothing: he who has laid up no materials, can produce no combinations.'[54]

The empiricist restriction of imagination to what, in some form or other, *has actually* been seen did not dismay Addison. For 'we have the power of retaining, altering, and compounding those images, which we have once received, into all the varieties of picture and vision that are most agreeable to the imagination'. So, with the faculty of imagination 'a man in a dungeon is capable of entertaining himself with scenes and landscapes more beautiful than any that can be found in the whole compass of nature'.[55] Not the least interesting word here is 'entertaining'. For whatever we mean when we speak of Romantic imagination, it is unlikely that we shall think of it as 'entertaining'. Entertainment goes with fancy, as Coleridge was eventually to define it, while 'imagination', as Beattie had perhaps anticipated, is reserved for something more fundamental.

Primary pleasures of the imagination, Addison continued, proceed from objects that are before our eyes, while secondary pleasures 'flow from the ideas of visible objects'.[56] These divide into two kinds: ideas of things that are absent and ideas of things that are fictitious.

Addison praised the imagination because we can 'immediately assent to the beauty of an object, without inquiring into the particular causes and occasions of it'. Thus the colours of a beautiful prospect 'paint themselves on the fancy, with very little attention of thought or application of mind in the beholder'.[57] Addison was faithful here to the Lockean picture of the mind as white paper. We have but to gaze upon a scene for it to impress itself upon the fancy.

However, Addison began to break away from Locke when he acknowledged that in looking upon 'huge heaps of mountains, high rocks and precipices, or a wide expanse of waters', we are not struck with their novelty or beauty, but 'with that rude kind of magnificence which appears in many of these stupendous works of nature'.[58] Addison had in mind here that great discovery, or rediscovery, of eighteenth-century thinkers, the sublime.

According to Addison the sublime fills the soul with an agreeable surprise, giving it an idea of which it was not before possessed, and thereby taking off that satiety we are apt to complain of in our usual and ordinary entertainments.[59] Addison stood near the beginning of more than two hundred years' theorizing about art which was to force the notions of art and entertainment further and further apart until, in our time, they are often represented as mortal antagonists (for example by R. G. Collingwood).[60] For it is not too big a step from Addison's claim that the sublime in its appeal to the imagination permits a deeper gratification than ordinary entertainments allow, to the claim, first prominent in Romanticism, that imagination is not a form of entertainment at all.

The sublime is central to the philosophy of Romanticism, so we shall have occasion to return to it. Much more central to Addison's own account of the imagination, however, is the way he managed to turn from defeat to triumph the discovery, quite commonly regarded as bleak, that light (as contrasted with shade) and colours are only ideas in the mind and not qualities that have real existence in matter. Referring his readers to 'the eighth chapter of the second book of Mr Locke's Essay on Human Understanding' Addison praised the distinction between primary and secondary qualities as 'that great modern discovery'.[61]

Earlier, I followed Burtt and others by representing the Lockean or Newtonian universe as a threat to poetry because of the monopolistic claims it made for reality as that in which everything is governed by mechanical laws and in which nothing lives. Addison did not share these fears. On the contrary, for him the world is an enchanting place, and it is a tribute to God who has arranged things thus that we should find it so.

> What a rough, unsightly sketch of nature should we be entertained with, did all her colouring disappear, and the several distinctions of light and shade vanish? In short, our souls are at present delightfully lost and bewildered in a pleasant delusion, and we walk about like the enchanted hero of a romance, who sees beautiful castles, woods, and meadows; and at the same time hears the warbling of birds, and the purling of streams; but upon the finishing of some secret spell, the fantastic scene breaks up, and the disconsolate knight finds himself on a barren heath, or in a solitary desert.[62]

George Berkeley (1685–1753), one of the outstanding philosophers of the eighteenth century, also celebrated the beauty of the
world. In the second of the 'Three Dialogues Between Hylas and
Philonous' (1713), Philonous, Berkeley's spokesman, says:

> Look! are not the fields covered with a delightful verdure?
> Is there not something in the woods and groves, in the
> rivers and clear springs, that soothes, that delights, that
> transports the soul? At the prospect of the wide and deep
> ocean, or some huge mountain whose top is lost in the
> clouds, or of an old gloomy forest, are not our minds filled
> with a pleasing horror? Even in rocks and deserts, is there
> not an agreeable wildness? [63]

Berkeley, however, reached a very different conclusion from
Addison's. For Addison, imagination can happily flourish in a world
where primary qualities only are real. Berkeley, on the other hand,
attacked the entire distinction between primary and secondary
qualities. He saw Newtonian physics, if interpreted materialistically
as it naturally was, though not by Newton himself, as constituting a
threat to religion. Later, Keats was to find it a threat to poetry.

Philonous asks: 'How should those principles be entertained, that
lead us to think all the visible beauty of the creation a false
imaginary glare?' [64] Notwithstanding Addison's optimism, this was
the intolerable conclusion to which Locke's principles led.

Later, Henry Home, Lord Kames (1696–1782) used the distinction between primary and secondary qualities for the purposes of
analysis and therefore more in the manner of Locke than of the
protesters. In his *Elements of Criticism*, published in 1761, he asked
if beauty was a primary or secondary quality of objects, but thought
there was no simple answer. [65] For example, the beauty of colour
must be considered distinctly from the beauty of regular form. And
in the former case, which is easy to settle, if colour is a secondary
quality so must the beauty of colour be. However, as Kames went on
to observe, 'a singular determination of nature makes us perceive
both beauty and colour as belonging to the object, and, like figure
or extension, as inherent properties', [66] notwithstanding proverbs
about beauty being in the eye of the lover (or, as we should say
nowadays, in the eye of the beholder).

Thomas Reid (1710–96), known as the philosopher of common sense, took his stand on this 'singular determination of nature'. In his essay 'Of Taste' (1785), he protested that the 'fashion among modern Philosophers, to resolve all our perceptions into mere feelings or sensations in the person that perceives, without any thing corresponding to those feelings in the external object' is contradicted by the language and common sense of mankind.[67] Later he complained that '[t]he spirit of modern philosophy would indeed lead us to think, that the worth and value we put upon things is only a sensation in our minds, and not any thing inherent in the object; and that we might have been so constituted as to put the highest value upon the things which we now despise'.[68]

Not only poets resisted the consequences of distinguishing primary and secondary qualities, then; some philosophers objected too. We must be careful, however, not to enrol philosophers such as Reid under the banner of Romanticism. Reid attacked the doctrine of primary and secondary qualities in the name of common sense, not of imagination. Likewise he was well aware of the difference between the immediate appeal of poetry to imagination and its intellectual analysis. His warning is as pertinent today as it ever was:

> A philosophical analysis of the objects of taste is like applying the anatomical knife to a fine face. The design of the Philosopher, as well as of the Anatomist, is not to gratify taste, but to improve knowledge. The reader ought to be aware of this, that he may not entertain an expectation in which he will be disappointed.[69]

So much then for Addison's account of imagination and issues it gave rise to.

Writers in the eighteenth century made a particularly rich contribution to that branch of philosophy which has since become known as aesthetics. Numerous treatises on such topics as taste, beauty and genius have come down to us from the period. Take, as a typical example, the works of Alexander Gerard (1728–95). Addison had identified two categories of things as not being 'before the eye', and Gerard attended to the second of these: imagination. In his *Essay on Taste*, first published in 1759, he said that imagination 'is, first of all, employed in presenting such ideas as are not attended with *remembrance*, or a conviction of their having been formerly in the mind'.[70] This kind of imagination only appears to be a 'wild and lawless' faculty;[71] or as David Hume had put it in *A Treatise of Human Nature* (1739): 'simple ideas may be separated by the imagination, and may be united again in what form it pleases'.[72] Nevertheless, ideas are related to one another by universal principles of association. Hume identified these principles as those of resemblance, contiguity in time or place, and cause and effect.[73] Gerard followed him, though with some variations.[74]

There is some account of the association of ideas in Locke's *Essay*, though it is only brief and schematic, and the topic did not originate with Locke. Aristotle had a highly developed theory of associationalism, as Coleridge pointed out in the *Biographia Literaria*. Associationalism, as it bears on aesthetics, was richly developed by Alexander Gerard, and by David Hartley (1705–57) in a version which was both psychological and metaphysical in form, and which was to have so signal an influence on Coleridge and Wordsworth. (This is explored by Stephen Prickett.[75])

Although Hume was centrally interested in the association of ideas, he was even more fundamentally concerned with the imagination. Unlike most philosophers he assigned to imagination a cardinal role in his own philosophical system. Since he thought reason to be much more limited in scope than philosophers had commonly supposed, Hume assigned to the imagination the task of carrying most of the burden of our capacity to understand the world. Hume shared with the Romantics the credit for putting imagination on the philosophical map. It was no longer to be dismissed, as philosophers had traditionally tended to do, as a minor but embarrassing manifestation of human error and irrationality.

Therefore Hume is quite often seen as the most important philosophical precursor of Romanticism, and certainly more important in this regard than, say, Locke. I cannot accept this view. Hume is a philosopher of the first rank but, unlike Locke, he is more a philosophers' philosopher with, historically speaking, much less general influence than Locke. Moreover, although Hume's emphasis upon the importance of the imagination ought to place him with the Romantic poets, he seems to have been known to them mainly for his views on religion. Furthermore Hume's view of art was entirely traditional and inimical to Romanticism. This in fact is no more than the then-commonplace view of the arts as civilized entertainments for the well-bred minds of gentlemen. Wordsworth, Blake and Keats, in their different ways, all express passionate hatred of this Augustan attitude.

I do not suppose that Wordsworth had Hume specifically in mind when he complained in the Preface to the *Lyrical Ballads* (particularly since the quotation that follows here is taken from the 1850 revisions and not from the 1800 version) about those 'who will converse with us gravely about a *taste* for Poetry, as they express it, as if it were a thing as indifferent as a taste for rope-dancing, or Frontiniac or Sherry'; [76] but Hume fits the part as do most philosophers and men of letters from Locke to Kant.

Gerard not only showed how fertile the principle of the association of ideas is when applied to aesthetics. We also find in his work an untroubled division between the arts and the sciences: 'As reason investigates the *laws* of nature, taste alone discovers its *beauties*.' [77] In his *Essay on Genius* (1774) he observed: 'Scientific genius addresses its discoveries to the understanding; their end is information: genius for the arts addresses its productions to taste, and aims at pleasing by them.' [78] Earlier in the same essay he had proclaimed: 'The Ends to which Genius may be adapted, are reducible to two; the discovery of truth, and the production of beauty. The former belongs to the sciences, the latter to the arts. Genius is, then, the power of invention, either in science or in the arts, either of truth or of beauty.' [79]

What the 'ends' or functions of art are, however, is a question that became problematic for the Romantics and remains so for us. Gerard's disjunct – truth or beauty – became in Keats a famous or notorious statement of identity – 'Beauty is truth, truth beauty'. Whatever the famous concluding lines of the *Ode on a Grecian Urn* do mean, it is evident that taste and beauty could no longer satisfy the Romantics as providing an adequate account of the foundations of art. The urbane words of a Gerard could not long convince, though something akin to Gerard's distinction between science and poetry was reintroduced in the twentieth century, principally by I. A. Richards.

Addison, as we saw, based imagination on the faculty of sight. Dugald Stewart grounded imagination more widely on perception while properly rejecting as arbitrary the 'limitation of the province of Imagination to one particular class of our perceptions', namely objects of sight. As Stewart rightly insisted, 'our other perceptive faculties also contribute occasionally their share'. Thus pleasing images may be 'borrowed from the fragrance of the fields and the melody of the groves'.[80]

To show how philosophy in the eighteenth century narrowed the intellectual gulf between Locke's empiricism and Romantic poetry, we should return our attention to the sublime. Addison recognized the sublime but did not give an extensive account of it. That omission was soon to be put right, and there are many treatments of the idea in eighteenth-century philosophy from which to choose.

Perhaps the most important account before Kant's, however, is Edmund Burke's. In *A Philosophical Enquiry into the Origin of our Ideas of the Sublime and Beautiful* (1757) he holds that the sublime excites ideas of pain and danger. The terrible is a source of the sublime, but in order for us to find delight in it, the threat of danger must be at a certain distance.[81] The sublime puts the mind in a state which Burke calls astonishment. In this state all the motions of the mind are suspended with some degree of horror. The mind is so filled with its object that it can neither reason about the object causing the astonishment nor entertain any other.[82] Thus the sublime hurries us on by an irresistible force exciting in us a state of mind whose object cannot be grasped adequately. Burke analysed qualities causally associated with the sublime, for example, fear, obscurity, power, vastness, infinity and magnificence.[83]

Burke, as the title of his *Enquiry* tells us, distinguished between the sublime and the beautiful. Each is based on a fundamental but distinct principle of human nature. Beauty is founded on our love for others, on the social affections including sexual appetite; the sublime on the egoistic need for self-survival. Given Burke's equal attention to these two principles, and the connexion he argued for between the sublime and the fearful, Wordsworth's lines in the first book of *The Prelude* (1805) are of especial interest:

> Fair seed-time had my soul, and I grew up
> Fostered alike by beauty and by fear: (lines 306–7)

A more extensive comparison is possible between Wordsworth and Burke, particularly if we do not restrict ourselves to the *Enquiry*. In their explorations of the human mind they both bring to the fore central aspects, particularly the imagination, which on Lockean principles must go unnoticed or undervalued. Burke, like Words-worth, brought into question the simple-minded dichotomy between reason and feeling. Both writers explored the emotions not so much in a spirit of opposition to reason but more against reason in its reduced and diminished forms as defined by philosophy. Burke opposed habits of thought which are reductive, that is, the taking of something and insisting that this is nothing but such-and-such, where this is a crude and distorted version of the original thing to be explained. Wordsworth's unhappy experience of reductionist modes of thinking is explored in the tenth book of *The Prelude* (1805). Here he is describing his application of Godwin's principles of social justice to society:

> I took the knife in hand
> And stopping not at parts less sensitive,
> Endeavoured with my best of skill to probe
> The living body of society
> Even to the heart.   (lines 373–7)

Experience does not have to be rejected or denied if it cannot be ex-pressed in intellectualistic terms. Romanticism opposes the dogma that what cannot be made intellectually perspicuous is nonsensical or unreal; it shows that experience must be wider than the limits of discursive understanding.

We have come full circle. We began with Locke whose enterprise was to stake out the limits of human knowledge so that we should not uselessly stray beyond them. Yet now we claim that experience must exceed these limits and validly so. Crucial to explaining this, which might otherwise seem an unpalatable irrationalism, is the philosophy of the greatest philosopher of the modern period, Immanuel Kant (1724–1804).

Kant Kant agreed with Locke that human inquiry must conform to the limits of what can be known. In his *Critique of Pure Reason*, published in 1781, he wrote that if we 'can perceive no limits to the extension of our knowledge' we are like the light dove. 'The light dove cleaving in free flight the thin air, whose resistance it feels, might imagine that her movements would be far more free and rapid in airless space.' [84]

Unlike Locke, however, Kant distinguished between understanding and reason. To understand an object is for the mind involuntarily to bring what is given in sensation under the control of a framework of necessary concepts or categories. To experience the world is necessarily to interpret or to understand what is given in sensation by the senses in terms of such categories of understanding as substance, and cause and effect.

The world, which is the object of knowledge or experience, consists of objects in various relationships, such as causality, with one another and with ourselves. So far this seems to have done little more than reinstate the Newtonian scheme of things offered to philosophy by Locke: the real world is the world known to physics. But Kant did not stop here.

Apart from understanding, there is also reason, in Kant's special sense of the term. The object of understanding is the world we experience. But the ideas of reason may *guide* the understanding. Certainly we cannot *know* what is not located in the framework of space and time. Hence reason goes wrong if it makes assertions about the nature of substance as such, or the age or size of the universe, say, where this means the totality of things. Such thoughts are discreditably metaphysical. Although we must understand, or experience, things in terms of the framework I have too crudely sketched, we can nevertheless *think* certain ideas *without understanding* those ideas.

Thus we cannot *understand* how nature as such is an ordered whole or a design. Such notions apply within experience, not to the totality of what is experienced. The corporation gardens are designed, but the sea and the beach beyond them are not. We experience things as designed within the wider context of things which are not. Nevertheless such ideas of reason as design play their part in guiding experience or in leading the understanding to look for connexions and relationships between things. Indeed, scientific understanding of the world would not be possible unless we believed that we lived in an ordered universe. Yet the proposition that nature *is* ordered can have no place among the propositions or the discoveries *of* science. Such notions as order as such are not categories of the understanding but are ideas of reason. These serve to guide our understanding of the physical world, while not themselves constituting elements of that world as discovered by the sciences. Physics could never *discover* that nature is ordered or orderly, but it could not proceed without the belief that it is. What belongs to physics is the province of understanding; what makes physics possible is guidance by the ideas of pure reason.

God, freedom and the immortality of the soul are the most famous ideas of pure reason. Thus we can *think* that we are free without understanding what such a claim could mean. Similarly God and the soul cannot be among the objects of understanding or experience. They cannot meet the requirements of human understanding: namely, that what is given in sensation must necessarily be united or subsumed under such intellectual categories as causality. The notion of 'being united' is important here. In the often-quoted formula: sensation without understanding is blind; understanding without sensation is empty. Thus any statement to the effect that God caused the world to come into existence does not make sense; as a proposition of the understanding, it must remain empty since there is nothing that can be given in sense experience to which it correlates. Here is a case where the mind has illegitimately trespassed beyond the limits of what can be known. The fault consists in mistaking ideas of reason for representations of reality. Reason, then, has 'regulative' force. It can guide the mind in cognitive constructions but cannot enter into judgements that belong to the body of knowledge.

The relevance to Romantic poetry of Kant's distinction between reason and understanding is that poetry gives us intimations of what, in Kant's sense, cannot be understood or conceptualized. That what poetry expresses cannot be understood discursively does not mean, however, that what is expressed is unreal or illusory. The point is put by Kant in his *Critique of Aesthetic Judgement* (1790) in one of the deepest insights philosophy has ever offered into poetry:

> The poet essays the task of interpreting to sense the rational ideas [ideas of reason, not of understanding] of invisible beings, the kingdom of the blessed, hell, eternity, creation, &c. Or, again, as to things of which examples occur in experience, e.g. death, envy, and all the vices, as also love, fame, and the like, transgressing the limits of experience he attempts with the aid of an imagination which

emulates the display of reason in its attainment of a maximum, to body them forth to sense with a completeness of which nature affords no parallel.[85]

Language Locke was not curious about such questions as whether language is used in distinctive or special ways in poetry (or more widely in literature). He was not interested in the nature of poetic meaning, unless perhaps to make disparaging remarks about rhetoric as the enemy of clarity and plainness of thought. But if Locke's naming theory of language is applied to poetry, there are at least two unfortunate consequences. First, it would follow that poetry is essentially descriptive in character; second, that the poet is naming ideas which have already occurred before he composes his poem or which already exist in some sense in the poet's mind. This follows from Locke's beliefs that thought consists in 'ideas' and that language is but the dress of thought. To clothe a thought is to name an idea.

These doctrines, applied to poetry, yield the consequences that a poem is the linguistic instrument by which poets communicate to their readers meanings which in their essential character are pre-formed and non-verbal 'ideas'. If the metaphor of dress is taken literally, a thought can be clothed in more than one way, in which case there is nothing necessary or essential about the particular language the poet *has* used. What the poet has said is but the selection of one from a number of possibilities.

The importance of this point is that it is at odds with the Romantic notion of the poem as something created and unique. Locke's theory implies that in principle the poet has before him different ways of saying the same thing, that is, alternative ways of communicating and transmitting his ideas to the public. The finished poem would then represent the poet's choice in favour of one of those ways, there being others which he had deliberately rejected. Furthermore, a poet must already know what he means before he has composed his poem, and the act of writing poetry would have to be interpreted as the poet's searching for words to match as closely as he can his already existing ideas.

Against this view of the nature of poetic language as contingent, Coleridge, in a remark in his *Biographia Literaria* that has caught the attention of modern critics, stressed the necessity of poetry. He did so when he set out as part of his philosophical definition of poetry the principle that 'nothing can permanently please, which does not contain in itself the reason why it is so, and not otherwise'.[86]

In defence of Locke, however, it may be said that Wordsworth wrote more than one version of *The Prelude* and Keats two *Hyperions*. But it does not follow, as from a Lockean view of language it must, that Wordsworth and Keats were both searching for the appropriate linguistic means to express or to match the meanings that were already known to themselves in the privacy of their own minds. It would follow from this view of the nature of poetic meaning that the task of the critic would be to say how nearly poems matched the ideas of their authors. Since this question, of its very nature, could never be answered, such a task would be impossible; and the Lockean theory of language which implies it must therefore be mistaken.

Berkeley and Burke both broke away from the Lockean view of language, Berkeley in theories which can accommodate uses of language in poetry, and Burke specifically in a contribution to the theory of poetic language. In *A Treatise Concerning the Principles of Human Knowledge* (1710), Berkeley, contradicting Locke, said that communicating ideas 'marked by words is not the chief and only end of language, as is commonly supposed'. Language has other ends too, such as the 'raising of some passion, the exciting to, or deterring from an action [and] the putting the mind in some particular disposition'.[87] More elaborately, in *Enquiry into the Sublime and Beautiful* Edmund Burke argued that the power of poetry does not 'depend for its effect on the power of raising sensible images',[88] or ideas in the mind; its 'business is to affect rather by sympathy than imitation'.[89] To understand this we have to abandon Locke's belief that primarily words signify ideas.

Burke considered how words influence the passions and why their influence in this respect is not 'but light'.[90] He gave examples of poetry which affect the mind without raising clear ideas. By reminding us that some of the most powerful poetry does not, in the Lockean sense, signify clear ideas, Burke also avoided the implausibility of having to suppose that poetry is typically an assemblage of ideas of fictitious entities such as dragons or centaurs.

Not surprisingly, Burke was interested in the sublime in poetry, and his account of the language of poetry anticipated Kant's insight that the poet can make us feel what will not lend itself to representation by the intellect. Burke distinguished between a clear expression and a strong one. This is crucial to a proper understanding of poetic language.[91]

Words can move the passions appropriate to real objects without having clearly to represent those objects. Clear expressions belong to the understanding, strong ones to the passions: 'The one describes a thing as it is; the other describes it as it is felt'.[92] Languages such as French which we praise for their clarity and perspicuity are lacking in strength, while the languages of 'unpolished people', by contrast, have great force and energy of expression.[93] 'Uncultivated people are but ordinary observers of things, and not critical in distinguishing them; but, for that reason, they admire more, and are more affected with what they see, and therefore express themselves in a warmer and more passionate manner.'[94]

Burke's account of the language of poetry inevitably brings to mind Wordsworth's pronouncements about the language of poetry made in his 1850 Preface to the *Lyrical Ballads* (albeit not in the earlier prefaces, and so nearly a hundred years after Burke's *Enquiry*): 'a selection of the real language of men in a state of vivid sensation';[95] 'a selection of language really used by men';[96] 'Humble and rustic life was generally chosen, because, in that condition, the essential passions of the heart find a better soil in which they can attain their maturity, are less under restraint, and speak a plainer and more emphatic language.'[97]

Burke's distinction between clear expressions and strong ones is a significant contribution to the philosophy of language, but more broadly speaking, it represents a collapse of the hitherto cultural commonplace that poetry, being a kind of picture, is the sister art to painting. Henceforth hierarchies of dominance would replace equality between siblings. Romanticism would acknowledge a supreme art, for some poetry, for others music, to which all the others must aspire.

One notion, or cluster of ideas, remains to be noticed. There is no mention of it in Locke, but it began to take shape in the century after him and in a recognizably modern form first came to prominence with the Romantics – namely, the idea of the work of art itself.

Works of art   With Romanticism, our characteristically modern idea of art began to take shape. The notion of the work of art as artifact or essentially product of craftsmanship brought into being through the exercise of particular skills was not systematically assailed before Kant and Hegel. Indeed it still survives in many uses of the term 'art': when we speak for instance of the art of doing or making something. Kant's *Critique of Judgement* (1790) was, however, a signal contribution to the process of separating out the ideas of art and craft and to identifying art with genius.

Lord Shaftesbury (1671–1713), sometime pupil of John Locke, is remembered for an aesthetic philosophy which is still of living interest. In his treatise, *The Moralists, A Philosophical Rhapsody* (1711), he distinguished between something which we should now call organic and something which comes about by accident. A tree, for example, is to be distinguished from the accidental patterns made by clouds, for the tree (and, inconsistently, for that matter the entire universe) 'all hangs together as of a piece'.[98] The tree displays 'a sympathising of parts', 'a plain concurrence in one common end, and to the support, nourishment, and propagation of so fair a form . . . a peculiar nature' belongs.[99] Similarly, the Romantics regarded a poem as if it were a totality, its elements necessarily and inter-supportively belonging together. A work of art is not a mere aggregation or collection of elements or parts contingently put together.

Coleridge criticized the empiricist theory of imagination (identifying its version of imagination more properly as fancy) precisely because fancy does seem to involve such contingency. By contrast, the poetic imagination creates works of art which are, as it were, alive. Like the tree in Shaftesbury's example, they are informed by a principle of life.

Thus it is not surprising that in Shaftesbury's *Moralists* there should occur some animated dialogue which brings the supposition that the world is 'mere body, a mass of modified matter' into speculative opposition to the unLockean possibility that nature as a whole is a self or being.[100]

In thinking about what a work of art is, we cannot avoid the issue of how art relates to reality. The nature of the relationship has been argued about since antiquity. Romanticism gave a new urgency to the problem. It insisted upon an intimate connexion between poetry and imagination; at the same time it seemed to distinguish the sense of 'imagination' thus involved from the common meaning of imagination as the unreal. For the Romantics imagination seemed to mean something more substantial, more serious, and certainly something which should be distinguished from the common implications of 'imagination' as what is untrue, fictitious or made up.

Coleridge's phrase the 'willing suspension of disbelief' has become proverbial, though the passage in which the phrase occurs is less commonly remarked upon in its entirety. Coleridge was speaking about the *Lyrical Ballads*. At first he seemed to fall in with the common assumption that the imagination *does* mean what is, if not unreal, then at least insubstantial. He began: 'my endeavours should be . . . so as to transfer from our inward nature a human interest and a *semblance* of truth *sufficient* to procure for these *shadows* of imagination . . .'. But, attempting to weaken the ordinarily supposed connexion between imagination and unreality, Coleridge continued his sentence: 'that willing suspension of disbelief *for the moment, which constitutes poetic faith*' (my italics).[101]

Coleridge's characterization here, though nowadays criticized by philosophers, is preferable to Hume's. Hume's unromantic bluntness startles: 'Poets themselves, *tho' liars by profession*, always endeavour to give an air of truth to their fictions.'[102] The inapplicability of the notions of lying and of fiction, which themselves should be distinguished, to the poetry of Wordsworth, Blake or Keats is another reason for not allying Hume with the Romantics. The passage quoted from *Biographia Literaria* suggests that Coleridge took seriously Hume's account of poetry as a semblance (an air) of truth. The famous phrase about suspension of disbelief is to be seen in its context: that is, as an attempt to deepen commonplace opinions about the nature of poetry.

In this matter Henry Home, Lord Kames is more satisfactory than his cousin David Hume. In *Elements of Criticism*, Kames developed a theory of the image as 'ideal presence'; the phrase is his.

> When I recall any thing to my mind in a manner so distinct as to form an idea or image of it as present, I have not words to describe this act, other than that I perceive the thing as a spectator, and as existing in my presence; which means not that I am really a spectator, but only that I conceive myself to be a spectator, and have a perception of the object similar to what a real spectator hath.[103]

This represents a significant attempt to account for art without reducing it either to imitation or to make-believe. Kames gave a dialectical account of ideal presence. 'In contradistinction to real presence, ideal presence may be termed *a waking dream*',[104] but ideal presence has also to be distinguished from reflective remembrance. Thinking of an event as past without forming an image is barely reflecting or remembering that I was an eye-witness; 'but when I recall the event so distinctly as to form a complete image of it, I perceive it as passing in my presence; and this perception is an act of intuition, into which reflection enters not, more than into an act of sight'.[105]

Ideal presence is important because it undermines the contrast between the real and the unreal. For if, as Kames said, ideal presence is the means by which our passions are moved, then it makes no difference whether the subject is a fable or a true history. Thus the meeting in the *Iliad* of Hector and Andromache or 'some of the passionate scenes in King Lear . . . give an impression of reality not less distinct than that given by [the historian] Tacitus describing the death of Otho'. In such cases 'we never once reflect whether the story be true or feigned'.[106]

Some fifteen years or so later James Beattie was to remark in his *Dissertations Moral and Critical*:

> In the language of modern philosophy, the word *Imagination* seems to denote; first, the power of apprehending or conceiving ideas, simply as they are in themselves, without any view to their reality: and secondly, the power of combining into new forms, or assemblages, those thoughts, ideas, or notions, which we have derived from experience, or from information.[107]

The first of the powers Beattie named is of interest to us here since it suggests a more adequate account of the poetic imagination than the second. The second will be recognized as the Lockean, or empiricist, theory of imagination.

Late in his *Discourses on Art* Sir Joshua Reynolds began to qualify what he himself has so lucidly elaborated: the doctrine that art is imitation or mimesis. Painting is not only to be considered as an imitation, operating by deception, but 'it is, and ought to be, in many points of view, and strictly speaking, no imitation at all of external nature'.[108]

Reynolds stressed the typical as the proper subject matter for art. By contrast, Romanticism is well known for its attaching value and significance to the individual and the particular. Just a hint of the distinction, which was to become so important, is to be found in Alexander Gerard's *Essay on Taste*:

> Tell us that a man is generous, benevolent, or compassionate, or, on the contrary, that he is sordid, selfish, or hardhearted, this general account of his character is too indefinite to excite either love or hatred. Rehearse a series of actions in which these characters have been displayed, immediately the story draws out the affections correspondent.[109]

Poetry, then, is the presentation of the particular and not description in terms that necessarily are general.

Turning from the question of subject-matter to that of form, many philosophers remained committed to the traditional notion of art as craft, whereas Coleridge stressed the organic nature of a poem. He did so in language which echoes the principle of sufficient reason maintained by the philosopher Leibnitz. This implies that everything is necessary and nothing haphazard or contingent. Dugald Stewart also invoked the principle of sufficient reason in his essay 'On the Beautiful'. He noted that we love regular forms 'where regularity and uniformity do not interfere with purposes of utility' [110] and added:

> there is one principle which seems to have no inconsiderable influence; and which I shall take this opportunity of hinting at slightly, as I do not recollect to have seen it anywhere applied to questions of criticism. The principle I allude to is that of the *sufficient reason* . . . in the philosophy of Leibnitz.[111]

Stewart, however, used the principle differently from Coleridge; he employed it to explain why 'in anything which is merely ornamental' irregular forms that do not profess to be an imitation of nature are displeasing. His answer was, 'at least *in part*', that since irregularities are infinite, 'no circumstance can be imagined which should have decided the choice of the artist in favour of that particular figure which he has selected'.[112]

More remarkable is the agreement, expressed in almost identical language in the attitudes of Stewart, Coleridge and, in our own time,

I. A. Richards (influenced by Coleridge), concerning the susceptibility of the imagination for growth and development. Stewart wrote:

> The mind awakening, as if from a trance, to a new existence, becomes habituated to the most interesting aspects of life and of nature; the intellectual eye is 'purged of its film'; and things the most familiar and unnoticed, disclose charms invisible before. The same objects and events which were lately beheld with indifference, occupy now all the powers and capacities of the soul.[113]

For Richards the effect of great art and, more specifically, poetry is to destroy the 'film of familiarity and selfish solicitude' which commonly hides nine-tenths of life from the ordinary person, making us feel 'strangely alive and aware of the actuality of existence'.[114]

The distinguishing of art from craft exhibits no steady or regular development. Very early in the eighteenth century we find glimpses of an aesthetics of organicism in Shaftesbury; but in the middle of the century we find in Hume a wholly traditional notion of art. This has been noted earlier specifically in connexion with Hume's account of poetry. Here our point is that the concept of art we find in Hume is to be found persisting late in the eighteenth century. We find it, for example, in the works of James Beattie and, for that matter, continuing into the nineteenth century in the philosophy of Richard Payne Knight. The third edition of Knight's *Principles of Taste* was not published until 1806; the fourth edition was published in 1808. By these dates much of the Romantic poetry to which we have had occasion to refer had already been written.

Hume, in his *Treatise of Human Nature*, used the term 'work of art' to mean useful object: 'This observation extends to tables, chairs, scritoires, chimneys, coaches, saddles, ploughs, and indeed to every work of art; it being an universal rule, that their beauty is chiefly deriv'd from their utility, and from their fitness for that purpose, to which they are destin'd.'[115] Later he said, 'Most of the works of art are esteem'd beautiful, in proportion to their fitness for the use of man.'[116]

Beattie was elaborating ideas of this kind and not rejecting them when he said in his *Dissertations*: 'The philosopher lays down a plan, and follows it; his business being only, to instruct. But . . . the poet, frequently, concedes his plan, and makes you expect something different from what he intends; because his aim is, to please, by working upon your passions, and fancy'.[117] The idea of art as a rationally-constructed object is antithetical to Romantic ideas of poetry.

Even into the nineteenth century, if only just, Richard Payne Knight could still speak in terms of 'the trains of ideas, which arise in the mind of the artist out of a just and adequate consideration of all such circumstances; and direct him in adapting his work to the purposes for which it is intended'.[118]

We must not look, therefore, for too orderly a development from the philosophy of Locke to imagination as it was understood and expressed in the poetry of the Romantics. Yet it is evident that the enormous changes in thought and sensibility between Locke and, say, Blake, were not achieved in sudden and inexplicable leaps for which the philosophy and the aesthetics of the eighteenth century leave us totally unprepared.

Notes

1 John Locke, *An Essay Concerning Human Understanding*, John Yolton (ed.), Everyman's Library, Dent, 1961, I, xxxii.
2 ibid., II, 248.
3 ibid., I, 6.
4 ibid., I, 131.
5 ibid., I, 77.
6 ibid., I, 15.
7 ibid., I, 89.
8 ibid., I, 92.
9 ibid., I, 129.
10 Geoffrey Keynes (ed.), *The Complete Writings of William Blake*, 2nd edn, Oxford University Press, 1966, 471.
11 Locke, *Essay*, I, 89.
12 ibid., II, 245.
13 ibid., I, 9.
14 ibid., I, 77.
15 ibid., I, 90.
16 A. D. Nuttall, *A Common Sky: Philosophy and the Literary Imagination*, Chatto & Windus, Sussex University Press, 1974.
17 William Blake, marginal note to *Discourse II* by Sir Joshua Reynolds, quoted from Keynes, *Complete Writings of Blake*, 456.

18 William Blake to Revd Dr Trusler, 23 August 1799, quoted from Keynes, *Complete Writings of Blake*, 793.
19 Locke, *Essay*, I, 106.
20 Alfred North Whitehead, *Science and the Modern World, Lowell Lectures, 1925*, Cambridge University Press, 1926, 80.
21 E. A. Burtt, *The Metaphysical Foundations of Modern Physical Science*, reprint of 2nd edn, revised 1932, Routledge & Kegan Paul, 1964, 78.
22 ibid., 79.
23 ibid.
24 Locke, *Essay*, I, 314.
25 ibid., I, 316.
26 David Hume, *A Treatise of Human Nature*, L. A. Selby-Bigge (ed.), Clarendon Press, 1888, book 1, part 1, section 3.
27 Locke, *Essay*, I, 126.
28 ibid., I, 240.
29 ibid., II, 119.
30 Lilian Furst, *Romanticism in Perspective: A Comparative Study of the Romantic Movements in England, France and Germany*, Macmillan, 1969, 31.
31 Keynes, *Complete Writings of Blake*, 97.
32 ibid., 153.
33 ibid., 149.
34 William Blake to George Cumberland, 26 August 1799, ibid., 795.
35 William Blake to Revd Dr Trusler, 23 August 1799, ibid., 793. My italics.
36 William Blake to John Flaxman, 21 September 1800, ibid., 802.
37 William Blake to Thomas Butts, postmark 23 September 1800, ibid., 803.
38 F. R. Banks, *Sussex*, The Penguin Guides, Penguin, 1957, 250.
39 See chapter 3, p. 143 ff. for a further discussion of this point.
40 Nuttall, *Common Sky*, 113.
41 Samuel Taylor Coleridge, *Biographia Literaria*, J. Shawcross (ed.), Clarendon Press, 1907, II, 11–12.
42 ibid.
43 Mary Warnock, *Imagination*, Faber & Faber, 1976, 111–12.
44 Joseph Addison, *Works*, 6 vols, Bohn's Standard Library, George Bell and Sons, 1902, III, 393; *Spectator*, no. 409.
45 Addison, *Works*, III, 394; *Spectator*, no. 411.
46 James Beattie, *Dissertations Moral and Critical*, London and Edinburgh, 1783, 72.
47 Dugald Stewart, *Elements of the Philosophy of the Human Mind*, 2nd edn, London, 1802, I, 286–7 (1st edn, 1792).
48 ibid., I, 288.
49 ibid., I, 289.

50 ibid., I, 287.
51 ibid., I, 340.
52 Addison, *Works*, III, 393–4; *Spectator*, no. 411.
53 Addison, *Works*, III, 394.
54 Sir Joshua Reynolds, Discourse II, delivered to students of the Royal Academy, 11 December 1769, in R. Wark (ed.), *Discourses on Art*, Yale University Press, 1975, 27.
55 Addison, *Works*, III, 394.
56 ibid.
57 ibid., III, 395.
58 ibid., III, 397; *Spectator*, no. 412.
59 Addison, *Works*, III, 398.
60 R. G. Collingwood, *The Principles of Art*, Clarendon Press, 1938.
61 Addison, *Works*, III, 403; *Spectator*, no. 413.
62 ibid., 402–3.
63 George Berkeley, 'Three Dialogues Between Hylas and Philonous', *A New Theory of Vision and Other Writings*, Everyman's Library, Dent, 1910, 243.
64 ibid., 244.
65 Lord Kames (Henry Home), *Elements of Criticism*, 4th edn, Edinburgh, 1769, I, 206 (1st edn, 1761).
66 ibid., I, 207.
67 Thomas Reid, Essay VIII, 'Of taste', *Essays on the Powers of the Human Mind*, 3 vols, Bell & Bradfute, 1803, II, 497–8.
68 ibid., II, 513–14.
69 ibid., II, 506.
70 Alexander Gerard, *An Essay on Taste*, 2nd edn, Edinburgh, 1764, 156.
71 ibid., 158.
72 Hume, *Treatise*, book 1, part 1, section 4, 10.
73 ibid., 11.
74 Gerard, *Essay on Taste*, 158.
75 Stephen Prickett, *Coleridge and Wordsworth: The Poetry of Growth*, Cambridge University Press, 1970.
76 W. Wordsworth, *Prose Works*, W. J. B. Owen and J. W. Smyser (eds), 3 vols, Oxford University Press, 1974, I, 139.
77 Gerard, *Essay on Taste*, 182.
78 Alexander Gerard, *An Essay on Genius*, London and Edinburgh, 1774, 319.
79 ibid., 318.
80 Stewart, *Elements of Philosophy*, I, 483.
81 Edmund Burke, *A Philosophical Enquiry into the Origin of our Ideas of the Sublime and Beautiful*, 2nd edn, London, 1759, 58–60 (1st edn, 1757).
82 ibid., 95–6.

83 ibid., 96 ff.

84 Immanuel Kant, *Critique of Pure Reason*, translation of 2nd edn, Everyman's Library, Dent, 1934, 29 (1st edn, 1781; 2nd edn, 1787).

85 Immanuel Kant, *Critique of Aesthetic Judgement* (1790), first part of *Critique of Judgement*, trans. James Creed Meredith, Clarendon Press, 1928, 176–7.

86 Coleridge, *Biographia Literaria*, II, 9.

87 George Berkeley, 'A Treatise Concerning the Principles of Human Knowledge' (1710), *A New Theory of Vision and Other Writings*, Everyman's Library, Dent, 1910, 107.

88 Burke, *Sublime and Beautiful*, 328.

89 ibid., 332.

90 ibid., 334.

91 ibid., 338.

92 ibid., 339.

93 ibid., 340.

94 ibid., 340–1.

95 Wordsworth, *Prose Works*, Owen and Smyser (eds), I, 119.

96 ibid., 123.

97 ibid., 125.

98 Anthony, Earl of Shaftesbury, *Characteristics of Men, Manners, Opinions, Times* (1711), John N. Robertson (ed.), Bobbs-Merrill, The Library of Liberal Arts, 1964, II, Treatise V ('The Moralists, A Philosophical Rhapsody'), 99.

99 ibid., 100.

100 ibid., 104–6.

101 Coleridge, *Biographia Literaria*, II, 6.

102 Hume, *Treatise*, book 1, part 3, section 10, 121.

103 Kames, *Elements of Criticism*, I, 90.

104 ibid.

105 ibid., I, 91.

106 ibid., I, 95.

107 Beattie, *Dissertations*, 74.

108 Reynolds, Discourse XIII, in Wark, *Discourses on Art*, 232.

109 Gerard, *Essay on Taste*, 191–2.

110 Dugald Stewart, *Philosophical Essays*, 3rd edn, Edinburgh, 1818, 281–2.

111 ibid., 282.

112 ibid.

113 ibid., 526.

114 I. A. Richards, *Principles of Literary Criticism*, 2nd edn, Routledge & Kegan Paul, 1926, 243 (1st edn, 1924).

115 Hume, *Treatise*, book 2, part 2, section 5, 364.

116 ibid., book 3, part 3, section 1, 577.

117 Beattie, *Dissertations*, 167.

118 Richard Payne Knight, *An Analytical Inquiry into the Principles of Taste*, 4th edn, London, 1808, 182.

Further reading

The works referred to in the chapter should of course themselves be studied by the reader who wishes to pursue further the philosophical, and particularly the aesthetic, context of Romanticism. In addition the following works may also be consulted:

Abrams, M. H., *The Mirror and the Lamp: Romantic Theory and the Critical Tradition*, New York, Oxford University Press, 1953.

Bate, Walter Jackson, *From Classic to Romantic: Premises of Taste in Eighteenth Century England*, Peter Smith.

Beardsley, Monroe C., *Aesthetics from Classical Greece to the Present: A Short History*, New York, Macmillan, 1966.

Hipple, Walter John, Jr, *The Beautiful, the Sublime, and the Picturesque in Eighteenth-Century British Aesthetic Theory*, Southern Illinois University Press, 1957.

Monk, Samuel H., *The Sublime: A Study of Critical Theories in 18th Century England*, rev. edn, University of Michigan Press, 1960.

Tatarkiewicz, Wladyslaw, *A History of Six Ideas: An Essay in Aesthetics*, The Hague, Martinus Nijhoff, 1980.

5 Romantic literature

STEPHEN PRICKETT

As we have seen, the subtle alterations in sensibility that we can associate with Romanticism in literature have direct counterparts in political and social thought, as well as in art, philosophy and theology. At the centre of this complex cultural shift we find emerging a new vocabulary – and in particular certain key words that express the new mood. As the Introduction showed, one such word was 'Romanticism' itself. In this, the concluding section, we shall be looking broadly at a number of other Romantic words, each with its own distinctive flavour, and trying to see a little of how they relate to the literature and criticism of the period.

The Gothick

Like 'Romantic', the word 'Gothic' first made its appearance during the seventeenth century as a term of abuse. Its root meaning, of course, was simply 'like or pertaining to the Goths and their language' – another word for 'Germanic' or 'Teutonic' – but right from the beginning it seems to have carried with it associations of the barbarous and uncouth. As we have seen in chapter 2, its commonest use was in architecture, and we find it being applied as a blanket term of dislike to almost all medieval works in the seventeenth and early eighteenth centuries. Yet in fact gothic architecture never quite died out in England.

In 1753 *The World*, a magazine dealing with taste and fashion, launched yet another attack on those who were misguided enough to cultivate such aesthetic crudities out of whimsy; but it concluded that the 'Gothic Revival' was now safely over.

> A few years ago everything was Gothic; our houses, our beds, our book-cases, and our couches were all copied from some parts or other of our old cathedrals . . . This, however odd it might seem, and however unworthy of the name of TASTE, was cultivated, was admired, and still has its professors in different parts of England. There is something, they say, in it congenial to our old Gothic constitution; I should rather think to our modern idea of liberty, which allows every one the privilege of playing the fool, and making himself ridiculous in whatever way he pleases.[1]

Horace Walpole, mentioned in chapter 2, is the man most often credited with having transformed the Gothic Revival with his extraordinary architectural fantasia at Strawberry Hill, near Twickenham, and with his no less extraordinary novel, *The Castle of Otranto*. Certainly it was he, more than any other single person, who turned the gothic from a modish, rather vulgar fashion, into an aesthetic sensibility. In his hands, the gothic became the *Gothick*. Walpole brought to a particular architectural style a matching emotional mood – partly fantasy, partly nostalgia, partly a craving for the unknown and irrational. 'I almost think', he wrote to a friend,

> there is no wisdom comparable to that of exchanging what is called the realities of life for dreams. Old castles, old pictures, old histories, and the babble of old people make one live back into centuries, that cannot disappoint one. One holds fast and surely to what is past. The dead have exhausted their power of deceiving – one can trust Catherine of Medicis now.[2]

Strawberry Hill was a lath-and-plaster exercise in domesticized nostalgia. With stone-patterned wallpaper, a 'Gothic ballustrade to the staircase, adorned with antelopes . . . bearing shields; lean windows fattened with rich saints in painted glass, and . . . niches full of old coats of mail', the 'castle' was an unashamed escape into an impossible antiquarianism, its elements collected from everywhere and anywhere and reused with no regard for context or scale.

The famous Long Gallery was only 56 feet long and 15 feet wide, but it was resplendent with gilt mirrors in gothic niches, and a ceiling of plaster fan-vaulting transposed and appropriately miniaturized from the Henry VII Chapel in Westminster Abbey (where Blake was later to study gothic designs). The fireplace in the Round Drawing Room in the Great Tower (each room had its proper name) was a copy of the tomb of Edward the Confessor. Even the ceiling decorations were based on the design of the rose window at Chartres.

In this 'little rural bijou' at Strawberry Hill, Walpole acted out a fantasy life with his amazing collection of art treasures and historical bric-a-brac; he was, in fact, a famous antique collector of his time. He would delight in wearing a pair of gloves which once had belonged to James I, and sleep with Charles I's death-warrant on one side of his bed, and Magna Carta on the other. It was in this bed in June 1764 that he dreamed that 'on the uppermost bannister of a great staircase' he 'saw a gigantic hand in armour'. The staircase was his own, but appropriately magnified. From this tableau in a dream grew the mysterious giant haunting the doomed Castle of Otranto. 'In the evening', he tells us, 'I sat down and began to write, without knowing in the least what I intended to say and relate.' As he himself pointed out, it was 'a very natural dream for a head filled like mine with Gothic story', and it is quite in keeping that Strawberry Hill was to provide the setting for the first gothic novel, since the place was itself such an essentially bookish creation.

The *Castle of Otranto* has a plot, but of such improbability and complexity that it scarcely matters. Its appeal lay in a series of memorable visual images (like the giant mailed fist upon the staircase) and a dreamlike atmosphere of mystery and passion. It was an instant success (much to Walpole's surprise), and these elements were to become the staples of a new literary genre. Its imitators used and reused the familiar elements of monsters, ghosts, murder, passion, intrigue and unspeakable villainy. William Beckford's *Vathek* (1786) concerns a Caliph of that name whose visage, when angry, was so terrible that he was obliged to control himself in order not to depopulate his dominions. M. G. Lewis's *The Monk* (1796) – which earned him the title of 'Monk-Lewis' – includes an incident when, owing to a case of mistaken identity, a character actually elopes with the ghost of a headless nun. It exhibited 'a mixture of the supernatural, the horrible, and the indecent', as one critic put it, and was, naturally, a best-seller, with a retinue of imitators of its own. Even more successful was Mrs Radcliffe, who never allowed her unspeakable horrors to offend the decencies of young ladies, or the managers of the circulating libraries that catered for their tastes. It was successes like these that made Wordsworth complain so bitterly of the public's 'degrading thirst after outrageous stimulation' driving the classics 'into neglect by frantic novels, sickly and stupid German Tragedies, and deluges of idle and extravagant stories in verse'.

Beckford was no less a connoisseur of taste than Walpole. He was a patron of the artist John Robert Cozens, and had a distinguished collection of paintings by Claude Lorraine. Moreover, like Walpole, Beckford was not content with writing gothic novels; he also built himself a gothic palace to live in on his estate at Fonthill in Wiltshire. Fonthill Abbey was the most fantastic building of its age, with vast vaulted state apartments and poky bedrooms, topped by an incredible octagonal tower 260 feet high – as unstable in reality as it was in appearance. It was a gigantic stage-set, designed to amaze, shock and awe. For its greatest (and virtually only) ceremonial occasion, when Beckford received Nelson as a national hero in December 1800, it was only partly finished, and had to be seen by night for fear of spoiling the effect. The great banqueting hall with its hammer-beam roof 80 feet high was totally impossible to heat, and the actual dinner had to be held elsewhere. Visually spectacular, architecturally unsound, and shoddily built of sub-standard materials, the tower collapsed in 1823, and within a few years most of the rest of the building had gone as well.

Walpole provides in many ways an interesting contrast with Beckford. As we have seen, Walpole had genuine scholarly interests, and from his somewhat dilettante antiquarianism was to grow a much more genuinely historical approach to the past. The early gothic novels, whether of Walpole, Lewis or Mrs Radcliffe, have no feeling of the periods in which they are supposed to be set, yet they do have a very strong sense of the past as being *different* from the present, and in that sense of difference begins the historical novel. With Scott, who also built himself a gothic house, Abbotsford, we find the first serious attempts at historical research as a background for literature. At first he was interested in understanding his society through its past in purely Scottish terms, as in, for instance, the

Waverley novels, but in such novels as *Ivanhoe* (1819) he turned his attention to themes such as the racial conflicts that have gone into the making of English society.

We have already mentioned the rise of Romantic historicism and its connexions with the gothic in chapter 2. There is, however, another way in which that sense of the differentness of the past finds expression in literature of the early nineteenth century. Jane Austen's *Northanger Abbey* was not published until 1818, but it seems to have been started as early as 1797 in direct response to Mrs Radcliffe's best-selling *Mysteries of Udolpho*. Unlike many contemporary gothic novels of the 1790s, *Udolpho* does not involve the supernatural in any way, though with a mysterious shrouded portrait, strange figures upon the battlements at dead of night, locked rooms and inexplicable noises, it has all the correct trappings of the supernatural horror story. In fact all these mysteries turn out to have naturalistic, if implausible, explanations, and much of the novel, with its lengthy landscape descriptions and complicated love-plot, falls more within the tradition of the sentimental novel than the horror story. Nevertheless, what interested Jane Austen in her parody is the *contrast* between such a world and that familiar to herself and her middle-class circle. When the full nature of Catherine Morland's lurid expectations burst upon Henry Tilney, he remonstrates with her thus:

> Dear Miss Morland, consider the dreadful nature of the suspicions you have entertained. What have you been judging from? Remember the country and the age in which we live. Remember that we are English: that we are Christians. Consult your own understanding, your own sense of the probable, your own observation of what is passing around you. Does our education prepare us for such atrocities? Do our laws connive at them? Could they be perpetrated without being known in a country like this, where social and literary intercourse is on such a footing; where every man is surrounded by a neighbourhood of voluntary spies; and where roads and newspapers lay everything open? Dearest Miss Morland, what ideas have you been admitting?   (chapter 24)

As D. W. Harding has shown, Henry Tilney's praise for the

respectability of his own society is more ambiguous than a first reading might suggest.[3] There is, perhaps, a different kind of horror in being 'surrounded by a neighbourhood of voluntary spies'. Behind Jane Austen's satire of Mrs Radcliffe's world where 'poison' and 'sleeping potions' were 'to be procured, like rhubarb, from every druggist', and where, 'among the Alps and Pyrenees . . . such as were not spotless as an angel, might have the dispositions of a fiend', lies a sense of her society as being at the end of a long process of evolution. She is often classified as being an anti-Romantic satirist, but this is only superficially true. In her feeling for the differentness of the past and the present, and of the tensions and contradictions within her society, she shared a common consciousness with her great Romantic contemporaries.

Beckford, in contrast, exhibits in his writing and his building a very different strand in the gothic from that of a dawning historicism. He always gives the impression of a man acting under compulsions he does not fully understand. For him the gothic's attractions are very clearly those of mystery, dreams and irrationality. The very luridness and impossibility of this new fictional form clearly held its own appeal for Beckford, and for a host of others, including some of the greatest artists of the age. In their own ways, Coleridge's *Ancient Mariner* and Keats's *Eve of St Agnes*, for instance, draw upon the world of the gothic as clearly as Mrs Radcliffe and Monk-Lewis. The reasons are not far to seek. Both are in search of alternative autonomous worlds remote from the immediate world to which Henry Tilney could appeal with such confidence. The 'Gothick Convention' (for such it was, in effect, by the beginning of the nineteenth century), for all its evident absurdities, offered the Romantics a symbolism and a language for talking about areas of human experience for which no alternative conceptual framework was available. The prevailing empiricist psychology of Locke and Hartley allowed no room for theories of the unconscious, for irrational deeds of guilt and expiation, or for the mysteries of pain and suffering with which the poets and writers found themselves confronted. The Ancient Mariner's experience is clearly at one level a story of breakdown and recovery (which does not, of course, preclude other symbolic levels), and it is not difficult to see in the spirit nine fathom deep beneath the keel of the ship an image of deep irrational and unconscious forces that were not to find clinical expression until the work of Freud almost a hundred years later.

Similarly, Mary Shelley's *Frankenstein* is in one sense the horror story it ostensibly claims to be: illustrating the dangers of man meddling with science or seeking to play God – a theme at least as old as Marlowe's *Faustus*. In another, and far more interesting sense, of course, it is the state of mind of the monster which is the focus of the story. He suffers from maternal deprivation – illustrating one of the great Romantic emphases on childhood that runs in growing streams through the thinking of such diverse figures as Rousseau, Wordsworth, Freud, Spock and Bowlby, or the artists Philip Otto Rünge and Kate Greenaway. The monster is not innately depraved: he desires love, but because he never receives it, even from his creator, Frankenstein, he is unable to give it either. He is the product of a bad environment in a true Godwinian sense, made and morally destroyed by harsh and unjust circumstances beyond his control. In short, he is the first *psychologized* monster. Mary Shelley's novel epitomizes the Romantic process of *internalization*: being a monster is a quality of mind.

The later gothic novels show an increasing psychological complexity. The black-and-white world of Mrs Radcliffe gave way by the 1820s to a world of the most subtle dialectic between unconscious impulses and conscious rationalizations. *The Private Confessions of a Justified Sinner* by James Hogg, published in 1824, concerns the psychological effects of Calvinist antinomianism. One of two identical twins is persuaded that as a member of God's 'elect' he can do no wrong. He is tempted by a mysterious and clearly diabolic stranger, Gil Martin, who oddly resembles him, and leads him eventually to the unforgivable sin – suicide. Gil Martin is clearly in some sense a doppelganger or 'double', and it is never clear in the story whether he is, in fact, an external figure at all, or merely a projection of the protagonist's own tortured consciousness.

Rarely can a literary fashion so unaesthetic, so implausible and at times so downright silly have had such an effect in helping to transform the sensibility of an age. That a novel as bad as *The Castle of Otranto* could have helped to create both a sense of historical perspective and pointed towards a symbolism for depth psychology is one of the most extraordinary ironies of literary history.

Nature and imagination

> And as imagination bodies forth
> The forms of things unknown, the poet's pen
> Turns them to shapes and gives to airy nothing
> A local habitation and a name.

It is a commonplace that Shakespeare is an anachronism – but nowhere is that extraordinary timeless quality of his thought and language better illustrated than in these lines from *A Midsummer Night's Dream* (v.i). His use of 'imagination' in this sense was not to be recaptured until the time of the Romantics, and in the intervening centuries the idea of the imagination as a creative and interpretative power was largely lost. By the beginning of the eighteenth century it was another low-status word like 'romantic' and 'gothic', with connotations either of madness or deception. As we have seen in chapter 4, however, 'imagination' became an increasingly important word in philosophy as the century went on. A closely parallel development was also taking place in literature, so that by the early nineteenth century 'imagination' had regained much of its Shakespearean force, but within a quite new intellectual context, becoming a key word in the critical vocabulary of the age.

Nevertheless it would be a mistake to assume the word had a single meaning for poets any more than it had for the philosophers of the period. Broadly speaking, uses of the word fall into two distinct groups. On the one hand, there were those like Wordsworth and Coleridge who employed 'imagination' principally in connexion with sense-perception; on the other were those who, like Blake and Keats, seemed to use the word to describe various forms of transcendent, visionary and supersensual experiences. Though these two ways of using it look in theory as if they are fundamentally incompatible, we shall see that both positions have blurred edges and even, at times, seem to meet and overlap.

The word 'nature' presents problems that are different in kind in connexion with Romanticism from any of the other words we are looking at. Clearly it too is a key word, yet it is a word of such blanket meaning that all attempts at definition seem to founder at the onset. It can, for instance, mean any one of the following:

1 The 'cosmos': the sum total of everything is clearly 'nature' in its broadest sense, but in fact the word is more normally used as *a contrast* with something else. For example:

2 The 'world of sense-perception' (as distinct from the 'super-natural');

3 The 'country' (as distinct from the town);

4 'What grows organically' (as distinct from an artifact that is made by man);

5 'What happens spontaneously' (as distinct from what is 'un-natural', either because it is laboured as contrived, or, as in 'unnatural vices', because it is held to be denying, perverting or thwarting a quality or instinct believed to be innate).

As we shall see, the last three notions – the 'rural', the 'organic' and the 'spontaneous' – are central to some aspects of Romanticism, and play a key part in the poetry of Wordsworth, for example. All three conceptions are what we might call inarticulate value words: that is, we have come to think of them somewhat vaguely as Good Things without, perhaps, having any very clear reason why. Indeed, poets as diverse as Pope, Wordsworth, Hopkins, Hardy and Lawrence all claimed they were in accordance with 'nature'.

Yet 'nature' can also be thought of in a much more active and manipulative role, as in:

6 'The life-force': This is a very ancient meaning indeed, going back to classical times and the Greek mystery cults. Two Latin tags bring out an ambiguity that has always haunted the word (see p. 156).

   (a) *Natura naturans:* literally 'nature naturing'. Nature is here experienced as an active, dynamic power in a constant process of change and renewal. It is in complete contrast with

   (b) *Natura naturata:* literally 'nature natured'. Here nature is frozen, is laid out on a slab for dissection and scientific investigation. The observer does not participate. It is against this view that Wordsworth was reacting in his famous line from *The Tables Turned*: 'We murder to dissect.'

Very often this idea of 'nature' as a dynamic power is personified:

7 'The Goddess': sometimes this is no more than old Mother Nature; sometimes she is further personified as in Kingsley's

Mother Carey in *The Water Babies* (1863); sometimes she is felt to be dignified, awe-inspiring, and remote; sometimes she is downright evil, as in certain classical nature-cults of Pan involving human sacrifice, the worship of Baal in Palestine, or, in Tennyson's modern evolutionary version, 'Nature red in tooth and claw'.

It is here, when we approach human responses to nature, that the latent ambiguity of the word becomes most apparent. It can be seen as morally neutral, as in:

8 'The thing in itself': from the clear-cut position where it is the 'nature' of wind to blow, rain to fall, or snow to be cold, this rapidly shades off through things like 'it is the nature of cats to play with mice' into implied moral judgement, especially in the case of

9 Human 'nature': here we find now fully developed a moral polarity between:

   (a) Man as fundamentally good. This is the view for instance of Rousseau, the early Wordsworth and Shelley.

   (b) Man as fundamentally bad. This section can again be divided between the religious pessimists, such as St Paul, Calvin, Dr Johnson, Coleridge and T. S. Eliot, and the atheistical pessimists, including Hobbes, perhaps Peacock, and Thomas Hardy.

We could go on. A. O. Lovejoy claims to have distinguished more than sixty separate meanings of the word 'nature',[4] but the complexity of the word and its connotations are apparent. Though we have somewhat arbitrarily divided Romantics into optimists and pessimists over human nature, it is clear, of course, that such a classification is far too simple. Both Wordsworth and Coleridge, for instance, were optimists in their youth, believing in human perfectibility and in the ideals of the French Revolution, but they later came, through experience, to believe in original sin and adopt a much more 'conservative' position. Wordsworth, however, turned towards nature (i.e. in the sense of meanings 2, 3 and 4) as he lost faith in human nature (9a) in the aftermath of the French Revolution. In Book X of *The Prelude* (1805) he speaks of how he was restored and made a poet through the influence of his sister, Dorothy, his friendship with Coleridge,

> And, lastly, Nature's self by human love
> Assisted, through the weary labyrinth
> Conducted me again to open day,
> Revived the feelings of my early life.   (lines 922–5)

Here, as so often for Wordsworth, nature is a semi-personified force, extended to man and possessed of healing powers (i.e. meaning 7).

Elsewhere, however, Wordsworth seems to think of nature not so much as an external power to man, but as proof of his involvement with his environment. In one of the now famous passages in *Tintern Abbey* he concludes:

> Therefore am I still
> A lover of the meadows and the woods,
> And mountains; and of all that we behold
> From this green earth; of all the mighty world
> Of eye and ear, both what we half-create,
> And what perceive; well pleased to recognise
> In nature and the language of the sense,
> The anchor of my purest thoughts, the nurse,
> The guide, the guardian of my heart, and soul
> Of all my moral being.

This clearly starts with meaning 2. But if we want to see what he means by 'half-create' we need look no further than a little poem he wrote in March 1802:

> My heart leaps up when I behold
> A rainbow in the sky;
> So was it when my life began;
> So is it now I am a man:
> So be it when I shall grow old
> Or let me die!
> The child is father of the man;
> And I could wish my days to be
> Bound each to each by natural piety.

In choosing the example of the rainbow as his touchstone of beauty, Wordsworth took his place in a controversy that had been raging ever since Newton had first explained what caused the optical phenomenon itself. In Lockean terms a rainbow is peculiar in that it consists *entirely* of secondary qualities: there is no quantifiable object there, merely the refraction of sunlight by water drops. For some, such as Addison and Thompson, it was a reminder of the 'pleasing delusion' under which we live our lives; for others, including Keats, it was rather a reminder of how science had destroyed beauty by explaining it away.[5] Wordsworth bypassed both parties. He was interested in the rainbow precisely because it *does* consist only of secondary qualities. The rainbow can exist only if there are certain conditions present in the atmosphere, *and* if there is an observer present. Without Wordsworth, the observing eye, there would be *no* rainbow. It is for him a perpetual reminder that nature, in all our senses, is something in which we participate, in the most literal manner. As Hopkins was to put it fourteen years after Wordsworth's death:

It was a hard thing to undo this knot.
The rainbow shines, but only in the thought
Of him that looks. Yet not in that alone,
For who makes rainbows by invention?
And many standing round a waterfall
See one bow each, yet not the same to all
But each a hand's breadth further than the next.
The sun on falling waters writes the text
Which yet is in the eye or in the thought.
It was a hard thing to undo this knot.

But in the passage we quoted from *Tintern Abbey* there was another very different attitude to nature coupled with this sense of participation. If nature is Wordsworth's own half-creation, how can it also be the 'soul' of all his 'moral being'? This was something that puzzled Blake as well. In Wordsworth's *Poems* of 1815 there is a poem with the long-winded but significant title: *The Influence of Natural Objects in Calling forth and Strengthening the Imagination in Boyhood and Early Youth*. Blake first read it in 1826 and scribbled furiously in the margin of his edition, 'Natural Objects always did and now do weaken, deaden and obliterate imagination in Me. Wordsworth must know that what he writes Valuable is Not to be found in Nature.'[6]

This was a point on which Blake was very clear. One of his earliest

pieces, written in 1788, ten years before the *Lyrical Ballads*, is
entitled *There is No Natural Religion*. Nature, he points out, being
perceived by the senses, is subject to the limits of sense-perception.
It cannot, by Locke's definition, point beyond itself to anything
greater: 'From a perception of only 3 senses or 3 elements none
could deduce a fourth or fifth.' To put it simply, our senses of
touch, taste or hearing would tell us nothing about sight if we were
born blind. There is nothing cumulative about the senses. How
much less then, can nature, the creature of sense (meaning 2), point
towards the 'infinite' which lies at the heart of religious experience?
On the contrary, it is what Blake (apparently following Lowth) calls
the 'Poetic' or 'Prophetic' which mediates revelation to man,
showing him that his perceptions are *not* finally bounded by the
limitations of sense, but as his desire is infinite (and ultimately *for*
the infinite), so the possession of that desire and he himself, the
possessor, are 'infinite'. Religion, by its very nature (meaning 7) is
opposed to nature (meaning 2).

Blake thus came to see the 'imagination' not as Wordsworth did,
as the power that links man to nature (meaning 2), but as analogous
to an extra sense reaching *beyond* sense-perception:

> Vision or Imagination is a Representation of what Eternally
> Exists, Really & Unchangeably. Fable or Allegory is Form'd
> by the daughters of Memory. Imagination is surrounded by
> the daughters of Inspiration. . . . The Hebrew Bible & the
> Gospel of Jesus are not Allegory, but Eternal Vision or
> Imagination of All that Exists.[7]

Though there are clearly Platonic elements in this, it is not classic
Platonism or even Neoplatonism. Blake is not interested here in particular philosophic systems (although as we have seen in chapter 4 he
did have a good grasp of current philosophical problems) but in
trying to describe a power that embraces nature by *transcending* it.
Values are not things that we find in nature, they are what we
approach nature with.

This meaning of the word 'imagination' is in some ways extraordinarily close to Kant's 'Reason' (see pp. 186–9). Not, it is true, as
Kant himself intended the word, but as subsequent German
Idealists and Coleridge came to use it. In spite of Kant's warnings
that Reason was regulative only, they seem to have interpreted him

to mean that it was possible to perceive God by direct mystical intuition. This power of Reason they described as being fundamentally 'poetic' in character. As Carlyle put it with characteristic enthusiasm;

> Not by logic or argument does it work; yet surely and clearly may it be taught to work; and its domain lies in that higher region whither logic and argument cannot reach; in that holier region where Poetry and Virtue and Divinity abide, in whose presence Understanding wavers and recoils, dazzled into utter darkness by that 'sea of light', at once the fountain and the termination of true knowledge.[8]

Yet there is a fundamental difference between this and Blake. For Carlyle and Coleridge, the world of Reason is fundamentally separate from the material and sensual world of the understanding. For Blake, the imagination, though it transcends nature, encompasses it. Another of Blake's marginalia to Wordsworth's 1815 *Poems* reads 'One Power alone makes a Poet: Imagination, The Divine Vision.' On this point Blake is, interestingly, more Kantian than the Kantians – though we have no evidence that he knew Kant at all.

Imagination is not a part of nature (meaning 2); it is, rather, the precondition with which we approach it. 'As a man is, so he sees.' Or, more explicitly: 'A fool sees not the same tree that a wise man sees.' Thus, for Blake, Wordsworth's claim to find *in* nature (presumably still meaning 2) values that belong to a different order of things is both puzzling and disturbing. Coleridge, similarly, showed an increasing distrust of nature (presumably 2 and 3) as a *source* of joy and inspiration, although he never ceased to take a delight in it. Some modern critics, David Ferry and Geoffrey Hartman for instance, claim to have detected a similar disillusion and even terror of nature in Wordsworth (meanings 2, 3, 4 and even 5).[9] Yet, as we have seen, tension and paradox are of the essence of Romantic poetry.

Wordsworth is essentially a dialectical poet, reconciling in his poetry what Coleridge called 'opposite and discordant qualities'. Thus, though I have so far been indicating which meanings of 'nature' seem most appropriate in each case, the reader will no doubt have noticed that part of Wordsworth's peculiar effectiveness lies in his ability to play off one shade of meaning against the next. His relationship with nature is not merely one of part-creation, but one that grows *through* creation. In Book II of *The Prelude* (1805 version) he described this process of growth as one of active interchange between the self and external world:

> Emphatically such a Being lives,
> An inmate of this *active* universe:
> From nature largely he receives: nor so
> Is satisfied, but largely gives again,
> For feeling has to him imparted strength,
> And powerful in all sentiments of grief,
> Of exultation, fear, and joy, his mind,
> Even as an agent of the one great Mind,
> Creates, creator and receiver both,
> Working but in alliance with the works
> Which it beholds. – Such, verily, is the first
> Poetic spirit of our human life . . .   (lines 265–76)

This growth of the mind, we notice, is described as 'poetic', which, for Wordsworth is a way of saying that it involves the whole person, intellect and feelings alike. Man's participation in nature is, of course, at a perceptual level entirely unconscious, but at a conceptual level – at the stage at which we begin to think about 'nature' – it involves both intellect and feeling. It is at this level that the discovery of values comes in. It is neither a process of simple 'projection', nor one of passive receptivity, but one of progressive and ever more complex confirmation and discovery.

Though, for some, this was no more than the 'naturalism' Blake feared he had detected in Wordsworth, for others, no less concerned with a transcendent vision than Blake, this was the source of one of Wordsworth's greatest strengths. For instance, George MacDonald (1824–1905), the poet, novelist, literary critic and mystic argued that:

> The very element in which the mind of Wordsworth lived and moved, was Christian pantheism. . . . This world is not merely a thing which God hath made, subjecting it to laws; but is an expression of the thoughts, the feeling, the heart of God himself. . . .[10]

You will find that he sometimes *draws* a lesson from nature, seeming almost to force a meaning from her. I do not object to this, if he does not make too much of it as *existing* in nature. It is rather finding a meaning in nature that he brought to it. The meaning exists, if not there.[11]

We have a good example of this 'discovery' of meaning in nature in a later book of *The Prelude*. At the beginning of Book XIII (1805) Wordsworth describes how he, with some friends, set out to climb Snowdon by moonlight. At first the mountain was covered in thick fog, but at last near the summit they suddenly burst through the 'sea of mist' into brilliant moonlight:

A hundred hills their dusky backs upheaved
All over this still ocean; and beyond,
Far, far beyond, the vapours shot themselves,
In headlands, tongues, and promontory shapes,
Into the sea, the real sea, that seemed
To dwindle, and give up its majesty,
Usurped upon as far as sight could reach.
Meanwhile, the Moon looked down upon this show
In single glory, and we stood, the mist
Touching our very feet; and from the shore
At distance not the third part of a mile
Was a blue chasm; a fracture in the vapour,
A deep and gloomy breathing-place through which
Mounted the roar of waters, torrents, streams
Innumerable, roaring with one voice!
The universal spectacle throughout
Was shaped for admiration and delight,
Grand in itself alone, but in that breach
Through which the homeless voice of waters rose,
That deep dark thoroughfare, had Nature lodged
The soul, the Imagination of the whole.   (lines 45–65)

The description of the mountain in moonlight, and the dark rift in the clouds is strikingly vivid, but, more than that, Wordsworth's final comment, linking 'Nature' and 'Imagination', suggests that the whole scene holds a special significance. It formed for him, he tells us in the next few lines, 'The perfect image of a mighty mind.'

This image of a mountain, all but its moonlit summit shrouded in mist, provides the model he has been in search of throughout *The Prelude* – the model by which he can describe the human mind. It corresponds in remarkable detail to the later (no less speculative) models offered by such clinical psychiatrists as Freud and Jung. The tiny illuminated area of consciousness is surrounded by the 'huge sea of mist' concealing what Wordsworth called 'an underpresence' (the words 'unconscious' or 'subconscious' belong to later psychiatry). The model is a familiar one: what is astonishing is to discover the detail with which Wordsworth has worked it out, and his feeling that nature had in some way put it there:

> above all
> One function of such mind had Nature there
> Exhibited by putting forth, and that
> With circumstance most awful and sublime,
> That domination which she oftentimes
> Exerts upon the outward face of things,
> So moulds them, and endues, abstracts, combines,
> Or by abrupt and unhabitual influence
> Doth make one object so impress itself
> Upon all others, and pervade them so
> That even the grossest minds must see and hear
> And cannot choose but feel.   (lines 73–84)

Here Wordsworth is describing existentially a certain type of experience of discovery. Kekule's discovery of the 'Benzine ring' is another example which comes to mind. Wordsworth did not (I think) believe that nature had actually staged a miracle for him: he saw the occurrence as perfectly normal. He was, however, able to see in it the answer to his problem of how to describe the intuitively observed fact that so many of our most influential mental processes are hidden from us. In one sense, I suppose, it was 'projection' on Wordsworth's part, but that was not how he felt it. He experienced it as an overwhelming discovery *outside* himself. Moreover he gives us a clue as to how this might be in his description of the gap in the clouds as the 'Imagination' of the whole. It represents, in his psychological model, the meeting point of the conscious and unconscious areas of the mind – and, by a brilliant piece of reflexive metaphor, it is by just such an 'imaginative' gap that his conscious mind is able to 'discover' in nature what his unconscious in some sense already 'knows'. In Coleridge's perceptive phase, Wordsworth receives 'The light reflected, as a light bestowed.'

This definition of imagination is, of course, very similar to Coleridge's own. His famous description of the imagination in chapter XIII of the *Biographia Literaria* is in many ways parallel to Wordsworth's:

> THE IMAGINATION then, I consider either as primary or secondary. The primary IMAGINATION I hold to be the living Power and prime Agent of all human perception, and as a repetition in the finite mind of the eternal act of creation in the infinite I AM. The Secondary Imagination I consider as an echo of the former, coexisting with the conscious will, yet still as identical with the primary in the *kind* of its agency, and differing only in *degree*, and in the mode of its operation. It dissolves, diffuses, dissipates, in order to recreate; or where this process is rendered impossible, yet still at all events it struggles to idealize and to unify. It is essentially vital, even as all objects (as objects) are essentially fixed and dead.[12]

More ink has perhaps been spilled over this passage than any other piece of Romantic theory. Much of it need not detain us here. The actual formulation is taken from Schelling, but Coleridge has made one or two important changes. The first is that it is fundamentally egalitarian. The 'Secondary Imagination', the creative power of the poet or artist (what Wordsworth in the Snowdon passage called 'That Glorious faculty / Which higher minds bear with them as their own') is of the same *kind* as the Primary: the unconscious process of what has been called 'making and matching', by which *all* perception takes place. In other words, the peculiar power of the artist is not something unique, but is an exaggerated or heightened form of something we *all* possess to some degree.

Second, Coleridge contrasts imagination with fancy. Fancy, for him, is no more than a scissors-and-paste job of the mind. 'The Fancy is indeed no other than a mode of Memory emancipated from the order of Time and Space.' It is, in short, Locke's 'imagination'. Coleridge is attempting to distinguish between mere passive reproduction, and the active power of the 'shaping spirit of imagination' which is a divine gift, reflecting the creative powers of God. Nevertheless, in spite of this association between poetic creativity and the divine, Coleridge's 'Imagination' remains very much a thing of this world, concerned with nature (in meaning 2) and sense-perception.

Perhaps the most thorough-going claim for the creative powers of the imagination, however, came from Keats. On 22 November 1817, in a letter to his friend Benjamin Bailey (afterwards a friend of Wordsworth), he wrote:

> I am certain of nothing but of the holiness of the Heart's affections and the truth of the Imagination – What the imagination seizes as Beauty must be truth – whether it existed before or not – for I have the same idea of all our Passions as of Love they are all in their Sublime, creative of essential Beauty. The Imagination may be compared to Adam's dream – he awoke and found it truth.[13]

The reference to Adam's 'dream' is to *Paradise Lost*, Book VIII, lines 460–90, where Adam is cast into a trance by God while he takes one of Adam's ribs to create Eve. Adam dreams of Eve, and then awakes and finds her real. As with the Knight at Arms 'alone and palely loitering' in *La Belle Dame Sans Merci*, Adam's dream was more 'real' to him than his waking surroundings, and had he not found Eve on awakening, life would thenceforth have been barren and meaningless. Clearly, therefore, though Keats's 'Imagination' is in some sense Platonic, like Blake's, its function is to transform our vision of *this* world rather than point to another.

This suggestion is reinforced by Keats's remark only a couple of lines later in the same letter: 'O for a life of Sensations rather than Thoughts!' Though this is sometimes quoted as being anti-intellectual, in context it has a quite different flavour: 'I have never yet been able to perceive how any thing can be known for truth by consequitive [*sic*] reasoning – and yet it must be. Can it be that even the greatest Philosopher ever arrived at his goal without putting aside numerous objections. However it may be, O for a life of Sensations rather than Thoughts!'

What Keats is saying here is very close to Blake's conclusion to *There is No Natural Religion*: 'If it were not for the Poetic or Prophetic character the Philosophic and Experimental would soon be at the ratio of all things, and stand still, unable to do other than repeat the same dull round over again.'[14] Logical reasoning, in the Lockean sense, is completely enclosed. It is unable *either* to provide values *or* to provide certainty. Without imagination, or what Blake here calls 'the Poetic or Prophetic', it is sterile and useless. It cannot create, it cannot innovate, it cannot satisfy.

Though they reached their conclusions by very different paths, it is clear that for all the Romantics the role of the 'poet' is crucial to human existence. Both religion and philosophy are ultimately dependent on it. Without the poetic imagination nature itself is dead. It is, therefore, to the role of the poet that we must now turn.

What is a poet?

Romantic literature is profoundly self-conscious. The forces of change we have been looking at in the course of this book – social, aesthetic, religious and philosophic – operating so cataclysmically within every level of British society meant that the act of writing itself, whether of poetry or prose, took on a new significance. Writers were, in effect, asking themselves 'What is literature?' with a quite new urgency. There was a need for critical theory in a way there had never been before, and one of the most characteristic pre-occupations of writers of the period is a questioning of their own identity *as artists*. The history of Wordsworth's Prefaces to the *Lyrical Ballads* shows the process in microcosm. In the first edition of 1798 he included merely a brief 'Advertisement' explaining that the following poems were 'experiments' written 'to ascertain how far the language of conversation in the middle and lower classes of society is adapted to the purpose of poetic pleasure'. Problems about 'Poetry, a word of very disputed meaning', could be shelved. By the 1800 edition this Advertisement had been abandoned in favour of a lengthy Preface which tried to examine and justify the collection of poems in a much broader context. 'It is supposed', admitted Wordsworth, 'that by the act of writing in verse an Author makes a formal engagement that he will gratify certain known habits of association . . .', but in discussing this relationship of author with audience, he found he could no longer avoid defining that word 'of very disputed meaning'. By 1802, however, even this 1800 definition of 'poetry' was apparently inadequate, and Wordsworth at last took the final step and asked 'What is a Poet?' It is, similarly, the question that animates the whole of *The Prelude*.

Wordsworth, however, though he was the most immediately influential, was not the first Romantic to concern himself with such questions. In the introduction, we looked at some useful definitions of Romanticism, including the idea that it involved an awareness of fundamental contradictions in human life, and that it is characterized by the asking of certain types of question. If this is so, then the first properly 'Romantic' manifesto in English was not that of Wordsworth, but of Blake. *The Marriage of Heaven and Hell* (1793) is not often treated as being a work of literary criticism, as a manifesto for an aesthetic position, yet that (among other things) is what it is. As we have already seen, it is one of the first works in English to draw on Lowth's biblical criticism, with its rediscovery of the close association of poetry and prophecy. It used to be fashionable to talk of Blake as if he were an auto-didact, a self-educated eccentric, yet the whole trend of recent Blake scholarship has been to demonstrate how widely read he was, not merely in arcane and hermetic mystical writings but also in the main movements of European thought. For instance, we mentioned (in chapter 3) how the effect of Blake's Swedenborgian connexions in the early 1790s put him in touch with currents of thought that were also, via Kant, running strongly through German thought, but were scarcely known at all in England at this period. Thus it should come as no surprise to discover that ten years before August von Schlegel's seminal essay on romanticism and classicism, Blake was writing in *The Marriage of Heaven and Hell* upon the experience of 'contraries' as the key to our mental development:

> Without Contraries is no progression. Attraction and Repulsion, Reason and Energy, Love and Hate, are necessary to Human existence.
>
> From these contraries spring what the religious call Good and Evil. Good is the passive that obeys Reason. Evil is the active springing from Energy.
>
> Good is Heaven. Evil is Hell.[15]

With this boldly ironic inversion of conventional definitions, we are ushered into a new world. The immediate source of Blake's imagery is a work entitled *Heaven and its Wonders, and Hell: From Things*

Heard and Seen by Emanuel Swedenborg; but Blake's use of Swedenborg's material is satiric. Swedenborg's premise is in the main tradition of hermetic writing, which asserts a secret 'inner' meaning to biblical and other texts – a meaning known only to the initiates: 'In every particular of the Word there is an internal sense, which treats of spiritual and celestial things and not of such natural and worldly things as appear in the sense of the letter.'[16] Yet Swedenborg's actual description of Heaven and Hell is extraordinarily prosaic and literal, with no suggestion of further layers of meaning. Blake, in contrast, is (as always) figurative and metaphorical. For Swedenborg, as 'the natural World . . . exists in a state of equilibrium', so Heaven and Hell are 'contraries' in a kind of spiritual equivalent of Newtonian physics, producing a perfect equilibrium of spiritual forces. But, just as Blake rejected Newton, so he rejects the stasis of Swedenborg's spiritual geography. For Blake, human existence is not an 'equilibrium', it is *progression*.

At one level, of course, this is primarily a theological assertion. The Bible is not an exposition of a static situation, but a record of development and growth. But it is also typical of Blake's thought that what is at one level a matter of theology is no less a statement of psychology and aesthetics. Attraction and repulsion, reason and energy, love and hate are not abstractions, or qualities of the 'spiritual worlds' described in such unconvincing detail by Swedenborg, but qualities of the human mind, which is alive, unified and dynamic, and therefore in a process of constant change. 'The cistern contains: the fountain overflows . . . Expect poison from the standing water.'[17]

Though he does not use the word 'romantic', Blake, no less than Schlegel, sees the Christian mind in terms of polarities. Blake's immediate time-scale, however, is somewhat shorter than Schlegel's. At the same time as Swedenborg was writing *Heaven and Hell*, in 1757, he was also at work on another book, *The Last Judgment*, in which he announced that the second Christian era, and the beginning of the new dispensation predicted in the Book of Revelation as 'the New Jerusalem', was to begin in that year. Since 1757 was also the year of Blake's birth, Blake clearly responded to the significance of this prophecy:

As a new heaven is begun, and it is now thirty-three years since its advent: the Eternal Hell revives. And lo!

> Swedenborg is the Angel sitting at the tomb; his writings are the linen clothes folded up.[18]

In 1790, when he began work on *The Marriage of Heaven and Hell*, Blake was 33. It marked some kind of psychological watershed in his life. Up to that year he had produced little, and what he had done had been painstaking and slow. After that year it seems as if he could scarcely keep pace in his painting, writing and engraving with the insatiable demands of his own overflowing creativity.

The 'new heaven' of Swedenborg is met by the 'Eternal Hell' of 'Energy'. Swedenborg is like the angel at Jesus's tomb: the message of his works is ironically simple: 'He is not here.' So much for Swedenborg.

The rejection of the Swedenborgian 'equilibrium' awoke Blake to the 'contraries' not merely within himself, but within his society, and within literature. Thus the aesthetic message of the *Marriage* is prophetic of changes that were transforming the whole sensibility of the age. Unlike Hegel's or Marx's dialectic, which come from the German, Kantian, tradition, Blake's is a perpetual tension or polarity between incompatible opposites. The metaphor of marriage is significant. Marriage is neither fusion nor synthesis; it is a tension between opposites which depend upon each other, just as the two poles of a magnet cannot exist without each other. If one pole of a marriage is removed or is submerged by the other, it ceases to be creative. This creativity of opposites is most obvious in the immediate sexual sense, but it has a range of figurative senses no less important for Blake.

> The reason Milton wrote in fetters when he wrote of Angels and God, and at Liberty when of Devils and Hell, is because he was a true Poet and of the Devil's party without knowing it.[19]

Blake used Milton's *Paradise Lost* to satirize the rigid spiritual geography of the neoclassical ideal. 'Heaven' is simply a reflection of the Augustan order. Its virtues were reason, decorum, elegance: all forms of conventional limitation. Energy, enthusiasm, desire, together with all *unlimited* emotions were banished to 'Hell', along with most of the qualities we have come to associate with the intuitive and non-cognitive sides of our being. In short, the division between Heaven and Hell (which, Swedenborg had declared, were both 'states of mind') had become a division between the conscious and unconscious.

Blake's choice of Milton as a 'true Poet' was significant. In *Paradise Lost*, Book VI, when the war in Heaven between God and Satan is at its height, God sends into battle his Son, the Messiah, for whom the victory has been reserved. This is one of the most puzzling passages for a modern reader, for whom the whole power struggle is inclined to seem ludicrously unreal. If God is omnipotent (as we have been assured he is in Book I) why doesn't he deal with Satan himself at once? Why even bother to send the son, whose 'victory' will by definition be a put-up job? The answer is that Milton is here following not the Bible (which in any case gives no account of the war in Heaven) but Aristotle. Milton's God is Aristotle's 'unmoved mover', the *primum mobile*. Perfection, runs the syllogistic argument, cannot be altered, since change or alteration implies that it was less than perfect in the first place. God, we know, is perfect. Therefore he does not act – since to act is to produce change. God is the ultimate stasis. As a piece of theology the argument is extraordinary in its belief in logic, and in its attempt to put Hebrew thought into Greek wineskins – but applied to aesthetics it is disastrous. In practice, as Blake pointed out in the case of Milton, it never was applied. But it is, perhaps, hardly surprising that so many of those we think of as most typical of Augustan writers – Swift, Pope or Johnson, for instance – were deeply neurotic figures torn between irreconcilable and unrecognized contradictions in their own natures. By this divine cosmology of Miltonic–Augustan metaphysics, the creativity of the artist, which is both rational *and* intuitive, had been fatally separated into a false antithesis. *The Marriage of Heaven and Hell* is thus a reassertion of the moral bases of human creativity.

How then was Milton, a great poet who was apparently bound by this crippling and blasphemous dichotomy, able to write such a great spiritual epic as *Paradise Lost*? Blake's answer is that he was 'a true Poet' and, like all artists, 'of the Devil's party without knowing it'. Milton's Satan, did his creator but know it, is really the image of the 'true Christ', the external 'contrary' of 'Old Nobodaddy up aloft' – who 'farted and belch'd and cough'd' – Blake's name for the cruel tyrant of the Old Testament who was 'Nobody's Daddy'.

As has already been suggested, *The Marriage of Heaven and Hell* is a fascinating work that cannot easily be classified. It is at once theological, philosophical, psychological and aesthetic – and it is this last category that specifically concerns us here. It lies, in time, between Blake's two best-known works, *The Songs of Innocence* (1789) and *The Songs of Experience* (1794), and provides the key to them. The sub-title of the combined *Songs*, published in 1794, says that they are 'Shewing the Two Contrary States of the Human Soul'. As if to reinforce this, many of the poems, such as 'Holy Thursday', or 'The Chimney Sweeper' are explicitly paired by title; others, such as 'The Tyger' and 'The Lamb' form equally obvious pairs of contraries. Clearly the two groups of poems are intended to form a single dialectical whole.

But what *kind* of a dialectic are the states of innocence and experience? If, as their names might imply at first sight, we simply grow through 'innocence' into 'experience' and so, presumably, at last to 'maturity', then they are hardly contraries at all. In fact the two states were clearly seen by Blake as *permanent* contraries; he was not interested in maturity but *growth*. This may seem obvious enough, but if we bear this distinction rigorously in mind when reading the actual poems, we get some interesting results. 'The Chimney Sweeper' is one of the most obviously problematic pairs of poems. The 'Innocent' version is very hard to read in innocence:

> When my mother died I was very young,
> And my Father sold me while yet my tongue
> Could scarcely cry "'weep! 'weep! 'weep! 'weep!"
> So your chimneys I sweep, & in soot I sleep.

> There's little Tom Dacre, who cried when his head,
> That curl'd like a lamb's back, was shav'd; so I said
> "Hush, Tom! never mind it, for when your head's bare
> You know that the soot cannot spoil your white hair."

Blake was not alone in his pity and indignation. The year before, in 1789, the first of many enquiries into the conditions of child chimney-sweeps had published its findings. It revealed, among other things, how few children survived to adulthood. Cancer of the scrotum and lung diseases – caused by the soot – seem to have been among the commonest killers. A bill was introduced in parliament to prevent 'climing boys' being apprenticed before the age of eight, and stipulating that they should be washed once a week, and not sent up chimneys where there was a fire burning. But reports of Royal Commissions were not Blake's only source. As Kathleen Raine has shown, there are a variety of Swedenborgian and Neoplatonic symbols in the poem.[20] The suffering dirty children 'locked up in coffins of black' are mankind as a whole, unenlightened and imprisoned within the mortal body. The dream of release by the angel, and the washing in the river, are traditional metaphors of death and rebirth. Yet for all the universal outreach of the symbolism and its optimism, what we are left with is something nonetheless very disturbing.

> And the Angel told Tom, if he'd be a good boy,
> He'd have God for his father, & never want joy.
>
> And so Tom awoke; and we rose in the dark,
> And got with our bags & our brushes to work.
> Tho' the morning was cold, Tom happy & warm;
> So if all do their duty they need not fear harm.

Are we meant to take this at its face value, or is it ironic? Kathleen Raine takes the 'social indignation' for granted: but in what sense? No one doubts Blake's indignation, but if it leads us to assume that the angel is to be treated ironically, in the manner of the pompous Swedenborgian angels of the *Marriage*, what are we to make of the clearly unironic lines of the *Experience* version of 'The Chimney Sweeper'?

> And because I am happy & dance & sing,
> They think they have done me no injury,
> And are gone to praise God & his Priest & King,
> Who make up a heaven of our misery.

In short, the problem is this: if the message of *both* poems is the same 'social indignation', where are the contrary states? We are forced back to the apparently less probable reading that the angel must be taken at face value. And when we think about it, this must be right. Otherwise we reach the absurd position of saying that the angel is lying: that Tom *cannot* have God for his father, and is to be *denied* all joy. In fact the cheerfulness of these climbing boys in the face of all adversity was often commented on. Lamb's essay *In Praise of Chimney Sweeps* (1822) exemplified the very sentimental attitude that Blake attacked in the second poem. Yet for all his bland patronizing of these 'innocent blacknesses', Lamb was right (and closer to Blake than to us) in his recognition of the genuineness of that innocence: 'for the grin of a genuine sweep hath absolutely no malice in it'. But though the innocence of Tom and the other sweeps may be spontaneous and unreflective, our understanding of it is not. We are, I think, invited to accept the less probable reading of the poem only *after* we have seen it as the less probable. To put it another way, the absence of irony in the *Innocence* poem is itself an achievement of high artistic irony. Blake's contraries are not a simple opposition, but contain yet further contraries within them. 'Innocence' for Blake was not a starting point that crumbles in face of 'experience', but a quality that was won through *recognition* of it. As he asked in 'The Tyger': 'Did he who made the Lamb make thee?'

With his elaborate Swedenborgian and Neoplatonic images, it is easy to see Blake, as many of his contemporaries did, as an eccentric figure, outside the main stream of thought of his age and not characteristic of anything but himself. Yet the astonishing thing is how representative of his age all his central concerns turn out to be. If we compare his critical thought with that of his nearest contemporaries among the Romantic critics, Wordsworth and Coleridge, it is amazing, once we penetrate under the very obvious differences, how similar they are. Though he had no such explicitly dialectical model, Wordsworth, for instance, was as much concerned with the growth of the mind as Blake. Like Blake, moreover, he saw that growth as being a fundamentally *moral* process, involving not a part, but the whole personality. The difference between them is in the shape of the philosophical scaffolding. Where Blake began with Swedenborg, who was little known outside the circle of initiates, and was in violent reaction to the British empiricist tradition of Locke and Hartley, Wordsworth in 1800 was still an avowed Hartleian – at any rate in his terminology.

Seen in context, the well-known precepts of the Preface to the *Lyrical Ballads*, which are often, rightly, quoted as ushering in a new critical era, in fact arise as natural extensions of the conventional Hartleian frame of reference. Wordsworth's famous Romantic definition of poetry, for instance, as 'the spontaneous overflow of powerful feelings', comes straight out of a discussion of our mental processes that is almost pure Hartley.

> For our continued influxes of feeling are modified and directed by our thoughts, which are indeed the representatives of all our past feelings; and as by contemplating the relation of these general representatives to each other, we discover what is really important to men, so by the repetition and continuance of this act feelings connected with important subjects will be nourished, till at length, if we be originally possessed of much organic sensibility, such habits of mind will be produced that by obeying blindly and mechanically the impulses of those habits we shall describe objects and utter sentiments of such a nature and in such connection with each other, that the understanding of the being to whom we address ourselves, if he be in a healthful state of association, must necessarily be in some degree enlightened, his taste exalted, and his affections ameliorated.[21]

Hartley's particular contribution to the Lockean empiricist tradition was his theory of association. The process by which complex ideas are built up in the human mind, he claimed, was not by any merely random process of association, but according to a divinely predetermined pattern. Starting from the passive Lockean *tabula rasa*, Hartley's model envisaged the development of the mind in seven stages from passive to an active and finally to a spiritual state. Simple Sensation led on to Imagination, Ambition, Self-Interest, Sympathy, Theopathy (that is, a responsiveness to God) and finally Moral Sense. As Hartley expounded his system, it was both 'necessitarian' and 'mechanical' in its operation. Though, in some unfortunate cases, it was possible to become 'stuck' at a point along the route, the associative powers of the mind led almost inevitably to its moral and spiritual growth.[22]

It is this process that Wordsworth was describing in the passage quoted. He stressed, as Hartley did, the cumulative nature of our thinking and the importance of repetition and association as a 'mechanical' process by which the poet 'must necessarily be in some degree enlightened'. This strongly traditional context of Wordsworth's pronouncement on poetry as 'the spontaneous overflow of powerful feelings' is reinforced by the word 'spontaneous', which still carries something of its older Latin meaning from *sua sponte*: 'of its own volition', or 'voluntary'. What is at stake here is the degree of conscious control. Does the word imply simply a voluntary process, or does it suggest the operation of forces deeper and stronger than those of the conscious mind? The answer is neither – or both. Once again – as in the case we encountered at the beginning of the introduction, with the meaning of the word 'romantic' itself for Percy – the new idea was framed and expressed in terms of entirely conventional concepts, and in the act of articulation those concepts were imperceptibly altered so that the old term conveyed a quite different charge. Thus, unlike Coleridge for instance, Wordsworth never seemed to have rejected Hartleian psychology outright. Instead, he progressively outgrew it, as Hartley seemed less and less able to account for the kinds of experiences Wordsworth observed in himself. For Coleridge, Hartley collapsed because in the end he was philosophically unsatisfactory; for Wordsworth Hartley simply became increasingly less relevant as he failed to describe his own feelings.

Similarly, Hugh Blair (1718–1800), mentioned before, had apparently anticipated the main thrust of Wordsworth's argument in his *Lectures on Rhetoric* (1783). Even his turns of phrase sound as if Wordsworth is echoing them: 'Our first enquiry must be, what is poetry? and wherein does it differ from prose?' His answer, that 'it is the language of passion, or enlivened imagination'[23] sounds even more as if it is the source of Wordsworth's ideas on the subject. Yet we must be cautious once again. Wordsworth had almost certainly read Blair, and it is impossible to imagine that he was not influenced by him. But if Wordsworth was doing no more than echo Blair (who was a well-known and respected critic), why did so many contemporaries find in Wordsworth an originality and a significance they failed to find in the older Scotsman?

Part of the answer lies in the second part of Wordsworth's argument: in the theory of poetic diction, with which his 'spontaneous overflow of powerful feelings' is coupled. Wordsworth took his poetic themes, he tells us, from 'low and rustic life' (already a growing theme in painting, as we saw in chapter 2),

> . . . because in that situation the essential passions of the
> heart find a better soil in which they can attain their

maturity, are less under restraint, and speak a plainer and more emphatic language; because in that situation our elementary feelings exist in a state of greater simplicity and consequently may be more accurately contemplated and more forcibly communicated; because the manners of rural life germinate from those elementary feelings; . . . The language too of these men is adopted . . . because such men hourly communicate with the best objects from which the best part of language is originally derived; and because, from their rank in society and the sameness and narrow circle of their intercourse, being less under the action of social vanity they convey their feelings and notions in simple and unelaborated expression. Accordingly such a language arising out of repeated experience and regular feelings is a more permanent and far more philosophical language than that which is frequently substituted for it by poets.[24]

Wordsworth's theory of poetic diction was thus not merely an aesthetic one, concerning the nature of poetry, but also a political one.[25] Behind it lay the cumulative experiences of his Cumberland upbringing and Cambridge education:

> For, born in a poor district, and which yet
> Retaineth more of ancient homliness,
> Manners erect, and frank simplicity,
> Than any other nook of English land,
> It was my fortune scarcely to have seen
> Through the whole tenor of my school-day time
> The face of one, who, whether boy or man,
> Was vested with attention or respect
> Through claims of wealth or blood; nor was it least
> Of many debts which afterwards I owed
> To Cambridge and an academic life
> That something there was holden up to view
> Of a Republic . . .   (*The Prelude,* 1805, IX, 217–29)

His already egalitarian instincts were strengthened by his visit to France and his involvement with revolutionary politics under the influence of his friend Michel Beaupuy:

> Man he loved
> As man; and, to the mean and the obscure,
> And all the homely in their homely works,
> Transferred a courtesy which had no air
> Of condescension;   (*The Prelude*, 1805, IX, 312–16)

The primitivistic and egalitarian strands in Wordsworth's thought are not the same, but they are connected. He saw in the rustic the basic human type from which all others are derived. Men like Michael in the poem of that name from the *Lyrical Ballads* are not a lowest common denominator of humanity, but the highest common factor. The task of the poet is to reunite sophisticated readers with their roots, and to show them purer and more simple ways of feeling and of expressing themselves. It is a mark of our social uprootedness, Wordsworth believed, that we have come to despise our deepest selves as being primitive. The oppression of the poor by the rich reflected the alienation of the rich from their own fundamental natures. Political, social and aesthetic principles form a single whole.

Yet it is easy to miss the fact that by insisting that 'there neither is nor can be any essential difference between the language of prose and metrical composition' Wordsworth was moving into a quite different realm from Blair, and balancing 'contraries' almost as startling as those of Blake.

In the 1800 Preface to the *Lyrical Ballads* this was not immediately obvious, but when, in 1802, he added the section on the nature of the poet, his argument became clearer. Blair's question 'What is poetry?' had been only half answered by the reply 'the language of passion'. *Whose passion*, we ask? It is unlikely that the question would have occurred to Blair as in any way ambiguous. It is clear when he goes on to talk of the origins of poetry in the cries of savages, bardic songs and the music of the dance, that he is thinking of poetry as an essentially communal activity, involving poet and audience in a single common activity. The poet is the mouthpiece of society. The 'language of passion' is as much collective as individual.

For Wordsworth, the ambiguity was much more real. As we have seen, 'the spontaneous overflow of powerful feelings' could be *either* a 'voluntary' activity on the part of the poet, who is therefore in control of his feelings, or a way of making the feelings themselves autonomous, in which case the poet is in the grip of his own passions. One is essentially a neoclassical theory still, the other highly Romantic. In *either* case we are talking of poetry not in terms of the audience, but in terms of the poet's *state of mind* alone. It is hardly surprising, therefore, that in the 1802 revisions to the Preface Wordsworth decided at last to turn his attention specifically to the poet. Blair's question, 'What is poetry?', was now being rephrased: 'What is a *poet?*' The question only becomes a burning one at the point when the poet's role can no longer be taken for granted. Blair was in no doubt as to what a poet was; it was the artifact that interested him. Wordsworth could no longer discuss the artifact without reference to the mind that created it. He could no longer take for granted the neoclassical assumptions of common ground between the artist and the audience.

It is significant, for instance, that Hartleian associationism makes no real allowance for new ideas or originality. To Hartley, it would not have been a problem that needed to be explored. He had little sense of change in his own society (*Observations on Man* was published in 1749), and therefore it does not enter into his psychological model except in the most general way. Wordsworth, in contrast, was conscious of the need for a massive reappraisal of human values, both political and aesthetic. 'If my conclusions are admitted,' he wrote confidently, 'our judgements concerning the works of the greatest Poets both ancient and modern will be far different from what they are at present.' Moreover, he was in no doubt that his was a minority view; 'a practical faith', in his opinion, he added, 'is almost unknown'. As a result he was interested in prophetic figures in advance of their time, or out of step with it, and his mind turned naturally to biblical models that recall Lowth's identification of the poet and prophet. He was fascinated by the outcast and the wanderer; pedlars and leech-gatherers became types of the poet, cut off from ordinary society by their prophetic role. From being the celebrant of common feelings, the poet has become the critic of social change.

It is against this background that Wordsworth set out to describe 'the poet'.

> He is a man speaking to men: a man, it is true, endued with
> more lively sensibility, more enthusiasm and tenderness,

who has a greater knowledge of human nature, and a more comprehensive soul, than are supposed to be common among mankind.[26]

Other Romantics, Schelling in Germany or De Vigny in France, for instance, were to assert the separation of the artist as a superior kind of being: isolated by his genius. This view Wordsworth rejected emphatically: 'Among the qualities which I have enumerated as principally conducing to form a Poet, is implied nothing differing in kind from other men, but only in degree.' His stress on the common humanity shared by the poet and 'other men' alike, with the common language of 'low and rustic life' shared by poet and peasant, is the opposite side of his assertion of the prophetic role of the artist. The two claims are not in conflict, but in tension: opposing sides of the *same* coin. 'The pleasure which the mind derives from the perception of similitude in dissimilitude' is a fundamental principle of aesthetics, and 'the great spring of the activity of our minds.'

Once again we can see in Wordsworth a metaphor in transition. 'Spring' can *either* mean the mainspring of a clock, or the source of a stream. When Hartley, for instance, stressing the mechanical nature of association, wrote of the 'springs of action' in man it is clear that he was thinking of a person in terms of a watch (the microcosm of the great 'watch' metaphor by which mechanist theologians from Leibniz to Paley had described the universe). Man is built to seek the happiness pre-set by the spiritual engineering of the Great Clock-maker.[27] Now Wordsworth's metaphor could well be as fully mechanized as Hartley's – from whom he might indeed have been quoting. Certainly many of his readers would assume that he was. Yet Wordsworth coupled his spring metaphor with the words 'and their chief feeder'. A 'feeder' for a watchspring is meaningless; but springs of water *do* have feeders, or a number of underground sources. Moreover, the key phrase of the whole discussion, 'the spontaneous overflow of powerful feelings', is undoubtedly a water metaphor. The difference in the two views of the mind is crucial. The former, the mechanistic, implies limitation, order, regularity and sameness. One watch is essentially like another. The latter suggests water breaking surface from unknown and unknowable depths, under irresistible pressure. It carries other associations, biblical and religious, of grace, inspiration and life. Edward Search, another eighteenth-century critic, somewhat perversely claiming the authority of Locke, had similarly compared the imagination to a mighty subterranean river, 'always . . . at work, and if restrained from roving in all that variety of sallies it would make of its own accord, it will strike into any passages remaining open'.[28] Similarly, Coleridge in his notebooks wrote (in connexion with poetic creativity) of 'the *Joy* . . . [as of a] fountain overflowing insensibly, or the gladness of Joy, when the fountain overflows ebullient'.[29] Wordsworth's and Coleridge's metaphors of the mind complete a revolution that had been unconsciously in progress throughout the previous generation, and offer a quite new way of seeing mental activity.

It is striking how similar Wordsworth's new view of the mind is to that of Schlegel or Blake, neither of whom he knew. As with them, his description moves in a series of tensional or dialectical statements. The poet is both prophet and outcast, and, at the same time, a sharer in the language of ordinary folk. Similarly, we find in Wordsworth's final definition of poetry a parallel tension between spontaneity and control. If, on the one hand, it is 'the spontaneous overflow of powerful feelings', on the other, 'it takes its origin from emotion recollected in tranquillity'. The creation of poetry is both spontaneous and free, yet, in the recollection in tranquillity, it is controlled, disciplined and distanced by the conscious judgement of the artist. Wordsworth's vision of the unified sensibility of the poet is dependent on the same dialectic that we have seen operating at every level of his thought.

Coleridge's part in the critical structure of the *Lyrical Ballads* has always been a matter of some debate. In one sense the debate is part of the *Ballads* themselves: they *are* a debate rather than an agreed poetic manifesto. The 1798, 1800 and 1802 editions all contain different selections of poems, reflecting the changing state of the relationship between the two poets. Coleridge's own account of the book illustrates the division:

> The thought suggested itself (to which of us I do not recollect) that a series of poems might be composed of two sorts. In the one, the incidents and agents were to be, in part at least, supernatural; and the excellence aimed at was

to consist in the interesting of the affections by the dramatic truth of such emotions, as would naturally accompany such situations, supposing them real . . . For the second class, subjects were to be . . . such, as will be found in every village and its vicinity, where there is a meditative and feeling mind to seek after them, or notice them, when they present themselves.

In this idea originated the plan of the "Lyrical Ballads"; in which it was agreed, that my endeavours should be directed to persons and characters supernatural, or at least romantic; yet so as to transfer from our inward nature a human interest and a semblance of truth sufficient to procure for these shadows of imagination that willing suspension of disbelief for the moment, which constitutes poetic faith. Mr. Wordsworth, on the other hand, was to propose to himself as his object, to give the charm of novelty to things of every day, and to excite a feeling analogous to the supernatural, by awakening the mind's attention from the lethargy of custom, and directing it to the loveliness and the wonders of the world before us; an inexhaustible treasure, but for which, in consequence of the film of familiarity and selfish solicitude we have eyes, yet see not, ears that hear not, and hearts that neither feel nor understand.[30]   (Chapter XIV)

Thus, according to Coleridge at any rate, the emphasis on low and rustic life is one side of a balance that was to be counterpoised by things marvellous, supernatural and 'romantic'. As his own definition of imagination makes clear, he did not disagree at all with the egalitarianism of Wordsworth's linguistic theory, but with his practical conclusions. It is one thing to say that in rural life 'our elementary feelings exist in a state of greater simplicity and consequently may be more accurately contemplated and more forcibly communicated'; it is quite another to say that the actual *speech* of rural people is more accurate and forcible than any other. In chapter XVII of *Biographia Literaria* Coleridge drew attention to the contradiction between Wordsworth's belief in the inherent superiority of the rural poor and his belief in the common humanity of man. Wordsworth's rustics are valuable not for their rusticity but for their universality. If their essential qualities are common to all people, these qualities cannot *also* be peculiar to one class. The question of how rustics actually speak is irrelevant to Wordsworth's theory. Said Coleridge:

> . . . I reply; that a rustic's language, purified from all provincialism and grossness, and so far reconstructed as to be made consistent with the rules of grammar (which are in essence no other than the laws of universal logic, applied to psychological materials) will not differ from the language of any other man of common-sense, however learned or refined he may be, except as far as the notions, which the rustic has to convey, are fewer and more indiscriminate.[31]

But, Coleridge went on, Wordsworth has ignored a very real distinction between the speech of the educated and the uneducated. The latter notoriously lack the vital qualities of discrimination, selection and generalization essential for clear communication. Thus the rustic 'aims almost solely to convey *insulated facts* . . . while the educated man chiefly seeks to discover and express those connections of things, or those relative *bearings* of fact to fact, from which some more or less general law is deducible'. The uneducated man lacks an organizing principle, a sense of relevance. Fortunately, as Coleridge pointed out with some satisfaction, Wordsworth does not allow his theories about language to interfere with 'the processes of genuine imagination' in his actual poems. *The Last of the Flock* and *The Thorn*, though they are supposed to reflect rustic speech, and do indeed use ordinary words, are far more lucid and compact than real conversation. Wordsworth's poems by *their artifice* create an impression of naturalness and colloquial ease, while at the same time keeping the dignity, compression, depth of feeling and clarity of ideas that we associate with the highest poetry. This apparent simplicity of Wordsworth's is not, of course, a product of any imitation of the speech-patterns of yokels, but of the most sophisticated poetic technique – just as, for instance, Shakespeare's blank verse gives an illusion of ordinary speech within the world of the play.

But behind Coleridge's criticism of Wordsworth's desire to use the language of 'low and rustic life' is a more fundamental disagreement about Wordsworth's major critical proposition that 'there neither is nor can be any essential difference between the language of prose and metrical composition'. 'Now prose itself', declared Coleridge, 'differs, and ought to differ, from the language of conversation; even as reading ought to differ from talking.'[32]

> The true question must be, whether there are not modes of expression, *a construction*, and an *order* of sentences, which are in their fit and natural place in a serious prose composition, but would be disproportionate and heterogeneous in metrical poetry; and vice versa, whether in the language of a serious poem there may not be an arrangement both of words and sentences, and a use and selection of (what are called) *figures of speech*, both as to their kind, their frequency, and their occasions, which on a subject of equal weight would be vicious and alien in correct and manly prose. I contend that in both cases this unfitness of each for the place of the other will and ought to exist.[33]

> (Chapter XVII)

Concluding a lengthy series of examples of metrical structure, Coleridge threw down his own counter-argument: 'that there is, and ought to be an *essential* difference between the language of prose and of metrical composition'.[34]

Since Coleridge is often seen as being the theoretical one of the pair, and Wordsworth the practical, it is worth observing that Coleridge's criticisms of Wordsworth in the second volume of *Biographia Literaria*, though they are sometimes couched within a framework of generalizations, are nearly always severely practical. It is Wordsworth who has allowed a doctrinaire egalitarianism to run away with him to the point of absurdity. Coleridge always starts with the poems. He is more certain of Wordsworth's stature as a poet than was perhaps any of his contemporaries, but this makes him the more puzzled by the apparent discrepancy between the greatness of Wordsworth's poetry and the obstinate wrong-headedness of some parts of his poetic theory. Coleridge's literary biography is not primarily about himself at all, but about Wordsworth. Its motivation is the need to reconstruct Wordsworth's aesthetics in such a way as to do justice both to the best parts of his critical theory and to his best poems. Thus the discussion of Wordsworth's Preface is not a digression from the main theme of the *Biographia* (which, in a narrow sense, has many) but a central stage in his own quest for an

answer to the question 'What is a poet?' His disagreement with
Wordsworth over the nature of metre and diction must be seen
against a background of common principles and poetic ideals which
they had shared in 1798, and still shared nearly twenty years later
when he wrote the *Biographia*. It is an extension of the creative
tension that had always been present in their relationship.

However, Coleridge *is* more theoretical than Wordsworth in his
attempt to see Wordsworth's poetic achievement within the context
of the time, and against the backdrop of English poetry as a whole.
Wordsworth's ability to create the illusion of ordinary speech is not
one peculiar to him, but is one of the great traditional skills of
English verse, linking him with Chaucer, Shakespeare and Herbert.
But, impressive as Wordsworth's ability to do this often is, it is not
the 'characteristic excellence' of his style; he has other and 'higher
powers'.

> To me it will always remain a singular and noticeable fact;
> that a theory which would establish this *lingua communis*,
> not only as the best, but as the only commendable style,
> should have proceeded from a poet, whose diction, next to
> that of Shakespeare or Milton, appears to me of all others
> the most *individualized* and characteristic.[35]
>
> (Chapter XX)

For all the claims about the language of ordinary men, in fact
Wordsworth's poetry is unmistakably individual and original – as
all great poetry is unmistakably individual and original to its creator.
As Coleridge said of Wordsworth elsewhere, in his poem *To
William Wordsworth, composed on the night after his recitation of
a Poem on the growth of an individual mind*:

> The truly great
> Have all one age, and from one visible space
> Shed influence! They, both in power and act,
> Are permanent, and Time is not with them,
> Save as it worketh for them, they in it.

Wordsworth was one of the really great poets, as original in his
own way as Chaucer, Shakespeare or Milton. 'The natural *tendency*'
of his mind, Coleridge argued, 'is to great objects and elevated

conceptions.' Where, in response to his own critical theory, Wordsworth attempted to give significance to the small and trivial, he was like a swan out of the water, which 'having amused himself, for a while, with crushing the weeds on the river's bank, soon returns to his own majestic movements on its reflecting and sustaining surface'. The contrast of grotesque waddling and natural grace is an apt image.

Coleridge was in many ways the most intensely self-conscious of all the Romantics. Behind his attempt to place Wordsworth in an ideal hierarchy of poets who stand outside space and time is Coleridge's perpetual interest in the nature of art and of poetic tradition. It is, perhaps, typical of his own myriad-mindedness that he should have been so fascinated by the attempts of others to define poetry and its social, religious and moral functions. Thus his own answers tend to come as footnotes, digressions and half-quotations from the ideas and work of others. *Biographia Literaria* is about everybody but Coleridge. The first volume, which is mostly philosophic, deals with Hartley, and Coleridge's rejection of the empiricist tradition of Locke. The culmination of what purports to be an account of Coleridge's own life and philosophical opinions is, however, a curious mosaic of unacknowledged quotations from Schelling. Yet even in his plagiarism (and much of it *is* inexcusably plagiarized), Coleridge is still capable of sudden illuminating shafts of originality. Schelling's 'imagination' is made Coleridge's by the alteration of a few lines. Similarly, it is in the second part of the *Biographia*, devoted to a discussion of Wordsworth, and much more practical in its approach, that we find Coleridge at last beginning to stalk the real question that so concerns him and his age: 'What is poetry? is so nearly the same question with, what is a poet? that the answer to the one is involved with the solution of the other.' [36] The significance of his answer is not that it is original, but that it so accurately sums up currents of thought that, as we have seen, had come to dominate his age:

> The poet, described in *ideal* perfection, brings the whole soul of man into activity . . . He diffuses a tone and spirit of unity, that blends, and (as it were) fuses, each into each, by that synthetic and magical power, to which we have exclusively appropriated the name of imagination. This

power, first put into action by the will and understanding
. . . reveals itself in the balance or reconciliation of
opposite or discordant qualities: of sameness, with difference; of the general with the concrete; the idea with the
image; the individual, with the representative; the sense of
novelty and freshness, with old and familiar objects; a more
than usual state of emotion, with more than usual order;
judgement ever awake and ready self-possession, with
enthusiasm and feeling profound or vehement; and while
it blends and harmonizes the natural and the artificial, still
subordinates art to nature; the manner to the matter; and
the admiration of the poet to our sympathy with the
poetry.[37]

Shelley's *Defence of Poetry* was, appropriately, one of the last things
he wrote. But though it was written in 1821, only about a year
before he was drowned, it was not published until 1840. Nevertheless, it is in many ways the culmination and explicit summing-up of
the debate about the nature of poetry and the poet that we have
been tracing since the end of the eighteenth century.

Shelley was provoked into writing his *Defence* by an article in a
new magazine, *Ollier's Literary Miscellany*, called 'The Four Ages of
Poetry' by his friend Thomas Love Peacock. *Ollier's* was one of a
number of ephemeral and ill-fated literary periodicals that sprang
up and died at that period. Shelley was unable to publish his reply
in it as he had originally hoped, because its first issue was also its last.
But Peacock's article, for all its urbane and playful style, was much
more than a piece of ephemera.

'Poetry, like the world,' Peacock began, 'may be said to have four
ages, but in a different order: the first age of poetry being the age of
iron; the second, of gold; the third, of silver; and the fourth, of
brass.'[38] The ages are defined primarily by their subject-matter.
'The poet of the age of iron celebrates the achievements of his contemporaries; the poet of the age of gold celebrates the heroes of the
age of iron; the poet of the age of silver re-casts the poems of the age
of gold'; and the poet of the age of brass, 'by rejecting the polish
and the learning of the age of silver, and taking a retrograde stride to
the barbarisms and crude traditions of the age of iron, professes to
return to nature and revive the age of gold.' To illustrate his thesis,

Peacock traced two cycles of poetry. The first, that of the classical world, begins with a pre-literate stage of bards whose job it was to celebrate the achievements of their 'employer' – the local chieftain or king:

> The natural desire of every man to engross to himself as much power and property as he can acquire by any of the means which might makes right, is accompanied by the no less natural desire of making known to as many people as possible the extent to which he has been a winner in this universal game. The successful warrior becomes a chief; the successful chief becomes a king; his next want is an organ to disseminate the fame of his achievements and the extent of his possessions; and this organ he finds in a bard, who is always ready to celebrate the strength of his arm, being first duly inspired by that of his liquor. This is the origin of poetry, which, like all other trades, takes its rise in the demand for the commodity, and flourishes in proportion to the extent of the market.[39]

With the coming of literacy, we get also the emergence of a national poetry, in which these first crude panegyrics are made into works of art.

> This is the age of Homer, the golden age of poetry. Poetry has now attained its perfection: it has attained the point which it cannot pass . . . Then comes the silver age, or the poetry of civilized life. This poetry is of two kinds, imitative and original. The imitative consists in recasting, and giving an exquisite polish to the poetry of the age of gold: of this Virgil is the most obvious example. The original is chiefly comic, didactic, or satiric: as in Menander, Aristophanes, Horace and Juvenal.[40]

Finally, we have the age of brass which is characterized by:

> a verbose and minutely-detailed description of thoughts, passions, actions, persons and things, in that loose rambling style of verse, which any one may write . . . at the rate of two hundred lines in an hour. To this age may be referred all the poets who flourished in the decline of the

Roman Empire. The best specimen of it, though not the most generally known, is Dionysiaca of Nonnus.[41]

Peacock illustrated his argument with a cool cynical intelligence and barbed wit. But his first cycle, based with considerable learning on the rise and decline of classical civilization, is only a stalking-horse for his real objective: the second cycle of modern poetry. This is developed precisely on the lines one might expect from the first cycle. The iron age of modern Europe is the world of the troubadours and Arthurian legends. Its golden age is that of Shakespeare and his contemporaries. After them comes the silver age 'beginning with Dryden, coming to perfection with Pope, and ending with Goldsmith, Collins and Gray'. So far, so good. Now, however, we come to the point to which Peacock, with a magnificent sense of inevitability, has been leading us: the modern age of brass. This is, of course, his own age – and that of his contemporaries – and he offers us a literary parallel to Fuseli's *Artist Moved by the Magnitude of Antique Fragments* (see above, chapter 2). In particular, he is aiming for

> that egregious confraternity of rhymesters, known by the name of the Lake Poets; who certainly did receive and communicate to the world some of the most extraordinary poetical impressions that ever were heard of, and ripened into models of public virtue too splendid to need illustration. They wrote verses on a new principle; saw rocks and rivers in a new light; and remaining studiously ignorant of history, society, and human nature, cultivated the phantasy only at the expense of the memory and the reason; and contrived, though they had retreated from the world for the express purpose of seeing nature as she was, to see her only as she was not, converting the land they lived in into a sort of fairy-land, which they peopled with mysticisms and chimaeras. This gave what is called a new tone to poetry, and conjured up a herd of desperate imitators, who have brought the age of brass prematurely to its dotage.[42]

Whether or not Shelley felt himself to be one of the herd of 'desperate imitators', this was fighting stuff, guaranteed to provoke a response from any of the few who actually read *Ollier's* – and, perhaps with premonitions about its disastrous circulation, Peacock made sure that Shelley was sent a copy in Italy. But before we dismiss Peacock's theory of literary history as merely an unusually witty way of goading some contemporary poets whose work he happened to dislike, it is worth looking seriously at one or two of his ideas.

To begin with, Peacock was, of course, providing his own answer to the contemporary question, 'What is a poet?', just as much as were either Wordsworth or Coleridge, of whose theory and practice he was so dismissive. Moreover, in spite of saying that he is describing the 'origins of poetry' in the ages of iron, what he is doing, like his contemporaries, is describing the role of the *poet*. The real difference is that he is offering a sociological account of the poet, rather than an aesthetic one. In other words, for all his ostensibly 'classical' pose, he turns out by some of the more important criteria we have been investigating, to be a 'Romantic' critic himself. In fact, when we get down to it, his opinion of the preceding 'silver' age of Augustan poetry is not very high.

> Good sense and elegant learning, conveyed in polished and somewhat monotonous verse, are the perfection of the original and imitative poetry of civilized life. Its range is limited, and when exhausted, nothing remains but the *crambe repetita* of common-place, which at length becomes thoroughly wearisome, even to the most indefatigable readers of the newest new nothings.
>
> It is now evident that poetry must either cease to be cultivated, or strike into a new path.[43]

Now this has a familiar ring to it, but it is a modern, not a neo-classical ring. Take, for instance, T. S. Eliot's famous remark about W. B. Yeats: 'It is my experience that towards middle age a man has three choices; to stop writing altogether, to repeat himself with perhaps an increasing skill of virtuosity, or by taking thought to adapt himself to middle age and find a different way of working.'[44] What is true of an individual is true of the tradition. Behind Eliot's judgement lay his whole concept of 'Tradition' as being a process not of repetition, but of progressive innovation and originality. Eliot was in this sense, of course, himself a highly 'Romantic' critic and not the classicist he would have us believe: his debts to Wordsworth,

Coleridge and Shelley are obvious. What is, perhaps, less obvious is the degree to which Peacock stood in the *same* camp – not, that is, so much the camp of Wordsworth, Coleridge and Shelley as the *modernist* camp of Yeats, Pound and Eliot.

As we have noted, Peacock offered not an aesthetic account of poetry, but a historicist and sociological account, linking the development of the art very closely to the needs of the particular society, and the relationship of the artist to his public. He did this at a number of levels, often so subtly that we do not at first see what he was driving at. For instance, his 'cyclic' theory of the rise and fall of poetry is *not* in fact properly cyclic at all, because the modern age is aware of the existence, and many of the works, of the preceding classical cycle. The second cycle is therefore inevitably more historicist than the first. We are reminded of Schlegel's distinction between the 'classic' and the 'modern', the more so when Peacock places Shakespeare at the centre of the modern golden age. But there is an important difference.

> From these ingredients of the iron age of modern poetry, dispersed in the rhymes of the minstrels and the songs of the Troubadours, rose the golden age, in which the scattered materials were harmonized and blended about the time of the revival of learning; but with this peculiar difference, that Greek and Roman literature pervaded all the poetry of the golden age of modern poetry, and hence resulted a heterogeneous compound of all ages and nations in one picture; an infinite licence, which gave to the poet the free range of the whole field of imagination and memory. This was carried very far by Ariosto, but farthest of all by Shakespeare and his contemporaries, who used time and locality merely because they could not do without them, because every action must have its when and where: but they made no scruple of deposing a Roman Emperor by an Italian Count, and sending him off in the disguise of a French pilgrim to be shot with a blunderbuss by an English archer. This makes the old English drama very picturesque, at any rate, in the variety of costume, and very diversified in action and character; though it is a picture of nothing that ever was seen on earth except a Venetian carnival.[45]

The first thing we notice, of course, is that Peacock is apparently advancing a *deteriorationist* argument. In his view, a knowledge of the existence and development of classical verse in the Renaissance did not, in fact, help to improve the art of the period, but actually made it worse. The second thing that strikes us is that he has given a very good description of the zany plotting of his own two historical novels, *Maid Marion* and *The Misfortunes of Elphin*. One of the reasons why Shelley could be so genuinely delighted by Peacock's wickedly skilful portrait of him and his love-life as Scythrop, in *Nightmare Abbey*, was that Peacock was no less quick to satirize himself and his own work, both as an official of the East India Company and as a writer. Yet, before we can even be sure this is deteriorationist satire, there is one other phrase that must give us pause. The reference to 'Shakespeare and his contemporaries, who used time and locality merely because they could not do without them', has, again, that curious, impossibly modernist ring to it. Is Beckett really waiting in the wings? Just what *is* Peacock suggesting here?

Throughout the brief essay one is haunted by the suspicion that Peacock, under the guise of putting forward a traditionalist attack on Romanticism as a process of steady degeneration, is in fact asking questions that none of his contemporaries could answer. As usual, we cannot be sure at what level his mind was moving. At its simplest and most knockabout, he seems to be able to anticipate and ridicule in advance Shelley's defence that 'Poets are the unacknowledged legislators of the world':

> [poets] are not only historians but theologians, moralists, and legislators: delivering their oracles *ex cathedra*, and being indeed often themselves (as Orpheus and Amphion) regarded as portions and emanations of divinity: building cities with a song, and leading brutes with a symphony; which are only metaphors for the faculty of leading multitudes by the nose.[46]

Yet behind this deflationary wit stalks another much more disturbing spectre. The progressive deterioration of poetry as an art form is not just a matter of the way in which fashion and the human desire for novelty operate. There are formidable intellectual reasons. It sounds at first as if he is merely echoing Locke: 'Feeling and passion are best painted in, and roused by ornamental and figurative language; but the reason and the understanding are best addressed in the simplest and most humanised.' But as his argument progresses we begin to see that he is hinting at a position much more thorough-going than Locke's suspicion of metaphor. As we have seen, Locke holds the metaphors of poetry to be an inaccurate and ambiguous way of expressing what might be put 'more plainly. He does not see the relationship between prose and verse as one of steady and inevitable *retreat* by verse. Peacock's view apparently involves an inexorable progression from verse to prose:

> As the sciences of morals and of mind advance towards perfection, as they become more enlarged and comprehensive in their views, as reason gains the ascendancy in them over imagination and feeling, poetry can no longer accompany them in their progress, but drops into the background, and leaves them to advance alone.
>
> Thus the empire of thought is withdrawn from poetry, as the empire of facts had been before.[47]

Now to later ears, and in a different setting, this is a very familiar argument indeed. It is, of course, a secularized version of the German Historical Criticism of the Bible, but whereas Eichhorn, Lessing and the others saw 'poetry' largely as the vehicle of primitive modes of *religious* thought, Peacock has brilliantly pushed the argument to its logical conclusion and used it as a weapon to attack poetry itself. Like Locke before them, the German critics merely saw poetry and prose as belonging to different orders of experience. Though Lessing, in fact, intended his arguments as an attack on the very basis of Christianity, he had no interest in attacking poetry as such. Peacock has swept away the barriers of genre and insisted that the truths of poetry must be judged by the same standards as any other kinds of truth – and if so judged, they will progressively be found inadequate. In short:

> Poetry was the mental rattle that awakened the attention of intellect in the infancy of civil society: but for the maturity of mind to make a serious business of the play-things of its childhood, is as absurd as for a full-grown man to rub his gums with coral, and cry to be charmed to sleep by the jingle of silver bells.[48]

Poetry is essentially the least sophisticated of the art forms, and as society develops it will have less and less place for the kinds of imagination and feeling poetry is best able to express. In our society, Peacock concluded,

> intellectual power and intellectual acquisition have turned themselves into other and better channels, and have abandoned the cultivation and the fate of poetry to the degenerate joy of modern rhymesters.[49]

What are we to make of this? Firstly, that Peacock is being ironic. We know from his novels that he did not believe in the kind of 'moral' and 'intellectual' progress he appears to be embracing here. Phrases like 'as the sciences of morals and of mind advance towards perfection . . . as reason gains the ascendency in them over imagination and feeling' are straight out of the sort of inane speeches he puts into the mouths of his madder progressives in *Melincourt* and *Crotchet Castle*. Peacock had no truck with notions of the moral improvement of mankind (he had been deeply upset over Shelley's desertion of Harriet and elopement with Mary Godwin), and he reserved his bitterest contempt for the

> mathematicians, astronomers, chemists, moralists, metaphysicians, historians, politicians, and political economists, who have built into the upper air of intelligence a pyramid, from the summit of which they see the modern Parnassus far beneath them, and, knowing how small a place it occupies in the comprehensiveness of their prospect, smile at the little ambition and the circumscribed perceptions with which the drivellers and mountebanks upon it are contending for the poetical palm and the critical chair.[50]

In other words, what we seem to have here is a piece of almost Swiftian irony: not an attack on poetry at all, but in fact a *defence* of it. Just as Swift in *A Modest Proposal* or *An Argument Against Abolishing Christianity* had pretended to advocate cannibalism and atheism in order to show how they (in a sense) already existed, so Peacock is proclaiming the imminent demise of poetry precisely because that (as a poet and critic) is what he most fears really *is* happening. It is not when he seems to criticize poets, but when he *agrees* with them that he is at his most dangerous. As, for instance:

when he sympathetically supports the poet's commercial need to 'please his audience, and most therefore continue to sink to their level, while the rest of the community is rising above it'.[51] Peacock is clear that once poetry is to be valued by the values of the market-place – by the values of chemists, moralists and political economists – then it really *is* doomed, and nothing can save it.

But to invert Peacock, as clearly in some sense we must do, is to invite other questions. If the answer to the question 'What is a poet?' is: a person out of step with society because of a wider, more comprehensive vision, in touch with the deepest and most primitive roots of human experience, then we begin to emerge with something that sounds suspiciously like the Preface to the *Lyrical Ballads*. Perhaps the deliberate singling out of Wordsworth and Coleridge for special attack is significant? But if Peacock really approved of Shakespeare's 'timeless' settings, and of the Lake Poets, what are we to make of his praise for Homer and Virgil, and contempt for Nonnus? We have apparently to conclude that the first cycle is *not* ironic, but that the second cycle *is*. What connects the two cycles, of course, is Peacock's sociological and historicist model, and at this point it begins to dawn on us that this is precisely the kind of model most favoured by the despised historians and political economists (not to mention German Historical Critics) who would seek to explain works of art in terms of economic motives and the state of society at one time. In other words, the whole massive historical inevitability by which Peacock leads us from the dawn of time down to 'that egregious confraternity of rhymesters known by the name of the Lake Poets' is nothing more than a parody of such works, applying historical arguments to areas where they have no jurisdiction at all.

But Peacock's irony is even here not that simple. From the evidence of his novels, and from the kind of neoclassical poetry he himself wrote, we have no reason to suppose that he *did* have *much* love for the ideals of Wordsworth and Coleridge at this period, though he did in his last novel, *Gryll Grange*, in 1861, make some amends for his early ridicule: 'Shakespeare never makes a flower blossom out of season. Wordsworth, Coleridge, and Southey are true to nature, in this and all other respects: even in their wildest imaginings.'[52] More disturbing is his argument that poetry will give way to prose by a process of historical inevitability. Let us take a twentieth-century quotation, from Ezra Pound:

From the beginning of literature up to A.D. 1750 poetry was the superior art, and was so considered to be, and if we read books written before that date we find the number of interesting books in verse at least equal to the number of prose books still readable; and the poetry contains the quintessence. When we want to know what people were like before 1750, when we want to know they had blood and bones like ourselves, we go to the poetry of the period.

But . . . one morning Monsieur Stendhal, not thinking of Homer, or Villon, or Catullus, but having a very keen sense of actuality, noticed that 'poetry', *la poesie*, as the term was then understood, the stuff written by his French contemporaries, as sonorously rolled at him from the French stage, was a damn nuisance. And he remarked that poetry, with its bagwigs and its bobwigs, and its padded calves and its periwigs, its 'fustian à la Louis XIV', was greatly inferior to prose for conveying a clear idea of the diverse states of our consciousness ('les mouvements du coeur').

And at that moment the serious art of writing 'went over to prose', and for some time the important developments of language as means of expression were the developments of prose.[53]

We have already mentioned Ezra Pound once before in connexion with Peacock's apparent modernism. Though Pound chose his examples from France, there is no doubt at all that something very similar happened in England round about 1820–30 with the death or silence of the great Romantic poets. Keats died in 1821, Shelley in 1822, Byron in 1824, Blake in 1827, Coleridge in 1834, and though Wordsworth lived on, incredibly, until 1850, his best work was all completed by the 1820s. As Henry Crabb Robinson, a friend of Wordsworth, put it (not unkindly) in a letter to Wordsworth's sister, Dorothy, in 1826: 'It gives me real pain when I think that some future commentator may possibly hereafter write – "This great poet survived to the fifth decennary of the nineteenth Century, but he appears to have died in the year 1814 as far as life consisted in an active sympathy with the temporary welfare of his fellow creatures." '[54] Whether he intended it or not, Peacock is quite prophetic in his feeling in 1820 that a poetic age was drawing to its close. In its narrow and conventional meaning at any rate, the Romantic period was almost over. Moreover, we note that Stendhal (1783–1842), whom Pound saw as being responsible for turning the main stream of creative literature in Europe from verse to prose, was a widely-cultured anglophile and an almost exact contemporary of Peacock (1785–1866).

However ironic Peacock's model was intended to be, it is also uncannily prophetic of the future development of literary sensibility. Though there was a great deal of prose being written at this period, and it included works by some of the greatest novelists and essayists in English literature – Scott and Jane Austen, Hazlitt, Lamb and de Quincey, for instance – it remains true that poetry was still thought of by contemporaries as the central literary art form of the age. Scott, for example, though he earned most of his considerable income from his novels, was thought of for most of the period primarily as a *poet*: author of *The Lay of the Last Minstrel* (1805), *Marmion* (1808) and *The Lady of the Lake* (1810). To some extent, of course, this is simply a matter of cultural time-lag. It is much easier to perceive literary trends in any period from a later vantage-point, and the richness of the age in prose writers would simply not have been apparent to those brought up to think of poetry as the dominant form. Yet this question of status is also connected with subject-matter. As we have seen throughout this volume, poetry was where the major aesthetic, religious and philosophic debates of the day were encountered. Prose merely reflected social reality – or escapism. Peacock himself, now remembered and read as an exquisitely subtle prose writer and author of some of the most sparkling satires in the language, had also published long poems (quite unknown today) such as *Rhododaphne*, and he was in no doubt that prose was the inferior form. Yet as his fears show, he was also sensitive to the shifting balance. Though it would have been hard to see the seeds either of historicism or a new psychology in the absurdities of the gothic or the excesses of the sentimental novel, that was where the growing middle-class readership was to be found. Social reality was itself becoming of increasing interest and the novel was helping to transform how people saw it. It is often remarked how little of the world of the Napoleonic Wars or social unrest finds its way into Jane Austen's novels. This is true, but in her last, and unfinished, novel,

Sanditon, there is a much stronger awareness of change. The new town of the title is a seaside resort on the south coast, and much of the plot hinges on land speculation. There is also a seducer who quotes Byron. We are only a generation away from the 'condition of England' question that was to haunt the early Victorian writers, Carlyle, Disraeli or Kingsley.

Nor when we are thinking of this movement from verse to prose, and the significance of Scott or Peacock, should we forget the even more startling example of Coleridge. We have already mentioned that his poetic career spans less than six out of his sixty years. To many contemporaries, as to many Victorians, he was principally a prose writer. The concerns of his early poetry were not abandoned as he moved into prose, they were simply transformed. He is, in a curious way, the paradigm example of Peacock's thesis – and it was a thesis for which his contemporaries had no answer. Tennyson and Browning are great poets, but I do not feel that they are as central to the Victorian age as, say, Dickens or George Eliot. When we wish to understand the Romantics, we read the poets; when we wish to understand the Victorians, we read first of all the prose.

Shelley's *Defence of Poetry*, written in reply to Peacock, is an ominous confirmation of Peacock's case, for the defence rests upon *including* prose as a form of poetry. The *Defence of Poetry* is a work of both brilliance and penetration, but it is essentially a summation of the arguments we have been following in various metamorphoses so far. In that sense it looks backward rather than forward. It does not attempt to face the future that Peacock proclaimed in grim jest and half-suspected in grim earnest. Indeed, its most puzzling feature is its apparent humourlessness. Though John Hunt, its first editor, deliberately removed specific references to Peacock's article which could only have been appropriate in a reply published by *Ollier's Miscellany*, it is still surprising that Shelley treated Peacock's arguments uniformly at their face value, without attempting to disentangle his friend's real position. The result is that Shelley follows through, with considerable passion, an argument not all dissimilar to the one implied by Peacock's irony.

Like all his contemporaries, including Peacock, Shelley's defence of poetry was achieved primarily by a discussion of the poet, not of poetry. He accepted his friend's suggestion that poetry is the most primitive art form, but then stood Peacock's argument on its head.

For 'primitive' equals 'primal': poetry is, therefore, the central art form from which all other kinds of literature are derived. Peacock's ironic 'sociological' description of poetry is thus taken up and re-argued on a historical basis.

We have already met briefly with Shelley's defence that 'Poets are the unacknowledged legislators of the world'. But Shelley also made the connexion between poet, legislator and prophet: 'Poets, according to the circumstances of the age and nation in which they appeared, were called, in the earlier epochs of the world, Legislators or prophets: A poet essentially comprises and unites both these characters.'[55] This is, in part, an echo of Sidney's *Apologie for Poetrie*. Sidney had written: 'Among the Romans a Poet was called *Vates*, which is as much as a Diviner, Fore-seer, or Prophet, as by his conjoyned words *Vaticinum* and *Vaticinari* is manifest: so heavenly a title did that excellent people bestow upon this heart-ravishing knowledge.'[56] But there are other sources of which Shelley may equally well have been thinking, like the description in Percy's *Essay on the Ancient Minstrels in England*, or the Norse 'Scalds', 'in whom the characters of historian, genealogist, poet, and musician . . . novelist and theologue' were united, and above all, of course, Lowth's *Sacred Poetry of the Hebrews* (Shelley specifically mentioned the importance of the translation of 'Hebrew poetry'). But these are also Peacock's sources, and he had made effective fun of them, both as we have seen in the 'Four Ages', and in *The Misfortunes of Elphin*, source of *The War-Song of the Dinas Vawr*, a parody so brilliant that it is still occasionally quoted in anthologies as if it were a translation of a genuine Welsh war-song. Shelley, however, combined this historical argument with an absolute one about the nature of language itself: 'a poet essentially comprises and unites both these characters'. Note the present tense.

> Poetry . . . expresses those arrangements of language and especially metrical language, which are created by that imperial faculty, whose throne is curtained within the invisible nature of man. And this springs from the nature itself of language, which is a more direct representation of the actions and passions of our internal being.[57]

Poetry is thus *primary*, not just in a historical sense, but in a psychological sense as well. It touches the deepest parts of a man and is therefore a fundamentally *moral* art:

> A man, to be greatly good, must imagine intensely and comprehensively; he must put himself in the place of another and of many others; the pains and pleasures of his species must become his own. The great instrument of moral good is the imagination; and poetry administers to the effect by acting upon the cause . . . Poetry strengthens the faculty which is the organ of the moral nature of man in the same manner as exercise strengthens a limb. [58]

Though this is no more than an extension of the kind of argument used by Wordsworth and Coleridge, it is an extension they hesitated to make in so many words. Shelley's boldness gives us the key. They did not doubt that the highest goodness involved imagining 'intensely and comprehensively', nor did they question that poetry was a 'moral' art, concerned with man's deepest self. But to leap from that to the statement 'the greatest instrument of moral good is the imagination' was neither acceptable to their religious beliefs, nor true to their practical experience, for Shelley was not slow to spell out the obvious corollary to this argument:

> A poet, as he is the author to others of the highest wisdom, pleasure, virtue, and glory, so he ought personally to be the happiest, the best, the wisest, and the most illustrious of men. As to his glory, let time be challenged to declare whether the fame of any other institutor of human life be comparable to that of a poet. That he is the wisest, the happiest, and the best, inasmuch as he is a poet, is equally incontrovertible. The greater poets have been men of the most spotless virtue, of the most consummate prudence, and, if we would look into the interior of their lives, the most fortunate of men. [59]

This is so staggering an assertion in the face of biographical fact that one wonders for a moment if Shelley is answering Peacock's irony with his own. But he is not. Shelley left others (like Peacock) to clear up the problems he scattered in the wake of the secularized anti-nomianism of his private life. Moreover, Shelley's entire argument is no less than a secularized religion. It is with Shelley in particular among English poets that T. E. Hulme's charge that Romanticism is 'spilt religion' makes most sense. Shelley, in effect, inverted Lowth's emphasis on the prophet as poet, and proclaimed the poet as prophet in a new religion of humanity. The whole tenor of his imagery is religious:

> Poetry lifts the veil from the hidden beauty of the world and makes familiar objects be as if they were not familiar.[60]

> Poetry is a sword of lightning, ever unsheathed, which consumes the scabbard that would contain it.[61]

> Poetry is indeed something divine. It is at once the centre and circumference of knowledge; it is that which comprehends all science [i.e. knowledge], and that to which all science must be referred.[62]

This framework of secularized religion is necessary for the next stage in Shelley's refutation of Peacock's ostensible thesis: the 'development' of poetry. Shelley accepted Peacock's idea of an internal and necessary process of development and change in the art, but in place of the four ages of poetry he inserted what is, in effect, a secularized version of the Old Testament prophetic tradition. The argument runs like a parody of Blake. Since we now see that what was once thought of as external 'religious' experience is really the internal 'poetic' faculty of mankind, we must look to poetry for the history of man's discovery of himself and of his moral world. Every great poet is an innovator, illuminating the tradition of his predecessors by changing it.[63] Shelley here has taken and developed an argument expounded by Coleridge (from German sources): that tradition consists not in imitation, but in innovation. This argument was later to be central to the modernist criticism of Yeats, Pound and, above all, T. S. Eliot.

In reply to Peacock's charge that progressively 'the empire of thought is withdrawn from poetry, as the empire of facts had been before', Shelley insisted that the tradition of poetry is also a tradition of philosophic and intellectual innovation. Following Wordsworth, he repeated that 'the distinction between poets and prose writers is a vulgar error'. But this now means that we can claim all great creative writers and thinkers within his definition of a 'poet'.

> Plato was essentially a poet – the truth and splendour of his imagery, and the melody of his language, are the most

intense it is possible to conceive. He rejected the measure of
the epic, dramatic and lyrical forms, because he sought to
kindle a harmony in thoughts divested of shape and action.

Lord Bacon, we discover, was also a poet, whereas Shakespeare,
Dante and Milton were 'philosophers of the very loftiest power'. In
short, Shelley insisted that 'all the authors of revolutions in opinion
are necessarily poets as they are inventors'.[64]

How are we to judge who makes up this 'poetic' tradition of great
innovators of thought? Shelley's answer was essentially the same as
that of Coleridge: 'the jury which sits in judgement upon a poet,
belonging as he does to all time, must be composed of his peers: it
must be empanelled by time from the selectest of the wise of many
generations'.[65] We are reminded of T. S. Eliot's dictum in *Tradition
and the Individual Talent*:

> No poet, no artist of any art, has his complete meaning
> alone. His significance, his appreciation is the appreciation
> of his relation to the dead poets and artists. You cannot
> value him alone; you must send him for contrast and com-
> parison among the dead . . . What happens when a new
> work of art is created is something that happens simul-
> taneously to all the works of art which preceded it. The
> existing monuments form an ideal order among them-
> selves, which is modified by the introduction of the new
> (the really new) work of art among them.[66]

Shelley's defence of poetry against Peacock's ironic questioning is
to answer the question 'What is a poet?' with greater boldness than
any of his contemporaries – or subsequent critics. Even Eliot
hesitated to include all creative writers in his poetic tradition. Yet
Shelley's strategy, if one can accept it, solves in a sense Peacock's
final fear that poetry will eventually be outmoded by prose as an
instrument for conveying 'the diverse states of our consciousness'.
Shelley slid, almost imperceptibly, from evidence that poetry is the
original literary art form to the claim that *all* literary art forms are
poetry. Given this premise he can state with some confidence that

> corruption must utterly have destroyed the fabric of human
> society before poetry can ever cease. The sacred lines of this

chain have never been entirely disjoined, which descending
through the minds of many men is attached to those great
minds, whence as from a magnet the invisible effluence is
sent forth, which at once connects, animates, and sustains
the life of all. It is the faculty which contains within itself
the seeds at once of its own and of social revolution.[67]

Shelley's ostensible purpose was to prove that 'Poets are the unacknowledged legislators of the world'. But he had a more immediate and personal task as well: to defend his own generation,
which Peacock had called the second 'age of brass'. It is one thing to
assert the enduring vitality and innovative power of the human
spirit; it is another to show that one's own age is not inferior to those
of the giants of the past. Shelley's defence here, too, is a part of the
seamless web of his whole argument. For him, poetry was not a
matter of verse-styles and metre, or of certain appropriate kinds of
subject matter, but embraced the whole world of ideas: philosophy,
religion, politics, social questions. With Shelley, the question
'What is a poet?' ceased to be a matter of literary criticism, and
became a much larger one about human nature as a whole. The
'march of the mind' that Peacock invoked, and so despised, is in
reality the march of *poetry*.

It is, in part, because of claims like Shelley's for the nature and
scope of the art of poetry that we have come to see the need for such
multidisciplinary studies as we have been attempting in this book,
however inadequate they may be. He simultaneously summed up
existing ways of thinking, and showed how the trend of Romantic
criticism was to open up yet further dimensions to the debate.
Whereas a poet like Gray assumed that change is essentially irrelevant, Shelley made the idea of change central to his notion of
poetry. His was the age when writers became aware of their true role
and destiny, and could proclaim with confidence what in fact they
always had been. Hence his certainty that

In spite of the low-thoughted envy which would under-
value contemporary merit, our own will be a memorable
age in intellectual achievements, and we live among such
philosophers and poets as surpass beyond such comparison
any who have appeared since the last national struggle for
civil and religious liberty.[68]

Notes

1 Cited by R. W. Ketton-Creamer, *Horace Walpole*, 3rd edn, Methuen, 1964, 315.

2 ibid., 231–2.

3 D. W. Harding, 'Regulated hatred: an aspect of the work of Jane Austen', *Scrutiny*, 8 (IV), March 1940.

4 A. O. Lovejoy, 'On the discrimination of Romanticisms', in M. H. Abrams (ed.), *English Romantic Poets*, Oxford University Press, 1960, 24.

5 See Stephen Prickett, *Coleridge and Wordsworth: The Poetry of Growth*, Cambridge University Press, 1970, ch. 1.

6 Geoffrey Keynes (ed.), *The Complete Writings of William Blake*, 2nd edn, Oxford University Press, 1966.

7 'A vision of the last judgment', in Keynes, *Complete Writings of Blake*, 604.

8 Thomas Carlyle, 'The state of German literature', *Critical and Miscellaneous Essays*, London, 1869, I, 96.

9 David Ferry, *The Limits of Mortality*, Middleton, Conn., 1959; Geoffrey Hartman, *Wordsworth's Poetry 1787–1814*, Yale University Press, 1967.

10 George MacDonald, *A Dish of Orts*, London, 1893, 245–6.

11 ibid., 252; see also Stephen Prickett, *Romanticism and Religion*, Cambridge University Press, 1976, ch. 3.

12 Samuel Taylor Coleridge, *Biographia Literaria*, J. Shawcross (ed.), Clarendon Press, 1907, I, 202.

13 Maurice Buxton Forman (ed.), *The Letters of John Keats*, Oxford University Press, 1935, 67–8.

14 Keynes, *Complete Writings of Blake*, 97.

15 ibid., 149.

16 Emanuel Swedenborg, *Heaven and its Wonders, and Hell: From Things Heard and Seen*, Everyman's Library, Dent, 1909, I, 2–3.

17 *The Marriage of Heaven and Hell*, in Keynes, *Complete Writings of Blake*, 151–2.

18 ibid., 149.

19 ibid., 150.

20 Kathleen Raine, *Blake and Tradition*, Routledge & Kegan Paul, 1969, 20–6.

21 W. Wordsworth, 1800 Preface to *Lyrical Ballads*, in R. L. Brett and A. R. Jones (eds.) *Lyrical Ballads*, revised impression, Methuen, 1965, 246–7.

22 David Hartley, *Observations on Man, his Frame, his Duties, and his Expectations*, London, 1749, I; see also Prickett, *Coleridge and Wordsworth*, 46–70.

23 Hugh Blair, *Lectures on Rhetoric and Belles Lettres*, Edinburgh, 1820, II, 212–13 (1st edn, 1783).

24 Wordsworth, *Lyrical Ballads*, Brett and Jones (eds), 245.
25 See Wordsworth's letter to Charles James Fox, quoted above in chapter
    1, p. 48.
26 Wordsworth, *Lyrical Ballads*, Brett and Jones (eds), 255.
27 Hartley, *Observations on Man*, I, 506; see also Prickett, *Coleridge and
    Wordsworth*, 83.
28 Edward Search, *The Light of Nature Pursued*, London, 1768, 12.
29 K. Coburn (ed.), *Notebooks of Samuel Taylor Coleridge*, Routledge &
    Kegan Paul, 1962, II, 2279.
30 Coleridge, *Biographia Literaria*, II, 5–6.
31 ibid., II, 38.
32 ibid., II, 45.
33 ibid., II, 49.
34 ibid., II, 57.
35 ibid., II, 77.
36 ibid., II, 12.
37 ibid.
38 H. F. B. Brett-Smith (ed.), *Peacock's Four Ages of Poetry*, Basil
    Blackwell, 1953, 3.
39 ibid., 3–4.
40 ibid., 7–8.
41 ibid., 10–11.
42 ibid., 14–15.
43 ibid., 10.
44 T. S. Eliot, 'Yeats', *On Poetry and Poets*, Faber & Faber, 1957, 253–4.
45 Brett-Smith, *Peacock's Four Ages*, 12–13.
46 ibid., 5–6.
47 ibid., 9.
48 ibid., 18.
49 ibid., 19.
50 ibid.
51 ibid.
52 Thomas Love Peacock, *Gryll Grange*, London, 1861, 204.
53 Ezra Pound, 'How to read', *Literary Essays of Ezra Pound*, Faber &
    Faber, 1954, 31.
54 Edith J. Morley (ed.), *The Correspondence of Henry Crabb Robinson
    with the Wordsworth Circle*, Oxford University Press, 1927, 153.
55 Percy Bysshe Shelley, *A Defence of Poetry*, H. F. B. Brett-Smith (ed.),
    Percy Reprints no. 3, Basil Blackwell, 1953, 27.
56 Sir Philip Sidney, *An Apologie for Poetrie*, Shuckburgh (ed.), London,
    1896, 5.
57 Shelley, *Defence*, 27–8.
58 ibid., 33.
59 ibid., 56.
60 ibid., 33.

61 ibid., 38.
62 ibid., 53.
63 ibid., 29.
64 ibid., 29–30.
65 ibid., 31.
66 T. S. Eliot, *Selected Essays*, 3rd edn, Faber & Faber, 1951, 15.
67 Shelley, *Defence*, 40.
68 ibid., 59.

Further reading

Abrams, M. H. *The Mirror and the Lamp: Romantic Theory and the Critical Tradition*, Oxford University Press, 1953.

Barfield, Owen, *History in English Words*, Faber & Faber, 1953.

Brailsford, H. M., *Shelley, Godwin, and their Circle*, Home University Library, Oxford University Press, 1913.

Butler, Marilyn, *Peacock Displayed: A Satirist in his Context*, Routledge & Kegan Paul, 1979.

Clarke, Colin, *Romantic Paradox*, Routledge & Kegan Paul, 1962.

Cooke, Katherine, *Coleridge*, Routledge & Kegan Paul, 1979.

Furst, Lilian, *Romanticism*, Methuen, 1969.

Furst, Lilian, *Romanticism in Perspective: A Comparative Study of the Romantic Movements in England, France & Germany*, Macmillan, 1969.

Hartman, Geoffrey, *Wordsworth's Poetry 1787–1814*, Yale University Press, 1964.

Jacobus, Mary, *Tradition and Experiment in Wordsworth's 'Lyrical Ballads' 1798*, Clarendon Press, 1976.

Jordan, John, *Why the Lyrical Ballads?*, University of California Press, 1976.

Levine, George, and Knowpflmacher, U. C. (eds), *The Endurance of Frankenstein: Essays on Mary Shelley's Novel*, University of California Press, 1979.

Lewis, C. S., 'Nature', *Studies in Words*, Cambridge University Press, 1960.

Lovejoy, A. O., *The Reason, the Understanding, and Time*, Johns Hopkins Press, 1961.

Mills, Howard, *Peacock, His Circle and His Age*, Cambridge University Press, 1968.

Moorman, Mary, *William Wordsworth: A Biography*, 2 vols, Clarendon Press, 1957.

Paley, Morton, *Energy and Imagination: A Study of the Development of Blake's Thought*, Clarendon Press, 1970.

Prickett, Stephen, *Coleridge and Wordsworth: The Poetry of Growth*, Cambridge University Press, 1970.

Prickett, Stephen, *Wordsworth and Coleridge: The Lyrical Ballads*, Edward Arnold, 1975.

Rader, Melvin, *Wordsworth: A Philosophical Approach*, Oxford University Press, 1967.

Raine, Kathleen, *Blake and Tradition*, Routledge & Kegan Paul, 1969.

Smith, Logan Pearsall, 'Four Romantic words', *Words and Idioms*, Constable, 1925.

Thorlby, A. K. *The Romantic Movement*, Longman, 1966.

Warnock, Mary, *Imagination*, Faber & Faber, 1976.

Willey, Basil, *The Eighteenth Century Background*, Penguin, 1964.

Willey, Basil, *Nineteenth Century Studies*, Penguin, 1964.

Index